STUDIES IN ROMANCE LANGUAGES: 43

John E. Keller, Editor

The
Three Secular Plays
of
Sor Juana
Inés de la Cruz
A Critical Study

Guillermo Schmidhuber

In Collaboration with
Olga Martha Peña Doria

Translated by
Shelby Thacker

THE UNIVERSITY PRESS OF KENTUCKY

Publication of this volume was made possible in part
by a grant from the National Endowment for the Humanities.

Editorial and Sales Offices: The University Press of Kentucky
663 South Limestone Street, Lexington, Kentucky 40508-4008

04 03 02 01 00   1 2 3 4 5

Frontispiece: Sor Juana Inés de la Cruz, portrait by Augustín
Velázquez Chávez, eighteenth century; in the Museo Nacional
de Historia, Mexico City

Library of Congress Cataloging-in-Publication Data

Schmidhuber de la Mora, Guillermo.
   The three secular plays of Sor Juana Inéz de la Cruz / Guillermo
Schmidhuber in collaboration with Olga Martha Peña Doria ;
translated by Shelby Thacker.
      p.   cm. — (Studies in Romance languages ; 43)
   Includes bibliographical references and index.
   ISBN 0-8131-2088-8 (cloth : alk. paper)
   1. Juana Inés de la Cruz, Sister, 1651–1695—Dramatic works.
2. Juana Inés de la Cruz, Sister, 1651–1695—Authorship. I. Juana
Inés de la Cruz, Sister, 1651–1695. Plays. II. Peña Doria, Olga
Martha. III. Title. IV. Title: 3 secular plays of Sor Juan Inéz de
la Cruz. V. Series: Studies in Romance languages (Lexington, Ky.) ;
43.
PQ7296.J6Z874   1999
862—dc21   99-25108

Contents

Figures and Tables

Figures

Tables

By Way of Prologue

The present book is aimed at scholars as well as graduate students who are analyzing Sor Juana's plays for the first time. I trust that the first group will find information about the secular plays that was previously unknown, and that it will serve as a foundation and motivation to further their critical research on Sor Juana's theater. For the second group I am including a study on Sor Juana's *Art of Writing Plays* and an analysis of the structures and language of the three secular pieces, as well as a synopsis of the plots and a summary of the primary critical contributions prior to the publication of this book.

In the Fourth Critical Act, I present my research hypothesis for determining that Sor Juana is the co-author of *The Second Celestina*; additionally, in the Sixth Critical Act, I include my proposition that Sor Juana not only wrote the first and third acts of *Love Is Indeed a Labyrinth* but also contributed partially to the second act, traditionally judged to belong in its entirety to Juan de Guevara.

This book is the first dedicated exclusively to the secular plays of Sor Juana, and the first in which three of her plays are treated, since prior to the publication of this book critics only noted one complete play, *The Trials of a Noble House*, and two acts of *Love Is Indeed a Labyrinth*. Now in the present volume three plays are recognized as hers, although the first and the last in collaboration. Thus from now on we will be able to say accurately: the three plays *by* Sor Juana.

The dramatic subgenre of *falda y empeño* [petticoat and perseverance] plays applies to the fundamentally different dramatic elements in the secular plays by Sor Juana, in relation to the Calderonian and post-Calderonian "cloak and dagger" plays, to which the Sorjuanian plays form a counterpart inasmuch as they present the perspective of the female protagonists and their efforts toward bettering the condition of women as thinking and social beings.

Just as ancient plays began with an encomiastic *loa*, so too this book has at the beginning a tribute to several scholars of Sor Juana and her era, without whose work this book would not have been possible. I wish to mention two Mexican books that were indispensable for understanding and attempting to re-create the dramatic world at the end of the Spanish baroque because they are worthy examples to follow in an age in which literary studies are plentiful: *Mexican Encyclopedia* (1755), by Juan José Eguiara y Eguren, and *Encyclopedia of Northern Spanish America* (1816), by José Mariano Beristáin y Souza; to these titles I would add a Spanish book, *A Bibliographical and Biographical Catalog of the Early Spanish Theater, from its Origins until the Middle of the Eighteenth Century*, by Cayetano Alberto de la Barrera y Leirado (1860). One must also include the three first editions of Sor Juana, published in 1689, 1692, and 1700.

I wish also to express my gratitude to Octavio Paz for his work on Sor Juana, for having believed in the research that led to my discovery of *The Second Celestina* in 1989, for his support of my idea that this play was authored by Sor Juana, and also for his prologue to the edition. I am grateful to other Sor Juana specialists whose contributions have shown me so much, especially Lee Alton Daniel and Georgina Sabat-Rivers. Together with them I must mention other critics whose studies have served me as both guide and inspiration: Ermilo Abreu Gómez, Luis Leal, Dorothy Schons, and Alfonso Méndez Plancarte, and especially those interested in Sor Juana's dramaturgy: Alberto G. Salceda and Rodolfo Usigli.

My studies on the works of Sor Juana have focused on her theater and her lost works. Both fields were linked with my discovery of *The Second Celestina*. In 1992, I found a *Declaration of Faith* by Sor Juana that was not included among her original works, nor in any of the modern editions; this text is being printed here for the first time. Lost Sorjuanian material for which I continue to search includes "The Moral Balance," which I suspect was taken to the United States during the middle of the nineteenth century, and the lost correspondence between Sor Juana and Father Diego Calleja, her first biographer.

I wish to thank the University of Louisville for grants that enabled me to carry out this research, especially in the Library of Congress in Washington, in the library of the University of Pennsylvania in Philadelphia, the New York Public Library, and the Hispanic Society of America, also in New York.

I dedicate this book to my family: to my wife, Olga Martha Peña Doria, who helped greatly with ideas during the research and editing of this book, and who also corrected the manuscript; and to my three children, Guillermo, Martha, and Erika, because they have shared my interest in the work of Sor Juana as well as the search for and discovery of two of her lost writings.

This study is our personal contribution to the baroque and postmodern festival for the third centenary of the death of Sor Juana, 1695-1995.

—Guillermo Schmidhuber

A Glossary of Literary Terms from Spanish

auto: a brief dramatic work of allegorical or biblical nature

canción: a varied number of lines of seven and eleven syllables, but often three quatrains of *redondillas;* the third repeats the theme and meter of the first

comedia: a three-act play in verse from the Spanish baroque

coplas de arte menor: quatrains with verses of eight syllables or fewer

décima: a ten-line stanza of octosyllabic verse

falda y empeño: "petticoat and perseverance," a reference to plays in which determined women are the protagonists

loa: a brief dramatic poem celebrating a famous person or event

mojiganga: a masquerade

ovillejo: three octosyllabic lines, each followed by a line of *pie quebrado* in consonant rhyme

pie quebrado: lines of four or five syllables alternating with lines of eight or more syllables

quintilla: a five-line stanza in octosyllabic verse with consonant rhyme

redondilla: an octosyllabic quatrain in which the first line rhymes with the fourth, and the second with the third

romance: a ballad in octosyllabic verse with alternate lines in assonance

romancillo: a short *romance*

sainete: a one-act intermezzo

sarao: a nocturnal gathering of persons of station for a dance or music *seguidilla:* a quatrain of alternating verses of five and seven syllables with second and fourth in assonance

silva: a varied number of alternating verses of seven and eleven syllables

silva pareada: a *silva* of rhyming couplets

suelta: an individually published edition of a work

villancico: a short poetic composition with a refrain, typically of a religious nature

First Critical Act

Introduction to Sor Juana's Dramatic Work

The Last of the Forgotten

The pendulum of favorable review has swung once again toward Sor Juana Inés de la Cruz. The cloistered obscurity of this nun has been increasingly lifted, bringing her into the light of the modern secular world. Today Sor Juana receives disproportionate praise, not because some of her work is inferior, but rather because of the focus on that part of her work as poet and her struggle as a woman intellectual. Less critical attention is given to her other contributions, such as her dramatic pieces or her religious prose. Today Sor Juana is first a woman, as evidenced in her thorough and abundant biography; then she is a poet, about whom an exhaustive list of critical works has been written in the twentieth century; and she is also a nun, a fact especially noted to exemplify her search for creative freedom in the convent and to describe her death while serving her sisters during an epidemic. However, attempts to define her have not taken into account Sor Juana as dramatist, in spite of all that her drama can contribute to a better understanding of her, both as an individual and as an author of a vast body of drama, poetry, and prose.

The high acclaim with which Sorjuanian poetry has been appraised has overshadowed, until today, any consideration whatever of her theater. This critical imbalance may be explained by the fact that in many instances her dramatic production has been confused with her poetry, without there existing any proper delineation of genres; for example, Sor Juana's *villancicos* and *loas* have traditionally been considered part of her poetic production; nevertheless, her *loas* and *villancicos* are part of her theater, as will be shown later. Another point of confusion among critics occurs when certain of her dramatic speeches are cited for their poetic quality, but without the context of their belonging to a theatrical work. The present study hopes to provide a general view of Sor Juana's dramatic works through critical evaluations derived by an examination of the plays in light of dramatic theory, as well as to present an individual analysis of the three secular plays. Thus she can be reconsidered not as a poet who wrote plays by commission, but rather as a dramatist of the first order, as much for the number of plays written—fifty-two dramatic works, according to the count we include in this First Critical Act—as for the quality that they display. Similarly surprising is the variety of types of plays to which she contributed: the *falda y empeño* (petticoat and perseverance), with its subgenres of plays of love and mythology; the *auto*, with its subgenres of sacramental *auto*, hagiographic *auto*, and biblical *auto*; as well as the *loas* and *villancicos* of dramatic nature.

The concept of the baroque has changed since the studies by Heinrich Wölfflin, in his book *Renaissance und Barock* (1888). Today it is no longer considered solely as the style that followed the Renaissance and preceded Classicism; rather it has been enriched through a greater appreciation and understanding. This period covers two aspects: baroque and mannerism. This is not the place to define the two styles, their similarities and their differences; it is enough to cite some of Sor Juana's attributes in relation to these styles. Undoubtedly Sor Juana is both mannerist and baroque, and sometimes she is both simultaneously. She is mannerist according to the characteristics for this concept pointed out by Arnold Hauser; for her vacillation toward reality; for providing an internal design in her work; for her deliberate alteration of the image; and for her decided affectation (2:17). On the other hand, she is also baroque, because in her work there is a coincidence of opposite principles and apparently divergent emotions; because thematically her philosophical sonnets are a meditation on the rapid passing of time and the resulting disillusion; because in all of her work she avoids the static; through her preference for disproportion; and through having adopted the chiaroscuro vision as a means of intellectual clarity. In a word, her courtly literature belongs to the domain of mannerism, while those works that have popular elements are essentially baroque. Sor Juana is especially mannerist in her poem *First Dream* ([26] 1:335–59), the *loas*, the plays, and the erudite poetry, whereas she is baroque in the *villancicos*, the *autos*, and popular forms of poetry. The reevaluation the baroque has undergone in the twentieth century and the advent of the mannerist concept doubtless favor the comprehension and the merits of Sor Juana's work, so much so that today the author may no longer be categorized in a derogatory way as post-Calderonian or Gongorist, epithets that should now be understood from the perspective of mannerism, that is to say, understood as a desire to follow the work of those predecessors with the intent of surpassing them.[1]

On the Question of Dramatic Genres

The *autos*, plays, and *loas* of Sor Juana have been understood by all the critics as part of the dramatic genre, but without exception the *villancicos* have not been included in her theater. Traditionally, the *villancico* is a popular poetic form with a refrain, primarily to accompany the music of a religious festival. The term derives from the diminutive of *villano*, which means a rustic sort, a villager. The words were understood in this way in the fifteenth and sixteenth centuries by such authors as Lope de Vega, Father José de Valdivieso, and Luis de Góngora. However, at the end of the baroque and mannerist periods, for writers such as Pedro Calderón de la Barca, Manuel de León Marchante, and Agustín de Salazar y Torres, the *villancico* acquired several elements of a dramatic nature: dialogue; the beginnings of a plot; a structure similar to that which the *loa* possesses; a conflict, on a conceptual plane, expressed through dialogue of two or more choruses; and the typification of characters with generic traits, such as the modus vivendi, nationality, habits of speech, and so on. Darío Puccini, in one of the best studies on Sor Juana's *villancicos*, queries, "Should the *villancicos* be restored to the realm of dramatic literature, as Pedro Henríquez Ureña suggests, or indeed to the realm of lyric poetry, as Alfonso Méndez Plancarte proposes?" (226). Puccini himself proposes a position that includes them in the genre of theater, although within the subgenre of musical lyric: "Recognizing the connection between the *villancicos*, sometimes as lyric works and sometimes as dramatic works of Sor Juana, we feel compelled to end the minor dispute with a 'Solomon's judgment': nor 'collective lyric' nor 'dramatic' work; rather, a work that at times (or at the same time) frees the lyrical moments, making them stand out in fragments of "pure poetry," and at times (or at the same time) stylizes the dramatic action in a musical evolution that foreshadows the eighteenth-century opera libretto" (230).

I suggest a reconsideration of the *villancicos*, utilizing a new definition of dramatic classification based on the three elements of all staging proposed by Richard Schechner in his studies on anthropological theater: in other words, audience assembly, performance, audience disassembly. Solidarity, not conflict, unifies the group, but only conflict is accepted if the public is willing to observe the performance with the resulting breakup of the group into audience and actors, and then again integrate them by the end of the play into a single group. Thus the essence of drama is not in the conflict between the characters, but rather in the *transformation* that the group experiences. This change can be understood in three categories, according to whether the change takes place (1) in the dramatic plot; (2) in the actors who undergo a psychosomatic rearrangement, a "transportation"; or (3) in the audience, with temporary changes if the drama is entertainment, or with permanent changes if it is a ritual ceremony. Thus the theater is defined in less limiting terms, which range from the ritualization of everyday life to extraordinary events such as family reunions, sports, ceremonies, and, obviously, theatrical works. The *villancicos* possess the three characteristics of performance: the popular gathering in a cathedral on a specific religious holiday; the performance by a group of actors—reduced to a chorus by the orthodox limitations of the epoch and not because of limitations of the text; and the subsequent dispersion of the group outside of the cathedral. If we compare the Christian Mass with *villancicos*, both are theatrical spectacles, the former being a theatricalized ceremony and the latter a dramatic celebration. Schechner also has provided another perspective on the analysis of drama regarding the degree of transformation: (1) ritual dramas, in which the subject is transformed by the ceremony; (2) social dramas, in which all the participants are transformed; and (3) aesthetic dramas, in which only the public is transformed. The *villancicos* possess elements of these three kinds of dramatic transformation: they participate in the ritual of Christmas or of a saint within a space considered sacred; they are social dramas because all the people attend (since it is a festival); and in some fashion the spectators are transformed by the spectacle, in spite of the fact that the performance is more auditory than visual.

As for the *loa*, it has not been accepted, in general, as a theatrical precept piece, not because there is some doubt as to whether it belongs to another genre, as is the case with the *villancico*, but because it has generally been considered part of *low theater*; from this scorn comes the scant critical attention it has received. Another factor that has prevented the *loa* from receiving valid appreciation has been the fact that this dramatic subgenre did not reach its structural and thematic height until the second half of the seventeenth century, that is, during the twilight of the baroque/mannerist era, with Calderón de la Barca and, precisely, with Sor Juana. Anthony M. Pasquariello wrote a clarifying study of the development of the *loa* in Spanish America, in which he includes Sor Juana's *loas* as the best among the production at the end of the mannerist period: "The best that can be said for the *loas* of Sor Juana is that they were less strained than most of the eighteenth-century efforts with their staggering multitude of mythological and allegorical characters, their complex elaboration of metaphors, and a versification which startles the reader with its twists and turns for effect" (9).

Lee Alton Daniel has defended the *loa* of Sor Juana with considerable success, giving it the same importance that is normally accorded the plays and *autos*, pointing out that this subgenre is one of the principal dramatic contributions of Sor Juana, since she exchanged the short and simple form based on monologues or dialogues for a greater structure with all the elements required by theatrical precepts ("A Terra Incognita," 143-47; "The *Loa*," 43). The *loa* should be considered a contribution to the charm of the "Sorjuanian mask": "She, as did Calderón, expanded the simple early form of the *loa*, elevating it to that of a brief one-act play. She is singularly important in the development of the independent *loa* form in Latin America. Sor Juana Inés de la Cruz has made her mark in drama and deserves to be considered in terms not only of the lyre but also of the mask" ("The *Loa*," 49).

All of the concepts discussed regarding the Sorjuanian *loa* are applicable to the *villancicos*, except that in the *loa* there was a separation between the actors and the audience, as in the aesthetic drama, while in the *villancicos* the audience remained part of the troupe and was even able to take part in the chorus of refrains or in the Aztec dances of the *tocotín* (Leal, 51-64), or in the danceable rhythms of the *conga* and *guineo*:

Chorus: Flacica, turu la Negla
        hoy de guto bailalá,
        polque una Nenglita beya
        e Cielo va gobelná.
     1:   ¡Ha, ha, ha
        buenu va!
     2:   ¡Cambulé,
        gulungué,
        he, he, he! ([26]2:315)

Thus the dark Virgin was changed into a "liberated Negro" by Sor Juana, and all the participants were transformed into Afro-Mexicans in the blink of an eye.

Therefore, the theater of Sor Juana should include the *loas* and the *villancicos*, along with her plays and *autos*, not solely for reasons of their literary excellence but especially because in these forms two of her contributions to dramatic art are found: (1) the evolution of the *villancico* realized by Sor Juana, to which she gave a complex dramatic structure, incorporating popular speech and the democratic representation of the society of New Spain with characters belonging to all levels of society; and (2) the giving of a specific, independent genre to the *loa*, since in its conception these dramatic works are not merely an appendage to a greater work.

Sor Juana's Dramatic Work

The body of Sor Juana's dramatic work is more voluminous than some critical studies might suggest, and it should be mentioned, at the risk of overstating the obvious, that the author wrote more lines of drama than of poetry. Lee Alton Daniel has had the skill and patience to count the lines of both productions. According to his count, there are 20,350 lines of drama and 22,250 lines of poetry ("The Loa," 43); but this count was made before the discovery of *The Second Celestina*, which adds at least another thousand lines to Sor Juana's dramatic production and does not include the *villancicos*. We must conclude that, at least in quantitative terms, Sor Juana was more dramatist than poet. She wrote fifty-two dramatic works (including original works and collaborations); and her authorship has been proven in the case of the *villancicos* attributed to her, in spite of their having been published anonymously.[2]

Following is a list of Sor Juana's dramatic production, divided into four genres: secular festivals, or *comedias;* sacred festivals, or *autos;* independent *loas* and *loas* that are part of a play or *auto;* original *villancicos* and *villancicos* attributed to her.

Secular Festivals (Three Plays)

- *The Second Celestina,* in collaboration with Agustín de Salazar y Torres
- *The Trials of a Noble House,* a *loa,* three songs, two *sainetes,* and a *sarao*
- *Love Is Indeed a Labyrinth,* in collaboration with Juan de Guevara, containing a *loa*

Sacred Festivals (Three Autos)

- *The Divine Narcissus,* a religious *auto,* with a *loa*
- *St. Hermenegildo, Martyr of the Sacrament,* a hagiographic *auto,* with a *loa*
- *The Scepter of Joseph,* a biblical *auto,* with a *loa.*

Villancicos (Twelve Original and Ten Attributed)

Original

- *Assumption,* 1676, Cathedral of Mexico City
- *Immaculate Conception,* 1676, Cathedral of Mexico City
- *St. Peter Nolasco,* 1677, Mexico City
- *St. Peter the Apostle,* 1677, Cathedral of Mexico City
- *Assumption,* 1679, Cathedral of Mexico City
- *St. Peter the Apostle,* 1683, Cathedral of Mexico City
- *Assumption,* 1685, Cathedral of Mexico City
- *Immaculate Conception,* 1689, Cathedral of Puebla
- *Nativity,* 1689, Cathedral of Puebla
- *St. Joseph,* 1690, Cathedral of Puebla

- *Assumption*, 1690, Cathedral of Mexico City
- *St. Catherine*, 1691, Cathedral of Antequera (today Oaxaca)

Attributed[3]

- *Assumption*, 1677, Cathedral of Mexico City
- *Nativity*, 1678, Cathedral of Puebla
- *St. Peter the Apostle*, 1680, Cathedral of Puebla
- *Nativity*, 1680, Cathedral of Puebla
- *Assumption*, 1681, Cathedral of Puebla
- *St. Peter the Apostle*, 1684, Cathedral of Puebla
- *Assumption*, 1686, Cathedral of Mexico City
- *St. Peter the Apostle*, 1690, Cathedral of Puebla
- *St. Peter the Apostle*, 1691, Cathedral of Mexico City
- *St. Peter the Apostle*, 1692, Cathedral of Mexico City

Loas *(Five in Plays/Autos and Thirteen Independent)*

In plays/*autos*

- A *loa* by Sor Juana appears in each of the Secular and Sacred Festivals except for *The Second Celestina*, whose *loa* was composed entirely by Salazar y Torres.

Independent

- *Loa of the Immaculate Conception*
- *Loa for the King's Birthday* [I] [Carlos II]
- *Loa for the King's Birthday* [II]
- *Loa for the King's Birthday* [III]
- *Loa for the King's Birthday* [IV]
- *Loa for the King's Birthday* [V]
- *Loa for the Queen's Birthday* [María Luisa de Borbón]
- *Loa for the Queen Regent's Birthday* [Mariana de Austria]
- *Loa for the Viceroy Marquis de la Laguna's Birthday*

- *Loa in the Gardens, for the Countess de Paredes* [María Luisa Manrique de Lara, Countess de Paredes and Marquise de la Laguna]

- *Loa for don José de la Cerda* [first-born son of the Viceroy Marquis de la Laguna]

- *Encomiastic Poem for the Countess de Galve* [Elvira de Toledo]

- *Loa for Fray Diego Velázquez de la Cadena*

In conclusion, as concerns the delineation of genres, Sor Juana's total production contains two poles: theater and poetry, and, of lesser importance, prose.

Early Editions and Dramatic Texts

Sor Juana Inés de la Cruz's *Obras completas* were published in three volumes. The first was published in 1689 in Madrid, with the mannerist title *Inundación castálida* [*Castalian Flood*] [1]; the second, in Seville in 1692 [2]; and the third, in Madrid in 1700 [3]. The first volume contains nine of the thirteen *loas* and six of the twelve sets of original *villancicos*, as an example of her dramatic work (Sabat-Rivers, "Introducción" [25], 58). In the second volume is the remainder of her dramatic creations, with the exception of *The Divine Narcissus*, which already had been published as a separate volume in 1690 [5]. There are no plays in the third volume. One should remember that the three volumes of this early edition did not follow any integral plan, since they resulted either from gathering manuscripts of Sor Juana's work on three different occasions or from transcriptions of her work that were available from a variety of sources. The editor of the third volume, Juan Ignacio de Castorena y Ursúa, complains in his "Prologue to the Reader" about the lack of any criteria for organizing the numerous works by Sor Juana, and he suggests a new editorial approach: "In the first, the poetry dealing with human themes, in the second, those dealing with divine themes, in the third, her prose writings on holy themes, so that her gifts could blossom in this intellectual springtime, paralleling vegetative order—leaves, flowers, and fruit" ([3], 82). The young editor signals his desire to reprint the three volumes in the order mentioned above, and later in that very prologue he lists the works by Sor Juana that he was unable to find and which, consequently, remained unpublished: "A gloss in décimas . . . The *Súmulas* . . . The Moral Balance . . . An unfinished poem begun by don Agustín de Salazar, and perfected with graceful artistry by the poetess whose original is much admired by don Francisco de las Heras, Knight of the Order of Santiago, Governor of Madrid,[4] and since it pertains to the first volume, I am not publishing it in this book, and it is being printed so that it can be performed before Their Majesties . . . Other writings on the fineness of Christ . . . The end of a laudatory ballad on the 'Swans' of Europe . . . And many other papers and letters"[5] ([3], 87).

This reference to the (dramatic) poem by Sor Juana and Agustín de Salazar y Torres served as a point of departure for the search for and discovery of *The Second Celestina* [27], found by Guillermo Schmidhuber in 1989, in the form of a *suelta* [separate volume], which is discussed in the Fourth Critical Act. The whereabouts of her other writings are still unknown today. In summary, Castorena y Ursúa understood the need for some future editing of Sor Juana's work by genre, with the plays logically grouped in the first volume, which would include those whose themes are human nature.

Sor Juana's original manuscripts have been lost; today we have only the early manuscript transcriptions of *The Scepter of Joseph*, *Love Is Indeed a Labyrinth*, and *The Trials of a Noble House*, all three in the National Library in Madrid. Some of Sor Juana's works that were suitable for staging were published as single volumes in Mexico before being included in the complete editions, as was the case with the two sets of *Villancicos for the Assumption* in 1676 [11] and 1679 [15], and those on the Immaculate Conception in 1676 [12], on St. Peter Nolasco in 1677 [13], and on St. Peter the Apostle [14], in the same year. In addition to the Mexican edition of *The Divine Narcissus* of 1690 [5], two early Spanish separate editions without dates ([26] 3:513) are known; this *auto* was incorporated into the first volume of early works when it was published again in Barcelona.[6] There is also a separate one-volume edition of *Love Is Indeed a Labyrinth* published in Seville, without a date [10]. There are three editions of *The Trials of a Noble House* published in Seville and one in Barcelona, also without dates [9] (Schons, "Bibliografía," 7, 31; Abreu, 261-65, 296). The loss of Sor Juana's originals may be explained, in part, by the fact that during the mannerist and baroque periods authorship was not considered of great worth; it has only been valued since the era of Romanticism, and so persists today.

Their loss may also be the result of negligence and indolence, "creator of our deserts," as Octavio Paz concludes (*The Traps of Faith*, 181).

Appreciation of Sor Juana's Theater by Her Contemporaries

Sor Juana's contemporaries also held her drama in less esteem than her other literary production. The well-known epithet "tenth muse," which was applied to Sor Juana, would seem only an echo of Erato, the muse of lyric poetry, and not of Melpomene, Talia, or Polimnia, the muses of tragedy, comedy, and mimicry, respectively. The concept of the dramatist as a social personage appears in France with Pierre Corneille (1606-1684), and it was not until 1839 that a Spanish author, Antonio García Gutiérrez, stepped onto the stage to thank the audience for its applause on the opening night of his *El trovador*. Thus we have to understand the baroque/mannerist dramatist from a secular perspective. The two collaborative dramas by Sor Juana are examples of the collective creation that was very common among two or more creative artists during the Golden Age, without there being any authorial responsibility for the entire piece, but only for some of the acts.[7]

In the early editions there is scant mention of Sor Juana's quality as a dramatist, which is more noticeable in comparison to the abundant commentaries and laudatory poems given her poetic production. The titles of some of the first editions of her dramatic works, which appeared during Sor Juana's lifetime, serve to demonstrate the lack of mention given her dramatic works, even though the author of the music is mentioned in the *villancicos*.

Anonymous Editions

1676   *Villancicos of the Assumption*. The authorship of the music, by the lawyer Joseph de Agurto y Loaysa, is stated.

1676   *Villancicos of the Immaculate Conception*. With a citation from the author of the music, Agurto y Loaysa.

1683   *Villancicos of Saint Peter the Apostle*. With music by Agurto y Loaysa.

1685   *Villancicos of the Assumption*. Set to music by Agurto y Loaysa.

1689   *Villancicos of the Nativity.* With music by Miguel Mateo Dallo y Lana.

Editions of Doubtful Authorship

1677   *Villancicos of Saint Peter the Apostle.* With the name of the author and a lengthy dedication by her. The first time Sor Juana's name appears on a title page.

1679   *Villancicos of the Assumption:* "Written by Mother Juana Inés de la Cruz," set to music by Agurto y Loaysa.

1689   *Villancicos of the Immaculate Conception:* "Written for the Holy Church by Mother Juana Inés de la Cruz," with music by Miguel Mateo Dallo y Lana.

1689   There is no explicit mention of Sor Juana's dramaturgy in *Castalian Flood,* nor in the appendices (the "Approval" by Father Diego Calleja; the "Prologue to the Reader" by an anonymous author; and the "Approval" by Luis Tineo de Morales) in spite of the fact that this volume includes nine *loas* and six sets of *villancicos.*

1690   On the cover of the 1690 edition of *The Divine Narcissus* [5] are the words "Sacred play . . . written by that singular numen and never adequately praised genius, the purity and nobility of the Castilian language of Mother Juana Inés de la Cruz . . ." and mention is also made of the desire to "take it to the Court at Madrid so that it could be performed there." This is the first praise of her theater.

1690   *Villancicos of Saint Joseph,* Puebla: "Devised by the unequaled erudition and always adept wisdom of Mother Juana Inés de la Cruz."

1690   *Villancicos of the Assumption.* Again, "Devised by the unequaled erudition and always adept understanding of Mother Juana Inés de la Cruz."

1691   *Villancicos of Saint Catherine.* Repeated for the third time, "Devised by the unequaled erudition and always adept understanding of Mother Juana Inés de la Cruz." This volume includes an effusive dedication to the "Prodigy of nature . . . Prototype of Knowledge . . . Oracle of America . . . Mighty Woman . . . unique among all women," but nothing is mentioned about her theater.

Included in the "Appraisal" for the second volume of *Obras completas* [2], signed by Fray Juan Navarro Vélez, is a commentary that we may consider the first critical apology for her theater, reproduced here in its entirety:

> *Regarding the comedias, I will only say that they seem to me worthy of being included among the best of the celebrated works by other skillful writers of this genre of poetry, and that in the theaters they will deserve the applauses they earn in their presentation. The sacramental* autos *are considered by some to be less artistic and less difficult than the plays (perhaps so by the precepts of the Theater), but by other precepts, their composition is doubtlessly more difficult and hazardous. They are more difficult and hazardous on account of the sacred material in which they had to be composed; in the truly difficult terms, which must be used in their composition; in the allegories, which must be woven together with great risk; and in being exposed to errors. A play, no matter how perfect, only requires for its composition matters which do not go beyond human affairs; but the composition of an* auto sacramental *requires joining the human and divine, because its fabric is woven from matters interwoven of both realms, of learning of the Holy Faith, of almost Scholastic and Theological terms; and a genius to manipulate all of these elements with elegance and skill, as required by the Theater, adjusting all of these elements to the level of truth and decency, without the slightest misstep, without the slightest error, all this is the product of a great genius, of great understanding and great judgment. And Mother Juana's* autos *have all of these qualities, because they are quite perfect, and they comply with all of the precepts of the Theater, with the truth of religion, with the purity of holy doctrine, and with the sovereign majesty of the Mystery. And if fulfilling all of this was a great achievement for a very great man, what would it be for a woman's wit and study to fulfill all this? Fray Pedro del Santísimo judges Sor Juana as "the phenomenon of women," paraphrasing Lope's nickname: "the phenomenon of geniuses." (De la Maza, 88-89)*

This commentary was the only one included in the original editions that makes reference to the dramatic work of Sor Juana.

It is surprising that Sor Juana's dramaturgy is not mentioned in the "Letter" by Bishop Santa Cruz [26], which precedes the *Athenagoric*

Letter [26], and especially in the *Reply to Sor Filotea* [26], which defends the intellectual freedom of women, perhaps because the "Letter" that motivated it did not indicate her dramatic activity nor evaluate the moral correctness of this activity. On the day Sor Juana died, Antonio de Robles noted her death in his *Diary of Notable Events* (3:166) and added this commentary: "Distinguished woman in all faculties and admirable poet . . . Two volumes of her works were printed in Spain, and in this city many *villancicos*"; but there is no mention of her plays, *autos*, or *loas*.

There is no commentary about Sor Juana's dramatic work in Father Calleja's "Imprimatur" to the third volume of *Obras completas* [3], which includes his famous protobiography; there is mention only of the *loa* to Holy Sacrament (today lost), which she wrote when she was a young girl. Stranger still is this silence because the biographer himself was a dramatist of such stature that he merited inclusion in the *Bibliographical and Biographical Catalog of Early Spanish Theater* by Barrera y Leirado (59-60). Regarding the drama of Calleja, we know of three original plays and three written in collaboration with Manuel de León Marchante.[8] Thus the first biography of Sor Juana that we know of begins the tradition of forgetting her dramatic work. Could this be the result of mere forgetfulness, or perhaps the desire to diminish the importance of one of the major achievements that the Mexican nun produced? Neither does Eguiara y Eguren include a commentary on the importance of Sor Juana's dramas, and only the *loa* written during her childhood is mentioned, along with a passing reference to the "*autos sacramentales*" (*Sor Juana*, 17).

The critical silence about Sor Juana's poetry began in 1725, when the last edition of her complete works was published. A century and a half had to pass before there was a modern edition of her poetry, when Juan de León Mera published in Quito *Selected Works by the Celebrated Nun from Mexico*. Her dramas, on the other hand, fared better, at least in print. *The Trials of a Noble House* was published as a separate work on four occasions [9], three in Seville and one in Barcelona, and even though these editions are undated, they belong to the eighteenth century. The play was subsequently published again in 1859, when Ramón de Mesonero Romanos included it in *Dramatists after Lope de Vega*, although not as a complete mannerist festival. There were also several editions of *The Second*

Celestina, also as a single-volume work, as is explained in the Fourth Critical Act; and at least one single-volume edition of *Love Is Indeed a Labyrinth*. Thus, during the eighteenth and nineteenth centuries, the theater of Sor Juana was fortunate to have seen so many editions, compared to the editions of her poetry.

The publication in 1910 of *Juana de Asbaje*, a collection of several lectures given by Amado Nervo in Spain, marked a new critical interest in the literary work of Sor Juana, an interest that has continued to increase year after year. Meanwhile, her theater has remained forgotten, and for many years it has only been cited for its poetic quality. The critical commentaries by Menéndez Pelayo are an example of this error: "The most beautiful aspects of her spiritual poems are found . . . in the songs inserted in the *auto, The Divine Narcissus*; they are so beautiful and so free from any affectation and *culteranismo* that they seem more likely composed by a disciple of Saint John of the Cross or Fray Luis de León than by a overseas nun" (75). Along with this reductionist point of view is the common critical failure of judging Sorjuanian theater through a narrow lens: the omnipresent influence of Calderonian theater and the predominance of *The Divine Narcissus* over her other dramas, without an analysis of the rest of her work, and as much from the perspective of drama theory as according to its stage merits.

Some of the critical evaluations of Sor Juana's dramatic work would make us suspect that her works were not read, not even by the critics themselves. Méndez Plancarte has traced typographical errors and omissions dating from the middle of the nineteenth century, which have endured for more than a century ([26] 3:viii-ix) because they have passed, like counterfeit coin, from critic to critic, without knowledge of the original work. The long list of errata discovered by Méndez Plancarte has continued to grow. To follow this genealogy of errors is a labor that seems to vacillate between fantasy and foolishness. In 1859 Mesonero Romanos initiates two errors: he attributes to Sor Juana only two *autos*, with no mention of *The Divine Narcissus*, and he alters the title from *El cetro de José* [*The Scepter of Joseph*] to "El cerco de Joseph" ["The Siege of Joseph"]. Both errors persisted for many years; the second error was repeated by Pedro de Alcántara (1884), Clara Campoamor (1944), and Sainz de Robles (1964). The Joseph in Sor Juana's *auto* is the son of Jacob, but he becomes Christianized as a saint: "El cetro de san José" ["The

Scepter of Saint Joseph"] is accepted by Enrique de Olavarría y Ferrari (1880),[9] Francisco Pimentel (1892), Carlos González Peña (1928), Ermilo Abreu Gómez (1940), Xavier Villarrutia (1942), and Anita Arroyo (1952), and it even becomes "El centro de Joseph" ["The Center of Joseph"] for Hildburg Schilling (1958). Some of the alterations become humorous, as when the Jesuit Alfonso María Landarech changes the title of *Love Is Indeed a Labyrinth*, spicing it up as "Love Is More Libertine" (1951), and when Ezequiel Chávez, without any apparent reason, renames *The Divine Narcissus* as "The Education of the Indigenous Race" (1931). And more than one critic has interpreted the title of the *auto St. Hermenegildo, Martyr of the Sacrament* as two *autos*, thereby spuriously increasing to four the number of *autos* said to be written by Sor Juana (Campoamor 1944). These errors make one doubtful of the complete reading of Sor Juana's dramas; perhaps these critics only partly read the works and presumed that they had read enough, secure in thinking that this was the least important part.

Today, the body of criticism on Sor Juana contains many pages of praise for her poetry and prose yet persists in dispensing only small doses of favorable criticism for her theater, perhaps because interest in Sor Juana was revived by a generation of critics who possessed a lesser degree of knowledge about the art of drama and scant appreciation for the theater of the later years of the baroque. Among the studies dedicated solely to the theater of Sor Juana, the work by Alberto G. Salceda excels, together with those of Lee Alton Daniel and María E. Pérez. Additionally, there are important articles alluding to the Mexican dramatist by José Juan Arrom, Raquel Chang-Rodríquez, Stephanie Merrim, Margaret Sayers Peden, Rodolfo Usigli, and Vern G. Williamsen, as well as a few others. Alfonso Méndez Plancarte, Alberto G. Salceda, and Georgina Sabat-Rivers, after re-editing the first editions of Sor Juana, have written indispensable material about Sor Juana's theater; the same may be said of the modern edition of *The Trials of a Noble House*, by Celsa Carmen García Valdés [28]. The present book is the first dedicated exclusively to the theater of Sor Juana and is a pioneering effort in utilizing as a critical apparatus the theory of drama. Prior to my work there was a thematic analysis (*The American Element in the Theater of Sor Juana Inés de la Cruz*, by María E. Pérez) and numerous generic studies whose criticism is oriented toward giving an overall vision of the life and work of the author, such as the study by Gerard Flynn. *The Traps of Faith*, by Octavio Paz, stands out among all the studies of a general nature; nevertheless, its specific interest is directed toward a historiography of Sor Juana in relation to the baroque society in which she lived and, as concerns genres, it gives preference to poetry over drama.

Dramaturgy and the Convent

Never before had there existed the precedent of a nun who wrote plays of such wisdom and quality, neither in the colonial Mexico of the *Splendors and Miseries of the Creoles*, a study by José Joaquín Blanco, nor in Golden Age Spain. It is possible that Sor Juana found a lack of understanding among some centers of opinion, since the activities of women religious were perfectly regulated, and the writing of plays was not among the acceptable activities.[10]

In the seventeenth century Mexico City had a population of approximately fifty thousand. Sor Juana lived in the convent of Santa Paula de San Jerónimo, whose building was located in what was then the outskirts of Mexico City and which had next to it a school for girls. The church still stands today, although it has been considerably rebuilt; it is located on San Jerónimo Street, between present-day streets 5 de Febrero and Isabel la Católica. There lie the remains of Sor Juana in a common ossuary in the center of the church's choir, "as was done with all of the nuns, even abbesses" (De la Maza, 117). Nothing remains of the original cloister; the building found today on the same location is a much later construction. The convent was a kilometer from the palace of the viceroy, which was located then on what is today the grounds of the National Palace, although the facade did not extend to Moneda Street (Atamoros, 41-44, 59-60).

In her excellent study *Women in Colonial Spanish American Literature*, Julie Greer Johnson presented evidence of the oppressive world in which women lived during the colonial era:

> *The most continuously influential component in the creation and transmission of attitudes toward women, however, was the Catholic Church, and its tradition not only dictated specific images but controlled the lives and destinies of the learned sector of the female population as well . . . The fact that such a genius as sor*

Juana Inés de la Cruz was able to overcome some of these ob-
stacles and effectively challenge men's image of women as well as
their position of superiority over them, leads scholars to conjec-
ture about how many women could have made outstanding con-
tributions to colonial culture had they been given the opportunities
granted to men. (186)

The *Reply to Sor Filotea* ([26] 4:694–97) is a document that presents
some of the limitations that the society of the viceroys imposed upon
a nun who defended her intellectual freedom and her creative rights.

In order to understand the regulations to which Sor Juana had to
adjust in her monastic life, it is worth commenting upon the aesthetic principles of her era, especially the writings by her confessor
of many years, the Jesuit Antonio Núñez de Miranda.[11] And in order
to understand the moral thought of Sor Juana's confessor, it is necessary to refer to his numerous pious books. In one he makes specific reference to the incompatibility of convent life and the writing
of plays and *villancicos*. In his *Primer of Religious Doctrine . . . for*
Young Girls Planning to Become Nuns, and Who Desire to be Per-
fect Nuns there are rules governing the use of drama in the convent.[12] This book is written in the style of a dialogue between a nun
and her confessor:

> *No. 153. "Father, are vows broken by listening to music and watch-*
> *ing plays and immodest dances?"*
> *"If you take delight in their obscenities, or if you desire them,*
> *as I said that* raro contingit, *then yes; but if it is just for recreation*
> *and not for the sake of scandal, then probably not." (45)*

Thus, recreation was permitted in the convent, but as soon as it
went beyond the cloistered walls, it became an unpardonable mortal sin:

> *No. 155. "Father, would it be sinful for the nuns to remove their*
> *habits in order to put on some play or other spectacle, such as for*
> *the birthday of an abbess, or during Carnival?"*
> *"I'll answer in the same manner, that if* recreationes causa
> *occurs inside of the convent, then there is no sin; but if it occurs in*
> *front of lay people, then it is a mortal sin." (46)*

The preceding excerpt in effect accuses Sor Juana of mortal sin, since
the following plays were performed publicly during her lifetime:

The Second Celestina was performed in 1679 (María y Campos, 98); *The Trials of a Noble House*, on October 4, 1683 (Salceda, "Introducción," 4:xviii); and *Love Is Indeed a Labyrinth*, on January 11, 1689 (Salceda, "Introducción," 4:xxii). The serious situation in which Sor Juana found herself as a result of writing and presenting secular plays was intensified by the audacity of publishing them, which, in the opinion of Dorothy Schons, must have been considered a crime by Archbishop Aguiar y Seijas, who detested the theater and did not permit plays to be printed during his pastoral appointment ("Some Obscure Points," 154). Similarly, the moral probity of the *villancicos* is denied in the *Primer of Religious Doctrine* by Father Núñez:

> *No. 311. "Well, Father, I have heard it said to learned men that what is prohibited is the singing of indecent things, but can holy songs be sung?"*
>
> *"All I know is that songs are not prohibited, from what I have read, and what you can read too [citing Pope Innocent XII] is that his Holiness has ordered that for Mass, Vespers, and Matins, nothing can be sung outside of the order of church rites because that would be a perversion of the order of the Church, which on the matter of rite, is the only one that can make decisions." (82)*

Consequently, the twenty-two *villancicos* by Sor Juana were a liturgical perversion, in spite of the fact that they comprise, without any doubt, the greatest literary expression of this author's religiosity.

In *Mystical Testament of a Religious Soul*, by Father Núñez de Miranda, the nuns who read this work are invited to reaffirm their *Declaration of Faith* on the anniversary of their taking of vows, before the image of "their spouse," with the renewal of their vows:

> *I will that my soul be given entirely into His hands, and that in everything and by every means it be treated as His, used for eternal purposes, without taking into account anything of this temporal world, let my mind only think, contemplate, and reflect on heaven, without concern for this world . . . [Let] my body be buried alive inside the four walls of the convent where I cannot leave even through my imagination. And as one truly dead to the World, let me not see, hear, speak, nor remember the things of the World. Let the world and its devices look after itself. It doesn't concern me; let it turn, let it fall apart. (n.p.)*

The palace parties, with their courtly *loas* and secular plays, the devices of this world, are far from this spiritual detachment. Even the *autos* themselves would seem part of this worldly noise.

In order to understand the period of crisis in which Sor Juana lived toward the end of her life, one would have to know something of the ulterior political motives of the religious groups. Undoubtedly, the Jesuits intervened in those crucial years and in the first years after her death, since Núñez de Miranda, her confessor, belonged to this religious order, as did Juan Ignacio de Castorena y Ursúa, the editor of the third volume of the early edition of Sor Juana [3], and from Spain, Father Diego Calleja, her first biographer and the person who granted approval for two of the early editions of Sor Juana [1], [3]. The archbishop of Mexico, Francisco de Aguiar y Seijas, was a great friend of the Jesuits and also an admirer of Father Antonio de Vieira, the Jesuit author of the sermon that Sor Juana criticizes in her *Athenagoric Letter* [26].[13] The period of attack on Sor Juana begins with the publication of this document carried out by Manuel Fernández de Santa Cruz, Bishop of Puebla, who concealed his identity under the pseudonym of Sor Filotea in a prefatory letter directed to the nun in which she was asked to dedicate herself more to matters of the spirit [26]. After her *Reply to Sor Filotea* [26], dated March 1, 1691, the last years of Sor Juana Inés de la Cruz are shrouded in uncertainty. What was the reason for the inexplicable change in her which took place during this crucial time? There is no single answer for this question, but there are two opinions: on the one hand, a group of critics claims that the reason Sor Juana rejected everything worldly was to proceed on her path toward spiritual perfection; the other group maintains that it was the result of the attack upon her by various powerful persons who sought to distance Sor Juana from her vocation of female intellectual. That is, it was asceticism or survival.[14]

In May 1992, Guillermo Schmidhuber located a *Declaration of Faith* by Sor Juana that is not included in the first editions nor in any modern edition; this text formed part of a devotional book, *Mystical Testament of a Religious Soul,* by Father Núñez de Miranda. For this ascetic, the four religious vows should follow this order: poverty, chastity, obedience, and perpetual enclosure.[15] Contrarily, when Sor Juana lists the four religious vows in the recently discovered *Declaration* she alters the order: obedience, poverty, chastity, and perpetual enclosure. Placing the vow of obedience before the others is perhaps an indication of how important she felt was obeying the orders of her superiors, among which was a tacit prohibition of writing secular works, especially plays. This is the same order of vows that she had written twenty-five years earlier in the *Book of Vows*, the day she put on the habit, February 24, 1669. By the end of her life Sor Juana's conception of freedom had completely changed. At the beginning of her vocation her own superiors had urged her to follow a path in literature, with their permission and even with commissions, as was the case with all of her dramatic works; nevertheless toward the end of her life the inexorable conflict of obedience arose because her spiritual leaders no longer permitted her to follow the paths earlier traversed with such freedom. Consequently, the core of the crisis was obedience. This recently discovered *Declaration* is recorded here for the first time in a modern book; for this reason, and for its importance, it is here included in its entirety:

Declaration of Faith and Renewal of Religious Vows Made by Mother Juana Inés de la Cruz, A Professed Nun of the Hieronymite Order of Mexico and Written in Her Blood[16]

Jesus, Mary, and Joseph. I, [Juana Inés de la Cruz], a professed nun in this convent of [San Jerónimo] in Mexico City, declare that I believe in God Almighty, three distinct persons in one true God, and I believe that the Word became flesh in order to redeem us, along with all else believed and confessed by the Holy Roman Church, whose obedient daughter I am, and as such I wish and declare that I shall live and die in this faith and belief, and let it be understood that it is not my will to do, say, or believe anything contrary to this truth, for which I am prepared to give my life a thousand times over and for which I would shed all the blood in my veins and thus as I write with it these lines, so I desire that all of it be spilled, confessing the holy faith that I profess, believing with my heart, and speaking with my mouth this truth at any cost and risk. I further declare that I ask confession for my sins, which cause me great pain, because they offend God, whom I love above all else, for only being who He is, in whom I believe, whom I love, in whom I hope, who will forgive my sins through His infinite mercy and through His precious blood [that] was shed for me, and through the intercession of my Lady, the Virgin Mary; all of which I offer to cleanse my sins. And so, as the professed nun that

I am (for which I give infinite gratitude to His Majesty), I renew the obligation of the four religious vows, and once again I vow obedience, poverty, chastity, and perpetual seclusion, and I reiterate to Christ, my Lord and my Spouse, the promise that I made to Him in my profession (which I have so poorly fulfilled, and which burdens my soul) not to have any other love, but only His, and to remain a true and faithful wife, correcting what until now I have done wrong. All of this I promise in the presence of the Holy Trinity and the Holy Virgin, my Lady, and all the Heavenly Hosts, before whom, as witnesses, I place this obligation, which I renew and compel myself to fulfill with the grace and favor of God and the intercession of His Holy Mother (whose Immaculate Conception may free her from any stain of sin in the first moment of life, I vow to believe in and defend until the end of my life) and I wish that these obligations be irrevocable for all eternity, and so I signed on ———.[17] (n.p.)

Reading this *Declaration* allows us to speculate about the real reason for the decrease in Sor Juana's creative labors toward the end of her life, both in the poetry and in the theater: her vow of obedience.

What could have happened in Sor Juana's soul? At the end of her life, how distant the palace festivals, the *villancicos* about saints, the nocturnal secular *loas*, and the cathedral *autos* must have seemed to Sor Juana. Her contemporaries kept silent in this regard, and they left only a few commentaries on her spiritual progress. While some accepted Father Núñez de Miranda's unsubstantiated commentary: "Juana Inés was not running but rather flying toward perfection," others suspected an imposition by her confessor, as Eguiara y Eguren affirmed in 1755: "It seemed to him that she was not running fast enough along the arduous path toward perfection, when instead he wanted her to fly," an expression that Beristáin ironically paraphrases in 1816: "He flattered himself with having sent to heaven as a white dove the one who had been the melodious swan of Mexico" (Oviedo, 281; Eguiara, *Sor Juana,* 469; Beristáin, 2:361). It goes without saying that in this period of importunement she distanced herself from the secular theater; her last play, *Love Is Indeed a Labyrinth,* premiered in 1689, and only the *villancicos* continued to appear sporadically, two in 1690 (*Assumption* and *Saint Peter the Apostle*). In the editions of the last two *villancicos* sung in the cathedral of Mexico City the name of the author was no longer included (*Saint*

Peter the Apostle, June 29, 1691 and 1692), and there were no more *villancicos* from her pen in the thirty-three months that remained of Sor Juana's life. In the last cycle of *villancicos* that bear her name and that were sung in the Mexican provinces, not in the cathedral of Mexico City,[18] Sor Juana had the courage to give witness to her personal beliefs, concealing her sentiments behind those of Saint Catherine in fragments shaded with her own biography, as she had done earlier in her plays with the characters of Beatriz, Leonor, and Ariadne:

> There once was a Girl
> as I now tell you
> whose years were
> ten and eight.
> Wait, wait,
> I will tell it.
>   This girl (how should I know
> how this could have happened),
> they say she knew a lot,
> even though she was a female . . .
> They envy her because she is beautiful,
> they emulate her because she is wise:
> Oh, controlling one's merits through sin
> has been around for a long time! . . .
> Never in an illustrious man
> have we seen comparable success;
> and it is because God wanted
> to honor the feminine sex in her. ([26] 2:179-80, 170, 172)

At the beginning of this First Critical Act we suggested that Sor Juana is today, for us, first of all a woman, then a poet, and finally a nun, her profession as dramatist not having defined her, perhaps because her labors as a dramatist, as has been shown, were the efforts least mentioned by her contemporaries. Sor Juana's boldness and her breaking with the norms imposed by the society in New Spain were of a different gravity. There are four areas where Sor Juana established a different manner of being woman. As a human being she demanded her right to education and intellectual endeavors; as a poet she demanded her freedom to express her sensibility; as a nun she declared her ability as a thinking woman to study theology and to make her religiosity compatible with her creative life; nevertheless, as a dramatist she committed something more than a transgression—writing, staging, and editing secular plays was a "crime," as Dorothy Schons calls it, one of the greatest transgressions that a cloistered nun could have committed ("Some Obscure Points," 154). There were antecedents of women who had broken with traditional norms of understanding their sex according to society, just as there had been poets of female gender and female religious who wrote poetry, but there is no example of any nun-dramatist writing secular plays, not in New Spain nor in any other part of the Spanish realm. Thus, to write the modern biography of Sor Juana and to understand the importance of her work we should include together with her successes as a woman, poet, and nun her achievements as a dramatist.

Second Critical Act

The Dramatic Itinerary of Sor Juana

Chronology for the Compositions and Performances

Sor Juana's three plays were written for the purpose of being performed at courtly celebrations—*The Second Celestina* for the royal court, and *The Trials of a Noble House* and *Love Is Indeed a Labyrinth* for the viceroyal court. The first play was begun by Agustín de Salazar y Torres (1642-1675) in honor of the Queen, Mariana de Habsburgo (1634-1696), and was completed by Sor Juana. *The Trials of a Noble House* was staged in order to pay homage to the viceroy Tomás Antonio de la Cerda y Aragón, Count of Paredes and Marquis of Laguna. And the third, *Love Is Indeed a Labyrinth*, written in collaboration with Juan de Guevara, was staged to honor the viceroy Gaspar de la Cerda Sandoval Silva y Mendoza, Count of Galve, also Viceroy of New Spain. We cannot be certain that the last two plays were written for the festivals during which they were first performed, since in the plays there is no mention that the piece was written at the same time as the corresponding *loa*, *canciones*, and *sainetes*, which do indeed make specific reference to the festival and those persons being celebrated and which would serve to prove why they were written.

The Second Celestina, in Collaboration with Agustín de Salazar y Torres

This play was to be performed on the occasion of the birthday of the queen, Mariana de Habsburgo, December 22, 1675, but its author, Agustín de Salazar y Torres, died on November 29 of the same year, leaving the work unfinished. (This work is discussed in detail in the Fourth Critical Act.) In 1989 Guillermo Schmidhuber presented the hypothesis that an ending—previously considered anonymous—for the play by Salazar, which had been published in a separate edition [7] under the title *The Second Celestina*, could have been the work of Sor Juana. In 1990 this play was published [27], with co-authorship given to Sor Juana, with a prologue by Octavio Paz and a critical study by Schmidhuber. Since then, several specialists on Sor Juana have accepted her co-authorship. There is not sufficient information about the first staging of this play to prove whether only the *loa*—by Salazar—or also the play was staged at the court of Queen Mariana, and whether with the ending by Sor Juana or another by Juan de Vera Tassis.[1]

In New Spain there was presumably a performance of this piece in the Coliseum of Plays in 1679 (María y Campos, 98). The stage was located in the cloister of the Royal Hospital for Citizens of the Realm and served to financially support the General Hospital of that city, as did the Corral de la Cruz and the Corral del Príncipe in Madrid. We do not know the year in which the Coliseum was built, but unlike the theaters of Madrid, the building in New Spain had been constructed especially for a theater; it had a roof and contained two levels, or tiers with box seats, with an entryway from the cloister of the hospital (Olavarría, 1:14).[2] The first Spanish production of *The Second Celestina* that can be historically verified took place in Madrid on Shrove Tuesday, March 6, 1696, in the Salón de los Reinos del Buen Retiro, by Carlos Vallejo's company (Varey and Shergold, 216, cited by O'Connor).

The Trials of a Noble House

The date for the staging of *The Trials of a Noble House* has been established by Alberto G. Salceda as October 4, 1683.[3] He arrives at his conclusion based on information included in the *loa* that precedes the play, and through a comparison of the events registered in the chronicles of the twenty-eighth viceroy of New Spain, Tomás Antonio de la Cerda, and his wife, María Luisa Manrique de Lara, Counts of Paredes and Marquises of Laguna (including the first son, José, born in Mexico on July 5, 1683). The *loa* mentions the occasion of the opening of the play when the character Joy says:

Joy: The happy arrival
     Of Most High María

> And the Mighty Cerda,
> May they reign long and live happily . . .
> And may generous José,
> Who, as robust succession,
> May the triumphs of the royal offspring be victorious.([26] 4:20-21)

Later, the characters of Fortune and Chance make additional mention of the viceroys being celebrated, with the rhetorical use of an oxymoron that joins two mutually exclusive concepts, arrogance and servility:

> *Fortune:* Welcome to
>   Most High María
>   Goddess of Europe
>   Deity of the Indies.
> *Chance:*   Welcome to
>   Cerda, who treads upon
>   the proud neck
>   of haughty America. ([26] 4:21-22)

It was Salceda who also noted that in the ending of the *loa* there is mention of the entrance of "His Most Illustrious Lordship" ([26] 4:xvii), a title of protocol for bishops, which refers to the entrance into the city of Mexico by Francisco de Aguiar y Seijas, the new archbishop for the city. In the second *sainete* the name of the owner of the house where the play was performed is given: "Who would be the one / to deceive poor Deza / with this play / so long and so dull?" ([26] 4:118). In the *Diary of Notable Events*, by Antonio de Robles, the following was written for an entry in October 1683: "Monday the fourth, day of St. Francis, the archbishop made his public entrance into the city through the arch; the viceroys came to the house of the tax collector, don Fernando Deza" (2:385). The play must have been written some time before its baroque/mannerist accompaniments—*loa*, two *sainetes*, three *canciones*, and a *sarao*—as Sor Juana's *décima* 131 proves. Here she refers only to the submission of a play, as has been suggested by Méndez Plancarte and Salceda ([26] 1:508, [26] 4:xx):

> There is little adornment
> for the play I have written
> although for our pleasure
> I do not know if my design is good.

If its length bothers you,
its long acts
are meant for you;
and it is not good that this frightens you:
for so much travel
three Acts are few. ([26] 1:26)

The lack of "adornment" accompanying the play does not correspond to the exuberance that is shown in the seven additional encomiastic pieces, which without any doubt embellish the play. Therefore, I conclude that the added pieces must have been written after the play, when it was going to be made part of a celebration with a precise motive and date.

Love Is Indeed a Labyrinth, in Collaboration with Juan de Guevara

Salceda also was able to date the staging of this play on Tuesday, January 11, 1689. In order to do this, he utilized information included in the *loa:* the feast day for the Count of Galve:

Age: And today is the day
        to wish for His Excellency
        many more years. ([26] 4:194)

The Countess of Galve, Elvira María de Toledo, is also mentioned, as well as the three children from the Count's first marriage:

Summer: . . . Wait, for me
          the acclamations sound
          from sovereign Elvira,
          at whose feet the roses
          acknowledge her entire being,
          with all their breath, the flowers! . . .
          José, Antonio and Josefa,
          their greater victories
          imitating, they will fulfill
          their high obligations. ([26] 4:204)

The Count of Galve had collaborated earlier in the theatrical productions organized for the regent at that time, Mariana de Habsburgo, by the writer, Fernando de Valenzuela, who in his role as director and costume designer collaborated with the Count of Galve, subdirector of the spectacle and future viceroy of New Spain (Paz, *The Traps of Faith* 351):

Age: First, because already
        most excellent care
        has directed the play
        which, being to their liking
        and sovereign choice,
        the celebrations in the Palace
        cannot exceed it. ([26] 4:194)

Who was able to select the play that could have warranted the epithet of great sovereignty? Only the queen with a piece about the same theme or the selection of the theme by the viceroy himself. Besides, the presence of the previous viceroy of New Spain, Melchor Portocarrero Lasso de la Vega, Count of Monclova, who on April 18, 1689, left Mexico to take charge of the viceroyalty of Peru, is mentioned:

Winter: And the very noble, illustrious
        victorious Count of Monclova,
        the palms of his family
        are laurels for his name;
        in the Temple of Fame,
        as an affront to the Twelve
        he surpasses their Caesars
        and exceeds their Scipios. ([26] 4:204)

In the *Diary of Notable Events*, Antonio de Robles notes similar information for the month of January 1689: "Tuesday, the eleventh, the birthday of the viceroy, the Count of Galve, was celebrated: there was a play in the Palace" (3:6). The *loa* can be dated with certainty because the year of its creation is written in one of the speeches that mentions, in baroque fashion, a hand game used to communicate numbers; the left hand shows the prime numbers and tens, and the right hand indicates hundreds and thousands, following a system utilized in antiquity, as the following discourse indicates:

Age: And thus, on his left hand
        fingers half-closed
        he indicated the Tens,
        and the palm, which a Denarius
        showed, came to
        Sixty, and then with

the middle finger folded over,
which makes the number Senarius,
the sum was Sixty Six;
and on the right there were indicated
with three joined fingers
the Hundreds making
Three Hundred and Sixty
Six the year accounted for. ([26] 4:192-93)

That is to say, the hands indicated the date of 366. Confronting this riddle, Salceda confesses, "We do not know where Sor Juana got the representation of 366 (instead of 365); nor can we explain why she may have preferred it here since the year in question (1689) was not a leap year" ([26] 4:574). This riddle is solved with the conjecture that Sor Juana wrote the *loa* in 1688, a year that was indeed leap year; that was the year in which the viceroyalty was given to the Count of Galve.

Another piece of information given in the *loa* is the fact that the Count of Galve had come to New Spain recently; according to the chronicles of the era his arrival was on November 11, 1688 (Robles, 2:505):

Winter: ... What can be done for him,
His Excellency being so
recently arrived, that even scarcely
admiration has given way
to applauding his gifts? ([26] 4:193)

There is no certainty that the play was produced together with the corresponding *loa*. The edition of 1692 [2] contains a title that suggests they were staged together: "*Loa* to celebrate the birthday of his Excellency, the Count of Galve, which apparently preceded the play that followed it"; and the idea is reiterated in the edition from Barcelona of 1693: "*Loa* which preceded the play that follows," which has been accepted by Salceda ("Introducción," 4: xxi). But the chronicles of the era discredit these interpretations: the *Diary of Notable Events* mentions a play in the palace on the 11th of January, and subsequently, a *loa*: "Sunday the 23rd ... there was a *loa* in the palace of the viceroy, Count of Galve, and another for the Count of Monclova" (Robles 1:6-7). Thus one can presume that the *loa* was staged after the play.

Dramatic Itinerary

Repertory of Works Performed during Sor Juana's Lifetime

The chronicles of the era preserve partial information about the following dramas performed during Sor Juana's lifetime. For a few, the title has been preserved and/or the name of the author; for others, only the fact that it was performed in the palace, without any information about the work or the author. The principal sources are two diaries from the era, the one of Gregorio Martin de Guijo, which covers the years 1648 to 1664, and the one of Antonio de Robles, which spans from 1665 to 1703. In general, they are plays by New World dramatists or by Spanish authors whose opening in Mexico was very close to the one in the peninsula.

Viceroyalty of the Duke of Albuquerque 1653-60

1656   (2 p.m., Sunday, February 6) Play performed by students from the university, as part of the entertainment for the dedication for the Cathedral (Usigli, *México en el teatro*, 45).

1658   (Thursday, November 28) Play and *sarao* in the palace. Celebration of first year of life for Prince Felipe Próspero (deceased in 1661), son of Felipe IV and Mariana de Austria (Guijo, 1:415).

1659   A play on the feast of Corpus Christi: *God's Elegant Man* by Luis Sandoval y Zapata (María y Campos, 95).[4]

1660   Feast of Corpus Christi with a play in the portico hall of the townhall (Guijo, 1:442).

Viceroyalty of the Count of Baños, 1660-64

1662   (May 25) In the palace. Play in celebration of the birthday of the Countess of Baños, performed by the servants of the viceroys (Guijo 1:482).
(Sunday, June 11) Play performed in the afternoon on the patio of the palace, for the vicereine and her servants, and later in the cemetery of the Cathedral (Guijo, 1:484).

Viceroyalty of the Marquis of Mancera, 1664-73

1665   "Toward the end of this year there came an extremely skillful aerialist, named Francisco de Morales, who was said to be from the Canary Islands" (Robles, 2:13).

1667   (February 2) A *loa* by the lawyer and presbyter Antonio Medina Solís, on Tepeyac hill, on the solemn installation of the Image in the new hermitage (Beristáin, 2:233).

1670   (Thursday, November 6, 8:00 p.m.) The king's birthday. "A masque of three groups, with different finery for each one, and two footmen for each gentleman, with torches . . . went through the plaza where there were many lights and many people on the stage" (Robles, 2:96).

1671   (March 12) Two plays on the beatification of Saint Rose of Lima (Robles, 2:104).

1672   (Sunday, February 7) A masque for the canonization of St. Francis of Borgia (Robles, 2:122), and on Sunday, February 14, another masque by the university students, "more than 400 actors turned out and there were also very splendid carts" (Robles, 2:123).

Viceroyalty of Friar Payo Enríquez de Ribera, 1673-80

1675   (Sunday, January 27) The students from the royal university "presented a play and farcical masque" in the celebration of the Immaculate Conception (Robles, 2:173).
(Monday, February 4) "On this day a company of actors went up to the coliseum" (Robles, 2:175); it was possibly *Handsome Don Diego*, by Agustín Moreto (Schons, personal archive).
(Wednesday, February 6) "There was a farcical masque with two carts and some fifty people" (Robles, 2:175).
(Wednesday, November 6) Play in the palace to celebrate the fourteenth birthday of the future king, Charles II; "it lasted until midnight" (Robles, 2:204).

1676   Masque on November 25 and 26, and on December 8 and 9 (Robles, 2:225).

1677   (August 9) The play, *The Great Cardinal of Spain, Brother Francisco Ximénez de Cisneros* [by Juan Bautista Diamante and Pedro Francisco Lanini y Sagredo],[5] on the occasion of the beatification of Francisco Solano and twelve martyrs, in the vestibule of the Cathedral (Robles, 2:241).

1678   (Sunday, November 6) *It Cannot Be*, by Moreto, in the Palace to celebrate the birthday of the king (Robles, 2:275-76).[6]

1677-79   In the Coliseum the plays of Salazar y Torres: *Choosing the Enemy, The Olympic Games,* and *Charm Is Beauty, and Charm without Witchcraft* (María y Campos, 98).[7]
1679   (November 6) *Trials through Chance,* by Calderón (Hesse, 15). The king's birthday celebrated in the palace (Robles, 2:291).[8]

Viceroyalty of the Count of Paredes and Marquis of la Laguna, 1680-86[9]

1680   (December 17) Performance of a Marian *auto* by Calderón [*The Noble Woman of the Valley,* according to María y Campos, 99] in the university, in the Literary Assembly Hall.
1683   (January, four times, at the celebrations of the Immaculate Conception) Marian *auto, The Greatest Triumph of Diana,* by Alonso Ramírez de Vargas (Sigüenza, 135).
(October 4) Play in the home of Fernando Deza, with the viceroys in attendance [*The Trials of a Noble House,* according to Salceda ([26] 4:xviii)].
1684   (Wednesday, July 5) Play in the palace to celebrate the birthday of the viceroy (Robles, 2:403).
(October 4) *Herald of God and Patriarch of the Poor,* by the lawyer Francisco de Acevedo, subsequently forbidden by the Office of the Holy Inquisition (María y Campos, 99).

Viceroyalty of the Count of Monclova, 1685-88

1688   (Tuesday, January 5) Play in the palace, the night before the viceroy's birthday (Robles, 2:491).

Viceroyalty of the Count of Galve, 1688-96

1688   (Saturday, December 4) (Robles, 2:507) A *loa* alluding to the arrival of the viceroy, the Count of Galve, by Alonso Ramírez de Vargas:[10] *Historical and Political Tale about a Prince concerning the Fable of Cadmus* (Eguiara, *Sor Juana,* 1:295-96; Beristáin, 3:3).
1689   (Tuesday, January 11) Play at the palace for the birthday of the viceroy, the Count of Galve [*The Trials of a Noble House,* according to Salceda ([26] 4:xxi)] (Robles, 3:6).

(Sunday, January 23) *Loa* at the palace for the viceroy and the Count of Monclova (Robles, 3:7).

(October 20) Play at the palace for the birthday of the vicereine (Robles, 3:24; Abreu, 265).

(November 6) Play at palace for the birthday of King Charles II (Robles, 3:25; Abreu, 265).

1690   (Wednesday, January 11) Soirée for the birthday of the viceroy (Robles, 3:30).

1691   (Wednesday, May 9) Masque or parade for the wedding of the king, which was organized in the name of the university by Fernando Valenzuela (Robles, 3:60).[11]

Information about the celebrations in New Spain disappears after the chronicles of the era; Usigli speculates that it was because theater activities were concentrated in the new theatrical locale called the Coliseum, which was built in 1671 (*Mexico en el teatro*, 47).

We know that Sor Juana left the viceregal palace for the convent of the Discalced Carmelites on August 14, 1667. Thus we can speculate that she attended on February 2, 1667, together with the viceroys, the solemn installation of the Image in the new hermitage of the Virgin of Guadalupe, on Tepeyac Hill, where a *loa* by Antonio Medina Solís was performed. One might speculate that Sor Juana had knowledge of some of these works, such as *It Cannot Be* and those of Salazar y Torres.

Sor Juana's Readings of Dramatic Works

The library of Sor Juana has been a concern of Sorjuanists since Abreu Gómez attempted to identify the possible titles in his pioneering *Bibliography and Encyclopedia* (331-46). Whether the number of four thousand volumes that Calleja cites [3] was correct, or whether it was fewer—as Schons and Paz believe—we cannot ascertain completely (Paz, *The Traps of Faith*, 323-40). Sor Juana's references to dramatists belonging to the ancient world are sparse, and these do not appear to come from original works.[12] Bacchus is mentioned at the beginning of the *First Dream* but is not mentioned in connection with the theater ([26] 1:336). Of the Greek tragedians, there is mention of Aeschylus ([26] 1:110) and Sophocles ([26] 1:110); and among the writers of comedy, she cites only Menander ([26] 1:110). In Sor Juana's work entitled *Reason for the Allegorical Creation,*

and *Application to the Fable*, which serves as the introduction to
The Allegorical Neptune, there is a citation about this god, according to Sor Juana, in Euripides' tragedy *Orestes*. Here I am making a
correction, since it is from *Ifigenia in Crimea*, in which Orestes is a
character who sacrifices bulls in honor of Neptune; as Sor Juana
writes, "If wisdom is represented in a cow, wise men were conceived
in a bull" (*The Allegorical Neptune*, [26] 4:364):

> ... Oceanus quem
> tauriceps ulnis
> Se flectens ambit terram. ([26] 4:364; *Teatro griego*, 1137)

> ... The ocean, whom with
> its arms embraces, reclining, near the
> land, the one who captures the bull. ([26] 4:604)

In the same introduction to *The Allegorical Neptune* one finds another reference to *Oedipus in Colonus*, the tragedy by Sophocles:

> Munus magni daemonis dicere
> gloriam maximam
> equis, pullis, mari bene imperitantem.
> O fili Saturni! tu enim ipsum in
> hanc ducis gloriam rex Neptune
> equis moderans fraeno. ([26] 4:368)

> *Proclaiming the gifts of the great god the greatest glory, which is*
> *to rule over horses, colts, and even the sea. Oh child of Saturn,*
> *Neptune, toward that glory you are guiding the horses with the*
> *bit!*[13] *([26] 4:605)*

Nevertheless, Sor Juana herself, as a good bibliophile, tells where
the citation comes from: "Natal, with the authority of Pausanias,
Mithol. lib. 2, fol. 163" ([26] 4:367), referring to the Italian writer
Natal Conti (1550-1582), author of *Mythologiae, sive explicationes
fagularum*, and to Pausanias, the Greek geographer of the second
century. The argument of the fourth section of *The Allegorical Neptune* mentions a citation, apparently directly from Venus, which is
included in "Trechiniis," that is, in the tragedy *The Thracian
Women*, or *Trachiniai*, also by Sophocles: "Magnum quoddam robur,
/ Venus, refert victorias semper" ([26] 4:381) (Mighty force / Venus,
you always achieve victory) ([26] 4:613).[14] In the argument of the

fifth part of *The Allegorical Neptune* there is a reference to Euripides with regard to the commentaries that this dramatic author makes about Hercules in his tragedy *Ifigenia* ([26] 4:383), but again the citation is with reference to the book by Natal Conti.

One of the books of the ancient world that most influenced Sor Juana was Ovid's *Metamorphosis*, which is cited twenty-three times and which served as a thematic basis for *The Divine Narcissus, Love Is Indeed a Labyrinth*, and *Loa in the Gardens*. Seneca is mentioned on thirteen occasions as a thinker, but not as a dramatic author. In addition, dispersed throughout Sor Juana's works there is reference to dramatic characters in Greek dramas, and we do not know if the nun was familiar with them through reading of original dramatic works or through epic and mythological works: Oedipus ([26] 1:174), Medea ([26] 1:10, 60, 154), Cassandra ([26] 1:236), the Cyclops ([26] 1:59) and Creon ([26] 4:227).

The writings of Sor Juana also include references to other Golden Age writers. Calderón de la Barca is mentioned on three occasions ([26] 3:312, [26] 4:119, [26] 4:136). The first mention is in the *Loa for the Birthday of the King [II]*:

Plebeian: Well, if my mind serves me
            well, all of you are familiar
            with the play,
            which is Calderón's,
            that says *In Life
            Everything Is Truth and Falsehood.*
            And so, your majesty,
            you will play the part of Cintia; loyalty
            will correspond to Libia;
            the role of nature
            belongs to Ismenia . . . ([26] 3:312)

There is allusion to the play by Calderón entitled *In Life Everything Is True and Everything Is False*, which Salceda speculates was performed on November 6, 1681 or 1682, with the *loa* by Sor Juana ("Cronología," 346), although historically this has not been proven because the chronicles of the era do not mention the celebration of the king's birthday on those dates. The reference compels one to think that Sor Juana at least read this Calderonian drama, since she refers to some of the characters in the drama: Focas, Cintia, Libia, and Ismenia. This work belongs to the Calderonian philosophical plays, along with *Life Is a Dream*, and, in the opinion of Everett W. Hesse, is based on *The Wheel of Fate* by Mira de Amescua ("Calderón in the Spanish Indies," 12-27).

Another mention of Calderón is in the second *sainete* of *The Trials of a Noble House*, as is discussed in the Fifth Critical Act: "One [play] by Calderón, Moreto o Rojas" ([26] 4:119). Calderón appears along with Rojas Zorrilla (1607) and Agustín Moreto (1618-1669), both belonging to the so-called Calderonian cycle (Ruiz Ramón, 258). The absence of Lope de Vega and the Mexican Juan Ruiz de Alarcón is worth noting. In the third act of *The Trials of a Noble House* one finds the third reference to the Spanish playwright: ". . . Let some part / that might resemble Calderón's inspire me / about how to get out of this entanglement!" ([26] 4:136). Other references by Sor Juana to the geniuses of the Golden Age are the following: the aforementioned Agustín Moreto and Francisco de Rojas Zorrilla[15] ([26] 4:119); Garcilaso de la Vega ([26] 1:321); Baltasar Gracían ([26] 4:455); and her beloved Luis de Góngora ([26] 1:174, [26] 1:269, [26] 1:355, [26] 4:369, [26] 4:372).

Among the many intellectual admirers of Sor Juana was a gentleman from Peru—a personage who has been identified as Luis de Oviedo y Rueda, Count of la Granja—who sent to Sor Juana a ballad that motivated her to write Ballad 49 as a reply to his missive ([26] 1:143). In the Peruvian ballad there is a reference to Sor Juana's dramaturgy in relation to Calderón's art:

> Only in Calderón do you follow
> the footsteps of de la Barca
> and you have made him greater
> by having competed with him. ([26] 1:151)

This is the only encomiastic reference to the dramaturgy of Sor Juana among the many praises that her contemporaries dedicated to her poetry during her lifetime and especially posthumously, and these were recorded in the editio princeps.

Comparative Study of the Three Plays

The Triangular Structure

The three plays possess a geometric structure (see fig. 1) by presenting three protagonists (two noblewomen and one favored suitor) who

The Second Celestina   *The Trials of a Noble House*   *Love Is Indeed a Labyrinth*

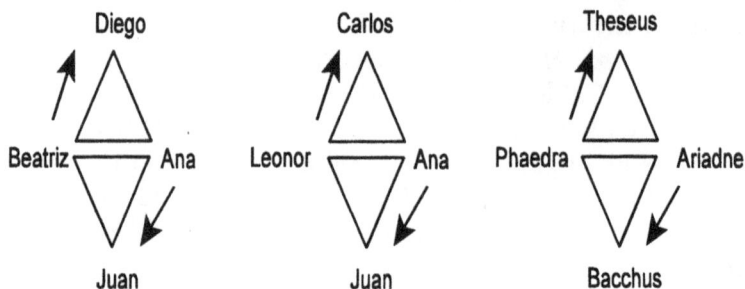

Diego   Carlos   Theseus

Beatriz ——— Ana   Leonor ——— Ana   Phaedra ——— Ariadne

Juan   Juan   Bacchus

Figure 1. The Double Triangular Structure of Sor Juana's Three Plays

can be exemplified by the vertices of a triangle. Another suitor of second preference—who is rejected by the female protagonist—forms, in turn, another triangle with the women. In several sonnets by Sor Juana these polarities, known as "opposing correspondences," have been identified: "Let not Fabio love me, since I love him, / my pain is without equal; / but let the abhorred Silvio love me, it's a lesser wrong, but no lesser annoyance"; and also the following: "Feliciano adores me, and I detest him; / Lisando detests me and I adore him" ([26] 1:288). Stephanie Merrim and Lee Alton Daniel have noted that the last two plays [*The Trials of a Noble House* and *Love Is Indeed a Labyrinth*] and *The Divine Narcissus* possess this same type of structure (Merrim, 98-110; Daniel, "A Terra Incognita," 94-96). Merrim has commented that in these "cloak and dagger" plays two noblemen usually court the same lady, whereas in Sor Juana's plays the ladies are the ones who have the amorous alternative of loving one nobleman and being courted by another (99). Beatriz, Leonor, and Phaedra triumph in their amorous pursuits and marry the noblemen of their choice, while the two Anas and Ariadne wed noblemen whom they had previously rejected for the love of the male protagonist.

The similar geometric structure in the three plays is an additional proof that Sor Juana was responsible for the plot and organization of all three plays, in spite of the fact that for the first and last she counted on the co-authorship of male dramatists.

Metric Study

The meter of the plays of Sor Juana illustrates her preferences in the use of versification and language. The three plays contain metrical forms characteristic of plays of the Golden Age, with occurrences of *romances* and *redondillas*. Table 1 compares the versification of the three plays.

The information in table 1 has as its base the studies by William C. Bryant and Thomas Austin O'Connor:[16] It is interesting to note that *The Second Celestina* does not have lyrics to be sung, in spite of the fact that Salazar y Torres was one of the initiators of the *zarzuela* (light opera). *The Trials of a Noble House* possesses one song and some verses in *arte menor* as musical accompaniment in the second act. And *Love Is Indeed a Labyrinth* has several songs, also in the second act. In comparison, in the three plays the *romance* (ballad) meter predominates at the beginning of the act (five times), the *silva pareada* (two times), and the *redondillas* (two times). Regarding the closings of an act, the ballad meter is used on eight occasions, and only in one closing are there *redondillas*. In general, the versification demonstrates a correspondence among the three plays, although with an increasing elaboration and variety of metrical forms. And the meter used in the *autos* by Sor Juana has an even greater elaboration.

Sor Juana's Art of Love

The three plays by Sor Juana are a treatise on the art of love that may be qualified as *Ars amandi* of baroque/mannerism. Salceda describes the amatory vocabulary of *The Trials of a Noble House* and *Love Is Indeed a Labyrinth* as a "treatise of love," and adds the following consideration: "Love appears as an object of study, analyzing with care and delectation its causes and motives, its development, its effects, its complications, its diverse types, the passions which with it covers every area of study: from divine love to the pretense of love; and it is always present, throughout the work, as a fundamental concern . . . pretexts for the author to continue her work on the philosophy of love" ("Introducción," [26] 4:xxii). Table 2 shows the amatory vocabulary of *The Second Celestina*, which is representative of the amatory vocabulary of the other two plays by Sor Juana.

Table 1. Versification of Sor Juana's Three Plays

Play	Act I	Act II	Act III
The Second Celestina[a] I: 1202 lines II: 1190 lines III: 1216 lines	Romance í-a Redondillas abba Romance á-a Romance é-a	Romances é-a Romances -ó	Silvas pareadas Romance á-o Redondillas abba Romances é-o Romances í-o Redondillas abba
The Trials of a Noble House I: 1042 lines II: 1049 lines III: 1280 lines	Redondillas Romance á-a Romance á-o Sonnet Romance í-a Silvas pareadas Romance á-a	Redondillas abba Romance ó-a Canción Coplas de arte menor Romance á-o Décimas Romance é-o	Romance é-a Redondillas abba Romance é-a Silvas pareadas Romance í-o Romance é-o
Love Is Indeed a Labyrinth I: 1274 lines II: 1093 lines III: 1264 lines	Romance á-a Dodecasyllable Romance á-a Sung romance Dodecasyllable Romance á-a Seguidilla Romance á-a Romance é-o Redondillas Romance -é Polimetric verses Romance -í Quintillas Romance á-o	Silvas pareadas Romance á-e Romance á-o Romance á-a Romance á-o with the intercalation of 2 Seguidillas 4 Canciones 4 Décimas 2 Redondillas Sonnet Romance í-o[b]	Romance é-e Prose letter Romance é-e Romance é-a Redondillas abba Romance í-o Prose letter Romance í-o Décimas Sonnet Romance ó-a Silva pareada Romance ú-a Romance -o Romance á-o Décimas Romance í-a

Canción: a varied number of lines of seven and eleven syllables
Coplas de arte menor: quatrains with verses of eight syllables or fewer
Décima: ten-line stanza of octosyllabic verse
Quintilla: five-line stanza in octosyllabic verse with consonant rhyme
Redondilla: quatrain in octosyllabic verse
Romance: ballad in octosyllabic verse
Seguidilla: quatrain of alternating verses of five and seven syllables with second and fourth in assonance
Silvas pareadas: rhyming couplets, alternating verses of seven and eleven syllables
[a] The ending by Vera Tassis has the following versification: *romances* í-a, *romances* é-o.
[b] The second act of *Love Is Indeed a Labyrinth* is written in different meters but with little variety of assonance: *silvas pareadas, romance* á-e, *romance* á-o, *romance* á-a, *seguidilla, romance* á-o, *seguidilla, romance* á-o, *canción, romance* á-o, *décima, canción, romance* á-o, *canción, romance* á-o, *décima, canción, romance* á-o, *redondilla, décima, romance* á-o, *redondilla, décima, romance* á-o, *sonnet,* and *romance* í-o.

Table 2. The Amatory Vocabulary of *The Second Celestina*

Absent one: person who is far away, 94

Adoration: maximum affection, such as toward God, 99

Affection: passion of the soul, 97, 99

Aloofness: indifference, harshness, displeasure, 56

Betrayal: breach of fidelity, 57, 97

Boldness: daring, 45

Cautiousness: precaution or reserve, 105, 107

Challenge: encounter or falling out; interesting event, 120, 205

Change: shift in amorous spirit, 120

Coarseness: discourtesy or lack of attention and respect, 53

Commitment: obligation or action for the sake of honor, 91, 135, 171, 177

Complaint: expression of pain and sorrow, 50, 122

Contempt: scorned love, disdain, 69, 180

Courteousness: expressions of affection and urbanity, 47, 109, 123, 140

Courtesy: action or effect of social fulfillment, 112

Decorum: circumspection or seriousness; purity or modesty, 99, 122

Diligence: care and effort of execution, 150

Disdain: indifference or coldness; diminished appreciation, 68, 69, 108, 109

Disillusionment: understanding of the truth behind a deception, 49, 214

Disloyalty: act against fidelity of love, 120

Distrust: mistrust or suspicion, 90

Favors: amorous actions, 52

Feigning: pretense; causing someone to believe what is not true, 97

Fineness: amorous activity or involvement, 11, 65, 76, 110, 133, 139

Flattery: affected praise, 107

Gallant: handsome man who courts a woman, 74

Grief: love pain, 67, 106

Honor: moral quality that leads us to strict fulfillment of our duties; reputation; decorum and modesty in women; good opinion of others, 103, 107, 121

Impertinence: irrelevant word or deed, 99, 118

Indecorum: lack of decorum or respect, 119

Insult: offense against honor, 45, 110, 202

Jealousy: anxiety when a beloved has changed his or her affections, 119

Longing: anguish or yearning, 67

Love: emotion by which the soul seeks the true good; passion that attracts members of the opposite sex, 107

Lovers: individuals in love, 111

Offense: act that offends or harms, 52, 107

Point of honor: personal honor and reputation, 149

Punishment: penalty imposed on one who has made a mistake in a love relationship, 85

Quarrel: trouble or falling out, 126, 190

Secret: something reserved or hidden, 72

Sophistry: use of sophist rationalizations or sophisms, 29

Spite: disaffection born of a lover's deception[a]

Suspicion: imaginary suspicion about love, 102

Sweethearts: lovers

Tyranny: excessive domination of an amorous passion, 49, 51, 97

Vengeance: satisfaction for an insult or harm, 74

Wild oats: mischief or disorderliness in young men, 182

Will: power to act by choice, 45, 61, 108, 110

Note: Numbers refer to pages in [27].
[a]*Spite* does not appear in *The Second Celestina*, but it is part of Sorjuanian language in the attitudes of the characters.

Paz has commented about the amorous poems of Sor Juana: "There are many and some are very profound. All reveal a perfect knowledge of what could be called the dialectic of love: jealousy, indifference, absence, forgetfulness, correspondence . . . The knowledge of the erotic that the poems and plays of Sor Juana reveal is, as much as or more than the result of an experience, a knowledge codified by tradition: a rhetoric, a casuistry and even a logic" (*The Traps of Faith,* 147). Because of their thematic relationship it is necessary to identify, together with the amatory poetry of Sor Juana, the ideas about love contained in her three plays.

Reception Codes for the Theater

When we read *The Divine Narcissus* or *The Trials of a Noble House,* we believe we have found a theater based on words, because it possesses beauty comparable to the best of the nondramatic poetry, but we forget that the baroque theater piece was a spectacle that had been written for a special festival, and that the mannerist spectacle was created for a feast day. The theological subtleties, the allusions to important persons and events of the time, and the mythological allegories were mere private games between the dramatist and some members of the audience, because if it is certain that the baroque works were theater productions for only one day—a Corpus Christi or another feast day—it is also certain that the dramatist knew, one by one, her audience's opinions and that the rest of their thoughts also were not strange to her.

The theater as a living phenomenon on the stage has been studied with success through semiology; hence it is indispensable to analyze Sor Juana's theater from that perspective. One must distinguish four codes of reception that serve as measuring instruments for the possible staging of her drama:

- Psychological code. It is worthwhile to study her theater in relation to the phenomenon of human perception and the means necessary for the message to be received.

- Ideological code. It is advisable to consider the knowledge of reality represented in Sor Juana's theater, with which the audience evaluates the world on the stage.

- Aesthetic-theatrical code. It is pertinent to analyze the public's understanding of the aesthetic aspects of the work within the genre of theater.

- Linguistic code. It is advisable to evaluate the effectiveness that the speeches in the text possess in order to be converted into meaningful words for the audience.[17]

These codes are utilized as criteria for the possible present-day staging of Sor Juana's plays, as will be seen in the corresponding Critical Acts.

The Greek theater, the Isabeline forum, and the playhouses of the Golden Age have been theatrical locations analyzed time and again by scholars. Architecture and drama are seen as unified in a single concept. Nevertheless, when today one thinks about the baroque theater, the first image that seems to come to mind is that of the tediousness of the interminable religious ceremonies—or in the mannerist theater, of the excessive protocols of life at court—failing to remember that they were, above all, festivals—the theater as a festivity—and that the sacramental *auto* came to include mixtures of piously religious and farcically pagan hagiography, with live dances and music, theatrical elements that contributed to the prohibition of the *autos* by Charles III in 1765.

In the seventeenth century an afternoon of theater in the palace included the presentation of a play, which would begin with a dramatic praise or *loa*, followed by humorous interludes or *sainetes* between the acts, and with original songs composed for the festival, and with a masque or *sarao* to conclude the spectacle. Eating and drinking were activities socially accepted as a complementary part of the spectacle, which changed the celebration into a gastronomical one. The *autos* were celebrations that remained for some time in the memories of those present. Plays were performed on carts or stages outside of the cathedrals, with as much pomp as that accorded today the solemn procession of Corpus Christi in the city of Valencia, Spain.[18] The baroque or mannerist festival was a celebration that brought together the arts that stimulated the senses: the ephemeral architectures and the adornments; the music and the songs; the dances and the masque; the visualization of the spectacle and the oral interpretation of the dialogues of the *loas*, the *autos*, and the plays with all their trappings; the floral arrangements and the pungent odor of the crowd; and the flavors of palace banquets or the fountains of wine and water and the distribution of sweets to the poor members of the audience (Díez Borque, *Theater and Festival*, 30). Just as at the dawn of the Golden Age the playhouse predominated as the location for plays, in the twilight of the baroque these theatrical celebrations took place in plazas and palaces.

Third Critical Act

Sor Juana's Poetics for Drama

The Dramatic Theory of Sor Juana

Just as Lope de Vega wrote an exposition of his dramatic theory in his controversial verse composition *The New Art of Writing Plays*, and just as Tirso de Molina left some written considerations about his dramatic art in *The Country Houses of Toledo*, so too did Sor Juana leave scattered, between lines and in the margins of plots, many commentaries on her artistic concept of writing plays.[1] Here, I propose a classification of these remarks by Sor Juana, in order thus to round out the discussion of her art of dramaturgy.

The Author's Criteria

For a definition of Sor Juana's concept of theater it is necessary to turn to the works themselves, especially the *autos*, because in them are found several clarifying remarks about Sor Juana's criteria as author, and since they are original commentaries, they yield insight into her dramatic theory. A speech in *The Divine Narcissus* serves as a paradigm of the dramatic criteria upon which Sor Juana based her dramaturgy and reveals her criteria:

> From here let the curious
> see if truth and fiction
> the meaning and the word,
> are reconciled. ([26] 1:33)

The audience receives the epithet of curious, of intellectually alive, of being able to judge the theatrical spectacle as an incipient critic, in order to be able to verify the equilibrium reached among the variables signaled by the author. This text allows us to identify four dramatic elements to which Sor Juana paid particular attention in her theater, *truth* versus *fiction* and *signified* versus *signifier*, which we can conceptualize as two polarities, one cognitive and the other semiotic. We can identify four elements of Sor Juana's theater: active intellectual perspective on the part of the audience based on curiosity; cognitive polarity between truth and fiction; semiotic polarity between signified and signifier; and dynamic equilibrium of the theater based on the above-mentioned polarities. Thus, according to the first polarity, truth (theology, in the case of *The Divine Narcissus*) and human fiction should be present without either predominating or being mutually exclusive elements, but rather as mutually subordinated elements, since fiction serves as a means for understanding truth. Allegory versus idea. The second polarity, between signified and the signifier, can be interpreted in current dramatic terminology as the effectiveness of the production in contrast to the dramatic text. Staging versus dramaturgy.

Table 3 shows two of Sor Juana's polarities and their definitions according to the *Dictionary of Authorities* (1726), which is almost contemporary with Sor Juana, as well as the modern meanings of semiotic theory for the theater. The three plays by Sor Juana, and especially the *autos* and the *loas*, are based on a dramatic conceptualization in which the elements of fiction and of *sentido de modo* (expression or performance) predominate over the elements of truth and symbol. Another significant text for understanding the scenic illusion is included in the *loa* of *The Martyr of the Sacrament*. There, she negates the possibility of magic and instead insists upon her intention of not wishing to have the audience deceived with verisimilitude:

> And this is the case, that I have
> the task of writing an *auto* . . .
> (which is not *Magic*, nor do I want
> to deceive you more
> with what is only *ingenuity*). ([26] 1:108-9)

Both dramatist and audience see creations borne of the ingenuity of fiction, which is intrinsically different from magic, since they are only *autos* and plays full of ingenuity, that is, of deceptive actions. This break from the theater that simulates reality is carried out by characters who know themselves to be theatrical entities; thus self-

Table 3. Two of Sor Juana's Polarities

	Cognitive Polarity		Semiotic Polarity	
	Degree of Truth vs	Degree of Fiction	Signified vs	Signifier
Definition in *Diccionario de Autoridades* (1726)	Conformity of something with reason, in such a manner that it convinces and persuades one to believe it as certain and infallible	Simulation with which one pretends to cover the truth or make one believe what is not certain	Perfect meaning of some proposition or clause	The note, cipher, and character that joined with others of the same kind, form diction or a word
Modern definition	Decoding of ideological elements (idea)	Decoding of imaginative elements (metaphor)	Scenic Semiotics; Decoding of the "density of signs" (Barthes)	Dramatic text

awareness gives way to metatheatricality, as is analyzed later in this Critical Act.

Theater as Visual Metaphor

Every dramatic work can be categorized in its conceptualization as a complete piece because of the three rhetorical tropes: (1) etonymy, if a character represents an individual without universalizing him, as in melodrama; (2) synecdoche, if a character is universalized to the point that he represents all of humankind, as in the best realist theater; and (3) metaphor, if the totality of the work is a simile for another totality, which may be the cosmos of the audience. The theater of Sor Juana is essentially metaphorical because it proposes a metatheatrical cosmos that is an allegory—a metaphor continued throughout the piece—of the world of the audience that attends the play:

Echo: I will tell you a story
         with the metaphor true,
         to see if the one by Echo
         corresponds to my tragedy. ([26] 1:32)

I.A. Richards has distinguished two elements in every metaphor: the tenor, which is the idea communicated, and the vehicle (Holman, 313-14), which is the semiotic medium it uses. The theater of Sor Juana uses the visual image as a primary vehicle and the word as a secondary vehicle. For the modern reader the ideological tenor and the secondary vehicle, the word, are the predominant elements in the reader's own decoding, as opposed to what a spectator used to experience at Sor Juana's plays, in which the visual vehicle was the primary one.

For the modern reader Sor Juana's dramatic works seem predominantly textual, given the excellent utilization of verse and the erudition of her lexicon, but that textual exuberance should be compared with baroque retables, in which detail is lost in order to give precedence to the overall effect. Let us imagine for a moment the productions of these baroque pieces, in the middle of the cathedral square or in a great hall of a viceroy, with the hubbub of a popular celebration, the coming and going of courtiers, without the advantages of modern sound systems. What would the audience in the plaza witness? Enough words to enjoy the plot of the *auto*, but most of all, the gestures and movements on stage. And what of the courtiers in attendance at a royal or viceroyal play? They especially witnessed the visual aspect, lacking modern programs and without any other information that was not spread by palace gossip. Unquestionably, the theater of the baroque and mannerist era was predominantly visual, although it also shared the literary refinement of pleasing the audience and the skillful representation of ideas.

Allegorical Characters and Human Characters

The theater of Sor Juana presents a spectrum of characters, such as Conjecture, that are theatrical entities lacking humanity and that personify virtues or qualities in metatheatrical space and time (that is, they can only exist on the stage), such as the characters in the sacramental *autos*, *loas*, and *villancicos*. These characters share their metatheatrical essence with the characters of the play, upon gaining consciousness of the metatheatrical world where they live and by not possessing an inventory of traits that bring them nearer to the human, because they were created so that they would never possess a complete humanity. Of all of Sor Juana's characters, the noblewoman is the character that most approaches the human being.

If one categorizes the characters of Sor Juana's theater according to their degree of humanity or lack of it, then four basic types are identified: (1) characters with complete humanity; (2) sentimental entities that are a composite of the sentiments of the protagonists of the play; (3) characters with complete external humanity but without interior humanity, such as the characters of the comic foils; and (4) mental entities that are the embodiment of concepts, such as Conjecture in the *autos*. In the palace celebration, chorus and song also appeared on the stage, but these royal men and women who sang or recited before the guests at the festival—who shared the same human nature with the audience—were in their time made theatrical, upon being presented together with the metatheatrical characters of the *loa* or play. Consequently, in this spectrum of characters the abstract reigned over the concrete, and the universal over the individual, a balance that is characteristic of baroque thought.

Figure 2 exemplifies the distribution of Sor Juana's characters according to their degree of humanization or fictionalization. Sor Juana describes the comic foils in *Love Is Indeed a Labyrinth* as jackanapes (*mequetrefes*) because they are characters without independent dramatic causality or a complete psychology:

Atún: And if perchance they ask me,
　　　　it will be easy to answer them
　　　　that I am one of those who
　　　　are always coming in and going out
　　　　without themselves knowing why
　　　　they come and why they go;
　　　　about whom, an author
　　　　of jokes and *sainetes*,
　　　　found no definition,
　　　　other than to call them *jackanapes*. ([26] 4:302)

The *mequetrefe* (jackanapes) is a meddlesome, quarrelsome, and somewhat useless man, according to this word of uncertain origin— Portuguese, Arabic, or Mexican.[2] The dialogue continues with humorous prattle:

Racimo: Hey, you there!
Atún: What do you want of me?
Racimo: Who are you?
Atún: I'm *Mequetrefe*.
Racimo: And whom do you serve?

Reality ————————————————————————→ Theatrical Fiction

Palace Celebration   Play   *Auto/loa/villancico*

Song→ **Chorus** → **Noblewoman** → **Gallant** → **Comic foil/Jackanapes** → **Conjecture**

Human ————————————————————————→ Allegory

Concrete and individual   Abstract and universal

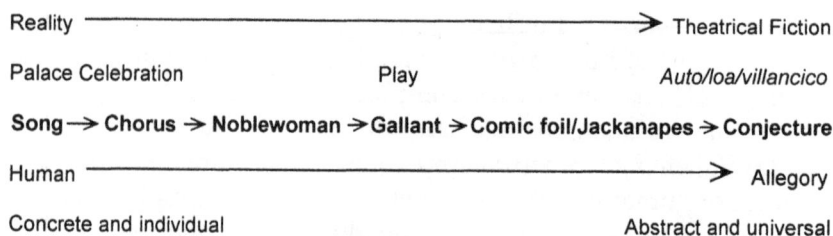

Figure 2. Distribution of Sor Juana's Characters

Atún:	I serve *Mequetrefe*.
Racimo:	Who is *Mequetrefe*?
Atún:	I am.
Racimo:	You're lying.
Atún:	I'm not lying.
Racimo:	Yes, you are.
Atún:	What are you saying, man! Look,
	you're offending many people;
	because the lineage
	of the Meques and the Trefes is very long. ([26] 4:302-3)

The comic foil lies twice, once about his personal independence and again about his noble ancestry stemming from a lineage from every aspect of Cretan society, which is a metaphor for the Hispanic environment. Another polarizing reference to the human being and the mental entity is found in *The Second Celestina* in a gradatory verse on the concepts of "Man, illusion or phantom," whose extremes correspond to the complete Human in contrast to illusory Conjecture ([27] 99), the former being a concrete and individual being and the latter an abstract and universal entity.

Conflicts of Thought and Conflicts of Action

Conflict as a dramatic element has been ubiquitous through the ages, being understood more as the collision of wills and actions rather than of ideas. The theater of Sor Juana employs conflicts of action in the plays, but it prefers the conflict of ideas in the *loas* and *sainetes*. One might think that ideas pertain more to the genre of the essay, but the baroque theater brings controversy to the stage with the personification of antagonistic ideas in conjectures (*conujeturas*) or fictional entities.[3] In the action plays, the confrontation between

two or more characters is followed until the conflict is resolved;
while in the plays of ideological conflict, the ideas are counterpoised
until a truth is reached by means of a dialectic, as in the Greek theater, where there existed an oratorical duel, or *stichomythia*, with
arguments and counterarguments until a resolution was attained
through the logic of a syllogism (Pavis, 463). The dramatic dialectic
of Sor Juana is related to baroque thought because it does not consti-
tute an irrefutable proof of the truth, but rather the opportunity to
demonstrate its ability for reasoning. While the conflict of action
requires the humanization of tensions that generate the struggle,
with the need for achieving the verisimilitude of the real world, the
conflict of ideas ought to create a dimension separate from the real
one, with the creation of dramatic entities that govern themselves
by their own laws. The first is based on the theatrical illusion that
presents actors as if they were real beings; the second is based on the
fiction that creates entities, that is, human creations who do not
submit to the laws of verisimilitude but instead proclaim their theatrical and metaphysical condition. In three words: Imagination over
fantasy.

In *The Scepter of Joseph* there is a dialogue that elaborates these
concepts of dramatic theory:

Conjecture: ... But (since
         license has already been *given*
         to make of myself a *visible object*),
         just like a human being
         I will act, using human *speech*
         necessary for the usage
         of the *style on the Stage*:
         so, to understand the *meaning*
         of the mode that is being used,
         they don't bother the intelligent man
         and the ignorant man needs them. ([26] 1:236)

The "*license ... given*" is nothing more than the theatrical convention that makes the character a visible object, as if it were human,
using dialogue or indispensable human speech for theatrical style
as a means of acquiring knowledge. Table 4 presents the observations of Conjecture expressed in the format of cognitive and semiotic
polarities in Sor Juana's theater, which were discussed earlier with
respect to *The Divine Narcissus*.

Table 4. Observations of Conjecture Expressed in the Format of Cognitive and Semiotic Polarities in Sor Juana's Theater

	Cognitive Polarity		Semiotic Polarity	
	Degree of Truth	vs Degree of Fiction	Signified	vs Signifier
Definition given by character of Conjecture	Substance of being and doing (behavior)	Style of the stage: license to make the object visible	*Sentido de modo* (expression or performance)	Human speech

Once again, now in a different work, Sor Juana refers us to the *sentido de modo* (expression or performance) in dramatic discourse, utilizing human speech as the means—a theatrical concept that we cannot interpret as the sole understanding of the theme, but rather as the sensitive perception of the spectacle. For this reason, her dramaturgy is predominantly visual, or stated with greater clarity, it is a theater in which the visual should surpass the verbal form and theme, as she expresses in poem 211: "Listen to me with your eyes, / since your ears are so aloof" ([26] 1:313).

Theatrical convention, in the words of Pavis, is the combination of ideological and aesthetic assumptions, explicit or implicit, that permit the spectator to understand the play correctly (97-99). Thus theatrical convention is subject to dramatic reception codes belonging to each generation of theatergoers. The baroque and mannerist codes, as discussed in later Critical Acts dedicated to the three plays, are only partially decodable for the modern spectator, especially the ideological code and the aesthetic-theatrical code. Nevertheless, if we accept the metatheatrical convention of dramatic entities, such as Conjecture and Mequetrefe, the theater of Sor Juana, and in general the theater of the end of the seventeenth century, takes on a new vitality and can once again provide an entertaining evening of theater more than three centuries after the first opening night.

Principal Dramatic Influences

The dramatic structure invented by Lope de Vega prevailed until the end of the baroque and is present in the theater of Sor Juana. Lope de Vega recognizes three phases of dramatic action, as Everett W. Hesse has pointed out:

- Act I. The expression, whereby the opposition of forces precipitates dramatic action. This serves as an introduction.

- Act II. The complication; this traces the development of the initial conflict to the point of greatest complexity, the climax that often appears with the arrival of the protagonist and antagonist.

- Act III. The denouement, the resolution of the conflict. This varies in duration; sometimes it is prolonged, and at other times it almost coincides with the climax. It is generally the briefest part of the plot. (Hesse, *La comedia y sus intérpretes*, 26)

The plays of Sor Juana adhere to these three phases of action. The first act begins *in medias res* in the first two plays. The first scene of *The Second Celestina* presents the fortuitous and unfortunate encounter of Beatriz, who is dressed as a huntress, with don Juan:

Beatriz: Sir, if you step
  forward, you will make my ire
  with the sound of this gun
  answer your audacity. ([27] 45)

The influence of Lope in this work is not limited to the dramatic structure; it is present also in the theme, since *The Trials of a Noble House* was inspired by his play *The Discreet Lady in Love*, as is discussed in the Fifth Critical Act. Lope's influence is also apparent in the poetic work of Sor Juana, as has been shown by Lucille K. Delano (79-94).

The Trials of a Noble House begins when doña Ana and Celia, her servant, are waiting for don Pedro: "*Ana:* Until my brother arrives, / Celia, we must wait for him" ([26] 4:27). By contrast, *Love Is Indeed a Labyrinth* has a slower introduction, as the Chorus tells of the misfortunes of Theseus, and it is not until the end of the second scene that the dramatic motive of the love of Ariadne and Phaedra for Theseus, the male protagonist, appears.

The second acts are very important in Sor Juana's works because the author carefully maneuvers the plot to the climax, which takes place before the close of the act. In *The Second Celestina*, the dramatic crux becomes complicated when the two noblewomen discover that they love the same suitor, which generates greater complexity of plot. In *The Trials of a Noble House*, the climax is in

Scene 2, with the gathering of all the characters under the musical backdrop of a lyrical song; and in *Love Is Indeed a Labyrinth*, in Scene 3, where the ball in the palace and the lyrical tone present an intercalated ballet that allegorizes the play. The denouement or disentanglement occurs in the final scene of the three plays; in the first two plays there is a multiple wedding with three couples, and in the last play there are four couples. The last scene is very similar in the three plays, as much as for the speed with which the noblemen decide to marry as for the even greater haste with which the servants, who are the ones to bring the play to its close, wed in parallel fashion.

At the end, the dramatic importance of the two servants is confirmed because the focus of the scene ceases to be on the happy noble couples, in order to observe the more serene and less elaborate wedding of the lower classes. The traditional appeal for forgiveness in the first two plays is spoken by the servants, Antonia and Castaño, respectively, but this is not the case in the third, since it is Captain Tebandro, who has just lost the war against the Athenians, who petitions forgiveness.

The last lines of the three plays by Sor Juana are shown in table 5 with the aim of making a comparison easier. In the endings of the first two plays reference is made to the title, as was the accepted custom, but this is not the case in *Love Is Indeed a Labyrinth*, which only presents the usual entreaty for forgiveness despite the fact that the phrase *Love Is Indeed a Labyrinth* contains only eight syllables in Spanish. *The Trials of a Noble House* achieves, in six Spanish syllables, a baroque apology. It is worth noting among the similarities, the servants' joyful, quick, and good-humored acceptance of marriage; this is a constant in the three plays by Sor Juana.

The influence of Calderón in the work of Sor Juana is great, but it would be more appropriate to identify this influence as coming from the so-called Calderonian cycle, since we do not know how much Sor Juana was influenced directly by reading or attending the staging of any of the *autos* or plays by Calderón. The influence could be due to her knowledge of the theater of Calderón's contemporaries, such as Francisco de Rojas Zorrilla and Agustín Moreto, or of the dramatists described as post-Calderonian, especially Agustín de Salazar y Torres.[4] The debt that Sor Juana's plays owe to those by Moreto has not yet been shown sufficiently, especially regarding the

Table 5. Sor Juana's Servants' Acceptance of Marriage

The Second Celestina	The Trials of a Noble House	Love Is Indeed a Labyrinth
Muñoz: I'm saying Antonia, give me your hand in marriage, since any old lackey can get married easily enough without getting ready at all. *Antonia:* Wonderful, even though you have been silent and there has never been the chance to become my husband, and to have wooed me, take this wonderful hand, which is the envy of soot, and here, my lords and ladies, ends *The Second Celestina.* ([227] 223)	*Castaño:* Tell me, Celia, some sweet words and see if you don't have a hand [for marriage] at hand. *Celia:* I don't have it with me, I left it in the kitchen; but will a finger be enough for you? *Castaño:* Give it to me, it's the bad finger, it's the one I find myself with. And here, most nobel lords and ladies, and here, discreet audience, *The Trials of a Noble House* ends. Forgive its errors. ([26] 4:352)	*Racimo:* Here I am. *Cintia:* And I'll accept you, because it would be foolish to lose this chance. *Atún:* Laura, it's not good that jealousy remain between us. *Laura:* You're right...and so here is my hand in marriage. *Tebandro:* And the writer, exhausted, begs your forgiveness for writing contrary to the genius that animates her, she wrote to serve you, without knowing what she was writing

idea of Sor Juana's comic foil. She perhaps read a manuscript copy or some of the first editions by this Madrid playwright that appeared in the second half of the seventeenth century, since *Disdain in Exchange for Disdain,* according to Méndez Plancarte, influenced the second *sainete* of *The Trials of a Noble House* ([26] 4:558). The names of Moreto's comic foils seem to have inspired those of Sor Juana: the comic foil in *Treason Avenged,* by Moreto, is named Castaño, the same as the comic foil in *The Trials of a Noble House;* also, in *The Look-Alike at Court,* by Moreto, Tacón is the namesake of the comic foil in *The Second Celestina.* In addition, Moreto's idea of the woman who advocates the freedom to choose a husband prefigures the female protagonists in Sor Juana's plays.

Elements of Sor Juana's Theater

Sor Juana uses a great variety of dramatic elements and techniques, some belonging to the genre of poetry and others pertaining specifically to the stage. These elements are grouped into four categories: dramatic elements; linguistic elements; dramatic rhetoric; and metatheater.[5]

Dramatic Elements

Dialogue. The use by Sor Juana of diegetic elements, recapitulation and asides, soliloquies, and monologues, shows the Calderonian influence in her work.

Diegetic Elements. The use of narrative or diegetic elements is an obligatory technique in the first act of the three plays by Sor Juana. With this she describes the events that have transpired before the act begins, for example, the long speech by doña Leonor with the autobiographical connotations about the author in *The Trials of a Noble House* ([28] 36-43) and the first speech by Theseus in *Love Is Indeed a Labyrinth* ([26] 4:223-30), which summarizes the wars between Athens and Crete.

Recapitulation. By means of this form of dialogue a summary of the events already staged or known to the audience is presented, perhaps because the audience did not follow the production in detail. An example is when doña Ana summarizes the dramatic action in the following soliloquy:

> Heavens, what a fix I'm in:
> in love with Carlos
> pursued by don Juan
> with my enemy in my home
> with disloyal servants
> and with my brother waiting for me! ([26] 4:61)

Another example of recapitulation is the long speech by don Carlos at the end of *The Second Celestina*, in which he summarizes the plot of the second and third acts ([27] 181). In this play, Celestina summarizes the dramatic conflict before the final denouement:

Celestina: Ladies, let's get to the heart of things
            the matter is a bit lively:

you are jealous of don Juan;
you feel the same about don Diego,
don Juan is jealous of don Diego. ([27] 205)

Asides, Soliloquies, and Monologues.[6] An aside is the oral expression of thoughts, and in Sor Juana's work there is abundant use of this dramatic element, for example: *Celia:* "For the envy that she feels toward her / I wouldn't want to be in her shoes" ([26] 4:35). A soliloquy is a discourse that a character has with himself, without being aware that the audience is listening to him. A shared soliloquy closes the first two acts of *Love Is Indeed a Labyrinth* with ten and eighteen asides, respectively, which exemplify the inner thoughts of the characters. The monologue is intrinsically metatheatrical, since the character is aware that the audience is listening to him, as in the magnificent monologue by Castaño, perhaps the most successful scene in all of Sor Juana's plays ([26] 4:135-38)—the parodical transformation of the comic foil into a noblewoman, with a humorous dialogue of great impact on the stage:

Now I am dressed. And who would doubt
that the moment they see me
four thousand of those handsome men
who go around flirting with whomever they can
will pursue me,
and they will fall madly in love with an image
not with the beauty that is present
but with that which they imagine? ([26] 4:138)

Interruptions of the Dialogue/Asides. Daniel has pointed out an element that appears in Calderón and that is utilized by Sor Juana: the interruption of the dialogue by continual asides in order to increase the dramatic tension ("A Terra Incognita," 115). For example, Calderón writes,

Well, how (I can't speak)
is it (my tongue goes mute)
possible (my voice becomes faint)
that you (my breath freezes up)?
(*Devotion to the Mass, Comedias,* 3:249)

Sor Juana writes,

in such a place (what torture!)
two women (what disrespect!)

disguised (what indecency!),
I find alone with two men?
Love Is Indeed a Labyrinth, [26] 4:341)

Structure. The plays of Sor Juana possess a linear structure, although in some cases she experiments with parallel scenes, as in the first act of *Love Is Indeed a Labyrinth,* or with analepsis or flashback based on narrated recapitulation—never staged, as was done in the subsequent theater.

Respect for the Classical Unities. The three plays by Sor Juana respect, more than their contemporaries', the unities of time, space, and action. Time is extended to cover more than one night, just as the space is reduced to several focused centers of attention, such as the interior of the house or the garden. The action is, in the three cases, the free will of women, exemplified by the sophisms of the female protagonists in order to escape the laws and limitations that the patriarchal society imposes upon them, and thus, by the end, to find love according to their own definition and personal desire.

Fusion of the Arts and Sciences. Sor Juana makes use of music in the *loas* that accompany *The Trials of a Noble House* and *Love Is Indeed a Labyrinth,* plays in which there is a lyric scene in the second act. The use of music in baroque plays came to be an obligatory element, to the point that Calderón and Salazar y Torres are pioneering authors of the *zarzuela. The Second Celestina* does not contain music, a contrast between the dramatic production of Sor Juana and that of Salazar. On the other hand, in many of the dramatic works by Sor Juana her interest in science and history is evidenced by the abundant astronomical and historical references scattered throughout her theater, as happens in the *loa* of *Love Is Indeed a Labyrinth,* with its allusions to different forms of the measurement of time. Her interest in theology is equally reflected in her *autos* and *villancicos.*

Stage Directions. Stage directions in Sor Juana's theater are sparse but indicative of a visual theater. One can identify a primary level of stage direction that signals the entrance and exit of characters and some minimal, pertinent information, as the following stage directions demonstrate:

- *The Second Celestina*: "Enter don Diego," "They exit," "Upon exiting Muñoz, doña Ana and doña Beatriz enter, veiled," "Doña

Ana goes over to don Juan and doña Beatriz goes over to don Diego," "Both exit, don Luis enters, from the wings." There are no stage directions at the close of the play.

- *The Trials of a Noble House*: "Enter doña Ana and Celia," "Enter doña Leonor, while don Juan is exiting," "Enter doña Leonor, wearing a cloak," "They draw their swords; and doña Ana and don Juan enter, holding hands, and through the other door Celia and Castaño, dressed as a noblewoman, enter." There is no final stage direction.

- *Love Is Indeed a Labyrinth*: "Singing the following song offstage, and Ariadne and Phaedra enter, as princesses; Laura and Cintia, as servants," "They speak in secret," "Drums play and Cintia and Laura enter, frightened," "Enter Licas, as a general, and Athenian soldiers." There is no final stage direction.

There are no stage directions of a secondary level referring to the emotions of the characters, so common later on; neither are there any that can be described as being of a tertiary level, in which the dramatist puts forward some idea about the aesthetics of the staging or about the perspective on the characters or the events on the stage.

The stage directions contained in the *autos* are more specific, as happened normally during the Golden Age, since the plays were staged in courtyards or at a palace, familiar theatrical locales, while the sacramental *autos* had to be improvised in New Spain by individuals less adept at the theatrical art. A sampling of stage directions will serve as an example:

Enter the West, a Gallant Indian, wearing a crown and America, at his side, as a splendid Indian woman: in native costume . . . (The Divine Narcissus, [26] 3:3)

[The executioner] is seen striking him a blow, and the cart closes up. The second cart opens, in which there is an altar with the Host and Chalice; and below, two Choruses of Music, and Faith and the other virtues . . . Martyr of the Sacrament, [26] 3:181)

Another cart opens; and in it is Jacob, asleep at the foot of the Ladder, and above, the Lord; and from inside, a Voice is singing . . . (The Scepter of Joseph, [26] 3:208)

These stage directions inform us of the mental preferences of the author, and they invite us to imagine what a contemporary theatrical director could create with these scenes, for example, a Grotowsky or a Peter Brook. According to the aesthetic code, the theater of Sor Juana is not only valid but favored by contemporary theories that support the theater as a visual spectacle, broadly based on advanced scenic technology that we rely on today.

Linguistic Elements

Linguistic excess has served as a basis for emphasizing the presence of Calderón in the dramatic work of Sor Juana.

Metaphor. Among the infinite similes and metaphors, there are some that are repeated, such as jealousy, described with the metaphors "Basilisk fire" ([26] 4:102); and for passion, "I have an Etna inside my soul" ([26] 4:106). Some of the metaphors bear a resemblance to Calderonian ones.

Oxymoron. This is the rhetorical antithesis that presents two terms that are mutually contradictory, it is also called antiphrasis.

Calderón writes, "Being a living skeleton," "being a dead animal" (*Life Is a Dream*, 46). Sor Juana writes, "Fire will freeze snowflakes," "ice will shoot out sparks" (*The Trials of a Noble House*, [26] 4:127).

Play on Words or Paronomasia. This is the inversion of the terms of a proposition into a subsequent one so that the sense of the latter forms the antithesis of the former. It amounts to a rhetorical balance.

Calderón writes, "I am a man among beasts / and a beast among men" (*Life Is a Dream*, 46); Sor Juana writes, "With my cunning in lying, my ability to feign / fed me at midday" (*The Second Celestina*, [27], 215) and "And here they sing about their sorrows / and there they suffer what they sing" (*Love Is Indeed a Labyrinth*, [26] 4:209).

Greco-Latin Mythology. Daniel has pointed out that the use of classical references in the plays by Sor Juana is not baroque ornamentation, as effectual as that was during that time, but rather an integral part of the dramas ("A Terra Incognita," 101), for example, "vassal of Venus" in the *The Second Celestina* ([27], 182); Ephebe and Hymen in *The Trials of a Noble House*; and the abundant references in *Love Is Indeed a Labyrinth*, itself based on a classical theme: Athens, Crete, and Thebes, from geography; Minotaur, Hercules, Creon, Sciron, Procrustes, the dog Cerberus, Pluto, and other references to the ancient world; as well as the characters in the play: Theseus and Phaedra, Ariadne and Bacchus.

Dramatic Rhetoric

The use of visual images based on words abounds in the plays; as does the use of irony, parody, the suppression of euphemism, and dialectic, as the following paragraphs illustrate.

Images. The Calderonian images are primarily visual (Hesse, *La comedia*, 35). The four elements of fire, air, earth, and water, so important in the conceptualization of the ancient world, are well known, and were utilized as a metaphor by Calderón on numerous occasions. In *The Second Celestina* we find these four images:

> So, I will adore your lights
> equally, as the one who saw
> in succession, the bright star,
> the pearl, the bird and the flower. ([27] 144)

Daniel has identified three of the four Calderonian images in one of the speeches by Leonor ([26] 4:127): fire in stars, water in the sea and waves, and earth in the fortress and sand, but the fourth element is missing, which signifies a disharmony in the life of the protagonist ("A Terra Incognita," 105).

Irony. This is an expression that exchanges the literal meaning for the opposite one. Three types of irony may be identified in the texts by Sor Juana:

- Linguistic irony. This is a play on words that uses irony, such as the commentary by Castaño in front of don Carlos with regard to his lady: "Well, if she's the sun, how could she be without any brilliance?" ([26] 4:79), with the double meaning of doubting whether or not she is his flame, and of affirming that just as the sun cannot lose its brilliance, so Leonor needs her cosmetics.

- Dramatic irony. When it is the audience and not the characters who know the truth about what is happening on the stage, as happens with the mistaken identities so common in Sor Juana's plays.

- Philosophical irony. This is an ironic consideration of the human condition, for example: "Let him die lowly / he who was born so high in life," ([26] 4:210). Another philosophical irony is the one referring to Theseus: "he who yesterday ruled a kingdom / now serves a kitchen helper" ([26] 3:212).

Parody. Parody is a burlesque imitation of an already existing work, as Sor Juana does in *The Trials of a Noble House* with the famous soliloquy by Segismundo (cited by Daniel, "A Terra Incognita," 94):

Carlos: Heavens! What's this I'm hearing?
          Is it an illusion, is it a spell
          that has come over me?
          Who am I? Where am I? ([26] 4:99)

Another example is in the same play, in which she parodies names cited in the story that appears in the puppet show in the second part of Cervantes' *Don Quijote:*

Celia: I'll do no such thing,
         I'll close the door,
         and I'll go tell Marsilio
         that Melisendra is leaving. ([26] 4:130)

Another example is when the servant Muñoz defines his master through the use of parody and with a Cervantine expression: "My master is a knight errant / who goes around righting wrongs" ([27] 181).

Additionally, there is a second type of parody that makes reference to the very play itself and its characters, as when Racimo, in *Love Is Indeed a Labyrinth*, parodies the story of the Minotaur: "There isn't much difference / between being a bull and Bacchus" ([26] 4:248), and when the same servant parodies the god of wine: "I'm really afraid that out of thirst / I'll have to drink up my master" ([26] 4:255). Furthermore, when the characters have the self-awareness of parodying their own play, they engage in metatheater:

Tacón: I didn't think that you were such a noble lady
         but let yourself love
         at least, and imagine
         that she is Prince Fedro
         and you are the Princess Tesea. ([26] 4:239)

Suppression of Euphemism. In some speeches, the characters present their ideas without seeking expressions of gentility or decorum highly esteemed in the mannerist period:

Castaño: Now I'm not amazed that
           women are so haughty,

because there's nothing that'll make a
woman conceited faster than her being begged. ([26] 4:140)

In Sor Juana's ending to *The Second Celestina* there appears a negative commentary about popular murmurings:

Beatriz: Circulating through Seville
the murmurings of the blind masses . . .
Because in similar cases
where the Common People is a severe judge
of what is reprehensible and what is praiseworthy
the Common People always choose the worst. ([27] 176-77)

The infrangible judgment by don Rodrigo is an example of the meager delicateness with which women were regarded in a world preponderantly patriarchal, as reflected in *The Trials of a Noble House*:

Rodrigo: Oh, women! Oh, poisonous monster!
Who trusts in you,
whether through insanity or boldness,
with the same degree
the ignorant woman and the wise woman are ruined? ([26] 4:48)

Dialectic. Sor Juana's characters seem to enjoy discussing ideas with positive and negative propositions, such as the first speech by Theseus in *Love Is Indeed a Labyrinth*, which begins as follows:

Theseus: Listen so that you will know
in two opposing actions
in the changeability of fate
what I lose and what you gain. ([26] 4:223)

Another model of the efforts at rationalization by the characters is a speech in the same play spoken by Ariadne:

How much better it is to
flee the cruel, amorous adventure,
since by fleeing
I free him from death
and myself from dying with him;
therefore I am faithful today
to our relationship,
as my love trusts in
his nobility, let it restore me,
seeing that I liberate his nobility,
as thus mine and his together. ([26] 4:319)

Metatheater

This element is one of the most often cited as defining the theater of Sor Juana; it is said to be a forerunner of the dramatic techniques developed by Luigi Pirandello in the twentieth century, a critical evaluation first mentioned by Francisco Monterde in his study *Sainetes of Sor Juana.* Paz, for his part, affirms that "the Renaissance and baroque theaters invented the theater within the theater, as Velázquez painted on canvas the very act of painting, but the dramatic poets of the sixteenth and seventeenth centuries, as best as I remember, never broke with the convention that separates the spectator from the stage" (*The Traps of Faith,* 435). The first critic who noted the true nature of this technique *Ad Spectatores* was Daniel, with a new definition of this form that "some consider . . . a modern technique, or a precursor to the future, [but that] should perhaps be considered rather as a continuation of the Greco-Latin theater" ("A Terra Incognita," 97).

This technique belongs to metatheater, according to the term coined by Lionel Abel in his book *Metatheatre,* or metadrama, according to the later definition by Richard Hornby. This last critic has identified several dramatic forms that allow a break with verisimilitude and achieve an intensification of the communication of the theatrical phenomenon, as one finds throughout the history of the theater, from the Greeks to the Isabeline theater, and from the Spanish baroque to modern authors such as Strindberg, Brecht, Beckett, and Pinter. Pirandello also is cited by Hornby for his metadramas, but with the difference that in his works one sees a change of roles that becomes reality: the characters move from voluntarily altering their personalities with a change of roles, to a change of roles that then becomes involuntarily an integral part of their personalities, as in *Henry IV.*

Many elements of Sor Juana's theater, and of the baroque/mannerist theater in general, possess metadramatic characteristics. The asides are words that the characters direct to the audience in order to express their intimate sentiments, without the other characters' hearing them. Using this element, the author arranges for the spectator/reader to participate within the work, since in many cases the characters directly ask them for help or understanding. As a result, the asides demonstrate that the characters are aware of the existence of the audience, and thus verisimilitude vanishes, since those being observed by their own kind are not human beings, but rather dramatic entities who change the norms of human perception upon becoming self-theatricalizing, with the consequent theatricalization of the audience/reader. Thus the work does not reflect life, but rather it reflects itself. In his excellent theoretical work *Drama, Metadrama, and Perception*, Hornby has identified five types of metatheatricality: theater within the theater; ceremony within the theater; change of roles within the character; references to literature and to real life; and self-reference (33).

Theater within the Theater. The format of the baroque festival is like a series of Chinese boxes that mark different levels of verisimilitude/metatheatricality. The *loa* and the *sarao* are highly metadramatic, given the use of characters like Conjecture, but since the performance takes place in space and time, the audience perceives the play within the *loa*, the songs, and the *sarao*. On the other hand, in many of the scenes the audience observes a character who, in turn, observes other characters. This we describe as the "audience" within the work, as happens in the third act of *The Trials of a Noble House* and in the first act of *Love Is Indeed a Labyrinth*. The same may be said of the scene with the mirror trick in *The Second Celestina*, in which the old woman manages to lead don Diego out of the house under the noses of the characters who are hiding ([27] 155-59).

Ceremony within the Theater. The *loa* is a ceremony exalting a powerful figure and is a community festival. The *villancicos* and the *autos* share the dramatic structure and the language of the Christian liturgy, which is the ceremony par excellence in the West. The entire mannerist festival is also a palace ceremony that borrows forms and words from the courtly protocol.

Change of Roles within the Character. This element takes place when a character dresses as another or pretends to be another, as does the comic foil Castaño in *The Trials of a Noble House*. He disguises himself as a woman, parodying the noblewoman herself and making a suitor fall in love with this false figure. In the baroque and mannerist theater the woman disguised as a man was very common. Thus Sor Juana inverts the change of roles, managing to parody the "cloak and dagger" plays and to ridicule male protagonists.

Another example is when, at the end of the third act of *The Second Celestina*, the noblewomen disguise themselves so that they will not be recognized by other characters, in order to go to the house of Celestina ([27] 186).

References to Literature and to Real Life. On many occasions there is a break with verisimilitude in order to direct a speech directly to a person in the audience, with an aside or a monologue, and with the consequent fictionalization of the audience, which is placed in the same circumstances as the characters. There are many references to personages from real life, historical as well as contemporary, as if the dramatic entities belonged to the time and space of the baroque audience. The mythological and literary references cause the plays to relate to other areas of human knowledge as if they pertained to a grand system that serves as a reference. The second *sainete* of *The Trials of a Noble House* is an example charged with references to real life: Cavite, a prison in the Philippines; Deza, owner of the house where the play was performed; Calderón, Moreto, and Rojas, authors whom the characters cite; mention of Celestina; calling the play itself a ridiculous work and considering it poor; reference to Silvanus and Arcadia; and the intertextuality of citing the ballad by Góngora: "So many boos, so many cat-calls!" ([26] 4:557).

Self-Reference. This element is observed when the characters of the play stop the dramatic action and for an instant possess a consciousness of their own metatheatrical quality, mentioning the structure or some other scenic element, with the total destruction of verisimilitude. It acts as a reminder to the audience that what it sees is not part of life, but rather part of theater:

Celestina: And let the audience beware
                that this play has been
                the first in which the old man has hidden himself. ([27], 161)

Another example is the closing of the second act in the words of Castaño in *The Trials of a Noble House*: "Come on, stop complaining / the act will be too long / if we stop here any longer ([26] 4:116). Or the famous monologue by Castaño that includes an almost magical invocation that compels one to think that the comic foil knows the author and Calderón:

Castaño: Oh, you, whoever you have been;
            oh, you, whoever you are,
            whether you wield a fan,
            or whether you carry a sword,
            let some trace reminiscent of Calderón
            inspire me,
            about how to get out of this spot! ([26] 4:136)

It would seem as if the comic foil were improvising the monologue and as if the end of the speech were still to be written.

The comic foils and servants often reveal themselves to be dramatic entities, as in the speech by Atún about the jackanapes, in *Love Is Indeed a Labyrinth* ([26] 4:302), which was mentioned earlier. This speech has a double self-referentiality; not only does it reveal the fact that the character knows himself to be a dramatic entity, but it also refers to Sor Juana herself ("an author / of jokes and *sainetes,/* found no definition / other than to call them jackanapes," ([26] 4:302). In another of her works, in a satirical sonnet, Sor Juana makes a pun with *jackanapes:* "Go on with that, jackanapes" ([26] 1:286). Other speeches serve as metadramatic stage directions, as when Racimo responds with a signal that pertains to the stage directions and with another self-reference to the world of the play:

Racimo: Here comes a servant.
            By heavens I hope that he
            manages to scheme well. ([26] 4:302)

At the end of *Love Is Indeed a Labyrinth,* after a long scene in which the chatterbox Atún has not had the opportunity to speak, the comic foil complains to the audience in an aside, so as to respond immediately to a question by King Minos:

Atún: Here I come.
            (Thanks be to Saint Lucy,
            that I've a place to speak!)
            —Yes, Sire, for my greed,
            thinking that it was Phaedra's,
            seized the role. ([26] 4:350)

Racimo also complains about the lack of dialogue endured by the servants in the play, because of not being the protagonists and because they know that they are, much to their regret, characters governed by the plot, of which they are not usually the agents:

Racimo: I'm going to make up for
all of the time I've been quiet,
since, I've come onto the stage
only to be quiet. ([26] 4:232)

The use of metadrama by Sor Juana is one of the most characteristic elements of her dramaturgy, above all because this self-
referentiality serves as a humorous element and gives it multiple
perspectives: while the audience observes the action, it simultaneously hears the ironic metacommentaries of the characters, as
much about the plot as about the play itself.

The Mexican Quality of Sor Juana's Theater

There has never been any doubt about the Mexican quality of
Sor Juana's theater. There exist studies that make this argument,
such as *The American Element in the Theater of Sor Juana Inés de
la Cruz*, by María E. Pérez, and *Toward an American Reading of the
Mexican Baroque*, by Rafael Catalá—a critical affirmation that con-
trasts with the never-settled debates about the Mexican quality of
Juan Ruiz de Alarcón's works. This study is not the place to illustrate how Sor Juana's work reflects the society of New Spain, with
its integration of Creoles, mestizos, Indians, and Negroes. Her theater is noteworthy for the occurrence of popular language in imitation of these groups in New Spain and of character types of Mexican
extraction, especially in the *villancicos*. Her theater is also known
for its incorporation of certain commentaries about the relationship
between the domineering person and the submissive person, bestow-
ing great dignity upon the Mexican of New Spain in a period in which
the Spanish Monarchy had great power over its colonies. In the *loa*
and in the *sarao* of *The Trials of a Noble House*, the author attempts
to concatenate two opposites that today seem irreconcilable to us,
the attitude of submission together with that of the national dignity
of New Spain:

Chance: Welcome to
Cerda, who tramples
the proud neck
of haughty America. ([26] 21-22)
Chorus 2: Come, Mexicans;[7]
come happy
to see in one sun

a thousand suns shine! . . .
If America, once
uncivilized and pagan,
tried to make
the sun her god . . .
. . . Happily let her
subdue haughty America's
proud neck. ([26] 4:180-81)

Together with these references to the feelings in New Spain toward
Spanish domination, there are many historical and everyday references that make one think that the "Toledan or Sevillian" setting
in her dramas is none other than the Mexican one, just as Spain is
hidden behind the Poland of *Life Is a Dream*, by Calderón.

The author makes few direct references that re-create an Ibe-
rian setting, as when Spain is mentioned out of historical and geo-
graphical context in *Love Is Indeed a Labyrinth*, in a mythological
play that takes place in Crete and Athens: "Let the Princes of Epirus
/ whom no one can remove / let them, like the princes of Spain, / be
chained" ([26] 4:305). This anachronism has no historical basis because no Spanish king has been put in chains, unless it was a reference to the Aztec kings, or perhaps to Columbus and Cortez who
returned to Spain in chains. To what country, if not Mexico, does
Sor Juana's autobiographical verse, spoken through the words of
Leonor, refer?: "Was the venerated object from my country?" ([26]
4:37). Thus, under the names of peninsular geography, one must
think that Mexican backgrounds are evoked in a baroque manner.

The psychology of Sor Juana's comic foils is Mexican, as Daniel
has noted ("A Terra Incognita," 91), but I would add that *mequetrefe*
(jackanapes) is Mexican. It is no coincidence that the etymology of
this word has been found in the Mexicanism "*meco*, meaning
wretched, low, as *mecada* means a blunder, an error or ridiculous
thing," according to Ramos Duarte, or as a contraction of *chichimeco*,
as Wagner explains (Corominas, 349-50). The study by María E. Pérez
makes coincidental remarks based on the behavior of the comic foil:
"Castaño [behaves] within the limits of the society in which Sor
Juana placed him: the Mexico of the era of the viceroys with all of
its vicissitudes, its vices, its coarse humor, its charm and spirit already different from that which existed in the theater for the purely
peninsular comic foil" (84).

The comic foils, Castaño, Atún, and Racimo, are representative
of the masses, given their behavior and their language filled with
popular sayings. Castaño cites some of the personages and events
that transpired in Mexico, as with the swindler Garatuza "about
whom they speak in the Indies / did many extraordinary things"
([26] 4:135-36). The entire spectrum of the Mexican character is ex-
posed in the theater of Sor Juana, but with detailed thoroughness in
her *villancicos*, where cultural, linguistic, and ethnic diversity of
the Mexican homeland are celebrated in baroque style.

Fourth Critical Act

The Second Celestina

Introduction

In 1990, as the result of the research and discovery carried out by Guillermo Schmidhuber, *The Second Celestina*, by Agustín Salazar y Torres, was published with the determination that Sor Juana Inés de la Cruz was the co-author. The edition [27] includes a prologue by Octavio Paz—"Chance or Justice?"—and a critical study by Schmidhuber. Prior to this find, several critics had suspected the existence of this lost play by Sor Juana: Ermilo Abreu Gómez in 1934, in *Sor Juana, Bibliography and Encyclopedia* (293); Alberto G. Salceda, in the introduction to her *Complete Works* ([26] 4:xxx-xxxii); Georgina Sabat-Rivers, in the introduction to *Castalian Flood* ([25], 51); Octavio Paz, in *The Traps of Faith* (435-36); and Carlos Miguel Suárez Radillo, in the first volume of *The Baroque Theater in Spanish America* (81-95). This last critic notes: "We wonder, sadly, what could have happened to the conclusion . . . ! All that remains is for us to hope that one day fate will bring it to light" (1:95). This chapter presents the hypothesis that guided the present discoverer and the reasoning that allowed him to establish beyond any doubt Sor Juana's co-authorship. A generic study of the play is also included here.

An anonymous ending for the play that Salazar y Torres left unfinished at his death had been noted many times, without these critics making any determination of authorship: Agustín Durán (1793-1862), in his *Indice general de piezas dramáticas del teatro antiguo español desde sus orígines hast mediados del siglo XVIII [General Index of Dramatic Works of the Early Spanish Theater from Its Origins until the Middle of the XVIII Century]* (Barrera, 361); Cayetano Alberto de la Barrera y Leirado, in the *Bibliographical and Biographical Catalogue of the Early Spanish Theater* (1860); Mesonero Romanos, who, upon editing the piece by Salazar in 1858-59, includes a note in which he claims to have read a "conclusion written by an anonymous author" (Salazar, *El encanto*, 241). This ending was also scrutinized by Menéndez Pelayo; in a note included in the *Origins of the Novel* he determined this ending belonged to "an anonymous poet," and he concluded that "the merit of the play would justify a new edition" (15:451). In the twentieth century, only Thomas Austin O'Connor, a critic specializing in Salazar y Torres,[1] and Donald G. Castanien (561) have written about the ending, although they never judged the conclusion to belong to Sor Juana, describing it as anonymous.

In 1989, Guillermo Schmidhuber put forward the claim that Sor Juana and Salazar y Torres co-authored *The Second Celestina*. The work entitled *The Great Play about the Second Celestina, Festivity for the Birthday of Our Queen, in the Year 1676* [7] only bears the name of Agustín Salazar y Torres and has no information about the place or year of publication. It was found by Schmidhuber in the library of the University of Pennsylvania (date of acquisition, 1954), forming part of a collection of twenty-four volumes of *Selected Plays* that had volumes from the beginning of the eighteenth century and that belonged to the counts of Harrach (Vienna) and previously to the *Bibliotheca Viennensi*, of the House of Austria. Volume 14 has other single plays by Tirso de Molina, Francisco de Rojas Zorrilla, Luis Vélez de Guevara, Lope de Vega, Agustín Moreto, Luis Belmonte y Bermúdez, and two by Calderón de la Barca. Only three individual plays from the collection have a publication date: 1687, 1719, and 1724 (Regueiro, 11; Reichenberger, 97-100). Because of these dates and the characteristics of the volume, we can fix the edition at the close of the seventeenth century or beginning of the eighteenth. Also, in the National Library in Madrid there are three single copies that show numerous alterations with regard to the original text of *The Second Celestina*; (they do not include the *loa*): T 9222, which has the title *The Famous Play of the Second Celestina*; R 12162, which carries the title *The Great Play about the Second Celestina*; and T-i 120, included in *The Pleasant Garden* (1794).[2] In the following section the reasons for determining Sor Juana to be the co-author of this play are given.

The unfinished play by Salazar y Torres came to have another ending from the one that was published in the second part of *Apollo's*

Lyre (1681), the posthumous edition of the complete works of this author, whose "Favorable Assessment" was written by Calderón de la Barca. The compiler was Juan de Vera Tassis y Villarroel, who finished the play *Charm Is Beauty, and Charm without Witchcraft*, which according to his own commentary was unfinished.

Research into the Authorship of The Second Celestina

A plan was designed for research, analysis, and confirmation of the three evidential components of the play in order to complete the study that proved Sor Juana's co-authorship of *The Second Celestina*: documentary and factual evidence; ideological and thematic evidence; and linguistic and statistical evidence. The arguments and their corresponding proofs are given here, starting from two working hypotheses:[3] (1) that Sor Juana wrote the last one thousand lines of *The Second Celestina*, and (2) that Sor Juana *perfected* the play in its entirety, not including the *loa*.

Documentary and Factual Evidence

Reference to Celestina *in* The Trials of a Noble House. Sor Juana herself left us an irrefutable proof of her co-authorship. In the second *sainete* of the celebration for *The Trials of a Noble House*, there is a dialogue in code that has no relation to the plot of this play and that would appear to be a private communication between the author and certain persons in the audience:

Arias: Was it not better to make *Celestina*
in which you were so witty,
that I am still afraid
—and it is right for me to fear—
that you are a sorceress dressed as a man?

Muñoz: Friend, *Celestina* was better
as a foreign play:
the ones from Spain are always better,
and in order for their humor to be understood,
they are light; because
things which pass over water are never heavy.
But the *Celestina* which caused you
so much laughter, was mestiza
and finished in fragments,
and if it lacked a plan, it had plot lines,

and with a diverse spirit
it was formed from a machine and a genius. ([26] 4:119-20)

This dialogue proves that Sor Juana wrote a play in collaboration: the apparently unnecessary mention of the *Celestina*; the reference to "mestiza" (co-authorship) and finished "in fragments"; describing Salazar as a genius—the faculty or person who subtly thinks up or invents plans, methods, machines, and artifices—and herself as a *trapiche*—the small machine used to make sugar (*Dictionary of Authorities*, 1726). The sentence "if it lacked a plan, it had plot lines" tells of the lack of a general plan and the presence of several lines or sketches, that is, Sor Juana's participation was not only in the conclusion but also in the delineation of the play. Besides, the word *trapiche* is a Mexicanism existing in our own day with the meaning of "contraband" (Ramos Duarte, 494).

Reference to a Collaborative Work in Reputation and Posthumous Works. A work in collaboration between Salazar y Torres and Sor Juana is mentioned in 1700 in the "Prologue to Reader," by Juan Ignacio de Castorena y Ursúa, editor of *Reputation and Posthumous Works* [3]. Listing the works still unpublished, he says: "An unfinished poem begun by don Agustín de Salazar, and perfected with graceful artistry by the poetess, whose original is much admired by don Francisco de las Heras . . . Since it pertains to the first volume, I am not publishing it in this book, and it is being printed so that it can be performed before Their Majesties" ([3] 87).

This prologue reveals the existence of a "poem" in collaboration, understanding *poem* in its broadest meaning (Salceda, "Introducción," [26] 4:xxx). It must have been a theatrical piece, as suggested by the remarks about performance[4] and about its pertinence to the first volume. According to the plan proposed by the editor, Castorena y Ursúa, there would be a future edition of the complete works of Sor Juana in which the dramatic works would compose the first volume. The collaborative piece mentioned by Castorena could not have been a poem, because Castorena decided not to include the work in his volume, which only included prose and poetry.

The claim by Castorena that Sor Juana *perfected* the unfinished work by Salazar has given rise to two interpretations: (1) Sor Juana as co-author wrote the ending and polished the rest, as proposed by

Paz (*The Second Celestina*, 7) and Schmidhuber ("Measurement of Style," 54-60); and (2) Sor Juana *alone* finished it from the point where the Spanish author had left it unfinished, as suggested at first by Alatorre ("*The Second Celestina*," 47) and as O'Connor states ("The Entanglements of a Play," 293-95). As a conclusive argument I propose keeping in mind the meaning of the verb *perficionar* (to perfect), which signifies, according to the *Dictionary of Authorities* (1726), "to completely finish something, giving it total perfection, or polishing it. Some say *perfeccionar*, to perfect, this verb being formed from the word *perfección*, perfection, but more natural is *perficionar*, from the Latin *perficere*, which means the same thing." In another part of *Reputation and Posthumous Works*, Castorena y Ursúa utilizes this term with the same meaning: "Having finished the Prologue for the Discerning Reader, be humane by favoring the first poems of this already *perfected* Book . . ." ([3], 105). Sor Juana also makes use of this meaning of the word: "If love is the cause producing / a variety of affections, / then, by producing all of them / it perfects itself" ([26] 1:9). Ignacio de Luzán has the same usage in his *Poetics* (1737): "The poet can make the story marvelous . . . perfecting Nature" (Luzán, 106). We conclude that this term meant the same in the seventeenth century as it does now. Consequently, Castorena y Ursúa, the editor of the third volume of Sor Juana's *Complete Works*, who knew the degree of collaboration by the Mexican playwright in the dramatic text, should have stated that "the poetess perfected it with graceful artistry" (87), meaning that the writing of the ending and the revision of what was written by Salazar y Torres result in the entire play's manifesting stylistic, thematic, and structural elements of the co-author.

Temporal Correspondence between Lives. A fundamental proof of the historical possibility of the co-authorship is Salazar y Torres's stay in New Spain, where he spent half his life at the viceregal court. Salazar was born in 1642, six years before Sor Juana, and died in 1675, when the nun was twenty-seven years old. Born in Almazán, Spain, he went to New Spain before his fifth birthday in the company of his uncle Marcos de Torres y Rueda, Bishop of Campeche and later viceroy in 1648 and 1649. Salazar studied humanities at the College of San Ildefonso and at the University of Mexico. He returned to Spain around 1660, under the generous protection of the Duke of Albuquerque, and he became one of the most important post-Calderonian playwrights. He died at the age of thirty-three, leaving unfinished the work that he was writing, according to the commentary of his biographer and editor Juan de Vera Tassis. There is no proof that the two authors knew one another personally, because when Salazar returned to Spain, the young Juana [Inés] was only twelve, although she had already been living in the capital of New Spain for four years. Between the ages of sixteen and twenty the young Juana Inés spent time in the court of the Marquis of Mancera, who was viceroy from 1664 to 1673. In 1669, Juana Ramírez decided to follow the way of perfection through conventual life (Paz, *The Traps of Faith*, 132s). *The Second Celestina*, the unfinished play by Salazar, is dated seven years later (1676).

Popularity of Salazar in New Spain. Salazar was one of the most admired literati of his time, as much in the peninsula as in New Spain. An important piece of information discovered by Armando de María y Campos is the performance of this play in the Coliseum of Mexico City in 1679, as well as of two other works by Salazar, which were presented on stage in 1677 and 1678 (*Choosing the Enemy* and *The Olympic Games*), premieres that prove the repute of Salazar in New Spain (María y Campos, 98). We know of the production in Peru during the colonial era of *One Also Loves in the Abyss*, by the same author, in 1711. José Simón Díaz remarks that "the numerous separate editions of the theater pieces produced in the eighteenth century are evidence of a maintained public interest, in contrast to the subsequent, complete disinterest" (245). In the literary Tournament of the Immaculate Conception, which took place in Mexico City in 1654, there is included a *loa* dedicated to Salazar y Torres, who is described as the "Second Anastasio Pantaleón [de Ribera] of our day," with reference to the Madrilinean contemporary of Lope who enjoyed equal popularity across the ocean ([26] 1:374). The numerous studies that O'Connor has dedicated to this playwright and poet have restored Salazar to his place in the history of Spanish literature.

The Date for the Creation of the Loa. The *loa* that precedes *The Second Celestina* carries in the title the date 1675, the year of

Salazar's death. I believe this *loa* is the exclusive work of Salazar y Torres. Notice that 1676 is *not* the year of the edition of the *loa*.

Posthumous Date on the Edition of the Play by Salazar. The date of 1676 included in the title of the play makes one think of the year in which the play was finished, or of an annotation by the editor to indicate its posthumous *perfection.* Notice that 1676 is *not* the year of the edition of the separate work. There is no information that proves that the collaboration by Sor Juana was written in 1676 as is indicated in the title of the play, because the latter must have been revised by the editor in Spain, since the premiere could not have been foreseen from New Spain: "Festivity to Celebrate the Birthday of Our Lady, the Queen" ([7] 43).

A Possible Intermediary for Sor Juana. The friendship between Sor Juana and the Marquis of Mancera, who held great influence at the court of Queen Mariana de Austria toward the end of the decade of the 1670s, makes one think of this personage as the possible intermediary who caused Sor Juana to finish the play, with the goal of having it performed before the queen. Queen Mariana de Austria reigned from 1649 to 1665. After the death of Philip IV in 1665 she was the regent until the majority of her son, Charles II (January 23, 1677), the last monarch of the House of Austria. Octavio Paz has suggested that "it was the Marquis of Mancera who had the idea of sending the play to Sor Juana so that she could finish it" ("Chance or Justice?" 9). On the other hand, several critical studies have noted the influence of Salazar in the poetic work of Sor Juana (Cossío, 27-47; Méndez Plancarte, [26] 1:374, [26] 2:xxxv; Paz, *The Traps of Faith,* 297, 407-10, 421; and Sabat-Rivers, [25] 51). At least two works by Salazar premiered to celebrate a royal birth (O'Connor, "On Dating the *Comedias*," 80-81). Later Sor Juana also dedicated *Loa* 380 to the queen: *Loa to Celebrate the Birthday of Her Ladyship, the Queen, doña Mariana de Austria,* which Méndez Plancarte dates as 1689 or 1690 ([26] 3:692).

The Dramatic Ability of Sor Juana in That Period. Among the dramatic works of Sor Juana, *The Second Celestina* is the first piece in three acts. By 1676 the budding dramatist was twenty eight years old and had already had the experience of writing several dramatic pieces: *villancicos (Assumption,* 1676, *Immaculate Conception,*

1676, and *Saint Peter Nolasco*, 1677); and the *loa* [I] dedicated to Charles II, which is dated by Méndez Plancarte as 1675.[5] As for her poetry, it is not possible to establish a chronology because we do not have the dates of composition, and when the poems were published they were not kept in chronological order. Several poems can be identified by the dates of the events they commemorate as being written prior to 1680, such as the sonnet on the death of Philip IV, in 1665, the three sonnets on the death of the Duke of Veragua, in 1673, and the three sonnets on the death of Leonor Carreto, Marquise of Mancera, who died in 1674. Paz puts forward the opinion that many of the works could have been written before the nun turned thirty years old: "It is plausible that other compositions pertain to this period, religious, erotic and philosophical, as well as satirical and courtly tributes. I am thinking about, for example, numerous laudatory poems, but, which ones?" (*The Traps of Faith*, 190).

Ideological and Thematic Evidence

Biographical elements of Sor Juana in Doña Beatriz. Doña Beatriz, the protagonist, is a worthy predecessor to doña Leonor in *The Trials of a Noble House* by Sor Juana (1683), and like her, she conveys the sentiments of the author. Paz has commented on the biographical similarities to the character of doña Beatriz, stating that "Sor Juana always desired to portray herself: how could she pass up the opportunity of doing so, surreptitiously, in a play that was not hers except in part and that did not bear the name of the author?" ([27], 8). At the beginning of the work, doña Beatriz is defined with a flash of wit that combines three adjectives that evoke Sor Juana:

Juan: Who has said
that there never was harmony among
shyness, beauty and genius?
Only the contrary is expressed
by vulgar opinions:
the portion of the soul being
preferred over the body,
imperfection would be unworthy,
a poorly fashioned pearl,
and a very polished shell. ([27] 56)

This female character expresses more than once her indifference toward the amatory life and her disposition toward her own free will:

Beatriz: I lived free from love
              without fearing its arrows,
              without fear of their feathers,
              scorn was my
              nature, because
              if it were not my nature
              it would have the appearance of flirtation.
              So in control of my free will
              I lived, that the forces
              of love, I am quick to say,
              I disdained. ([27] 107-8)

Like Sor Juana, doña Beatriz does not enjoy the courtly life, and she
states she "exchanged, for the tumult of the wild, the delights of the
Court" ([27], 108). Paralleling the attitude of Sor Juana, doña Beatriz
ponders the power of reason over that of sentiment:

Beatriz: Rather because of the grief which today
             afflicts me, better you know
             the one who always explains herself more
             than the one who is less passionate. ([27] 140-41)

This same balance is found in the following speech, in which Beatriz
reproaches don Diego for having courted her and also doña Ana:
"Wouldn't you like, traitor, / to pass off as a refinement / the wooing
of two women?" ([27], 144). Reason does not justify the excesses of
passion, not even the jealousy "which outlasts their thoughts" ([27],
136), in the opinion of Celestina, the expert on "Procurement" ([27],
63). There exists, then, a privilege of the use of judgment and free
will, while passion and jealousy, which cloud reason, are censured.

The Female Protagonists as Central Characters. The Second Celestina
is an amatory play with the characters from the *Tragicomedy of
Calisto and Melibea,* but without the tragic ending of the work by
Fernando de Rojas, since the new dramatic crux does not lead to the
murder of Celestina, nor to the death of the lovers, but rather to a
happy marriage.

     A singular aspect of this play that makes it correspond to the
two other plays by Sor Juana is the dramatic tension that stems from
the development of the plot and allows the denouement to be moved
forward by the female characters—the love of Beatriz and the false
arguments of Celestina—while the male characters, don Diego, the

lover, don Juan, the beloved of Beatriz, and don Luis, the father of one of the noblewomen, are merely receivers of the dramatic action. This novel dramatic balance, favoring female objectives, constitutes a genuine "pulpit for noblewomen" ([27], 112, 127), exactly the opposite of what happens in the majority of Golden Age plays. Table 6 presents a conceptualization of the protagonists as one of the most valid proofs for confirming the two hypotheses about Sor Juana's coauthorship. If she had only finished the play [alone], she would not have had the opportunity to *perfect* the female psychology, thus rendering the similarities between this play and the other two only linguistic but not foundational to the play's conception. Besides, the presence of androgynous elements throughout the play has been demonstrated by Kristin Routt (45-54). It is also coincidental that in the three plays two noblewomen appear as protagonists, without either of them dominating the scene, as happens with Beatriz and Ana in this play, and with Leonor and Ana, and Phaedra and Ariadne in the other two.

Allusions to the Freedom and Intelligence of Women. The play has several speeches by doña Beatriz and Celestina that are an apology for the thinking woman, an unusual fact for works of this epoch written by talented men, with the exceptions of some plays by Rojas Zorrilla and Agustín Moreto:[6]

Celestina: God bless so much good;
            this pair of beauties can
            give lessons by noblewomen.
Doña Ana: Is being a noblewoman a science?
Celestina: And a great one it is, though
            they learned in Athens
            about philosophy,
            by being ladies they learned
            what the Seven Sages of Greece could not. ([27], 112)

Even Celestina, a character so unlike Sor Juana, acquires an awareness of her intellect in this play; she no longer believes in astrology or magic, but rather in knowledge from books:

Celestina: I cannot find a cure in my books
            for blinding the suspicions
            of a father: now if it were
            a husband . . . ([27], 206)

Table 6. Sor Juana's Dramatic Balance, Favoring Female Objectives

Characters	Older Generation	Young Nobles	Young Commoners
Strong	Celestina	Beatriz and Ana	Inés and Antonia
Weak	Don Luis	Juan and Diego	Tacón and Muñoz

It is ironic to present female protagonists who use their intellect alongside of gallants who, beneath their "cloak and dagger" exterior, conceal a high degree of stupidity, for in spite of the use of violence they do not resolve the conflict. It is the perspicacious noblewomen and the intelligent intermediary who, in order to persevere in their goals, bring about a denouement in the play.

This Celestina, "daughter of Celestina / and heir to her works" ([27], 58), is no longer the witch that her famous predecessor was: instead of spells there are schemes of female ingenuity. This new *Celestina* bears witness to the evolution of the Medieval and Renaissance ideas that served as a foundation for the original work, since we can assume that it takes place at the close of the seventeenth century because it stages different social conditions. Several speeches by Celestina ridicule witchcraft from a predominantly rationalist perspective:

Celestina: The business of love
is not very rewarding;
the most faithful lover
pays very little.
But I invented a fanciful scheme,
which has served me well;
and it is that I myself have pretended
that I am such a great witch,
that I know the spot where
fortune lies, and I understand
astrology, lying
even about the heavens.
In this matter of the Stars
the surest thing is to lie,
since no one can go
up to ask them about it.

> Lying like a Gypsy,
> I take the hand of everyone
> and give them a going over
> while I read their palms;
> I pretend to know what is happening with an absent loved one,
> whom I will make fall in love in an instant:
> and this is believed by the lovers,
> who are such gullible people. ([27], 64)

In the third act Celestina includes among her achievements taking advantage of human credulity, thanks to her talent or "cunning for lying":

Celestina: Well, know, that I never
learned my science
because my good fortune
has been to be credible.
With the pleasant air blowing over me,
with my cunning in lying,
my ability to feign
fed me at midday.
What I was hearing from some
I gave to others as an answer
and thus with others I gained
credibility as an astrologer. ([27], 215)

Other Allusions. Of the servants, Tacón and Muñoz, the first stands out for being a predecessor to the famous Castaño in *The Trials of a Noble House*. In the ending by Sor Juana, Muñoz makes a reference with a Cervantine flavor: "My master is a knight errant, who goes around righting wrongs" ([27], 181), which should be compared to the *villancico* of the Assumption, 1676, which says of the Virgin: "Righter of wrongs, destroyer of insults" ([26] 2:11).[7] The names of the characters were of necessity given by Salazar, and thus it is worth noting that the character of Inés, one of the servants, disappears in the third act of Sor Juana's version (although she does appear and even marry in the ending by Vera Tassis).[8] Would Sor Juana discreetly hide her name so that it would not appear in the multiple wedding that closes the play?

As a closing for the arguments supporting the ideological and thematic evidence, it is fitting to cite the commentary by Paz, included in the prologue to the edition of *The Second Celestina*, in which Sor Juana "did not limit herself to writing the ending since traces of her appear in the part Salazar had written" ([27], 7).

Linguistic and Statistical Evidence

Correspondences to Other Plays by Sor Juana. The linguistic and statistical similarity of *The Second Celestina* to the other two plays by Sor Juana is conclusive, as is its consequent disparity with the rest of Salazar's dramaturgy,[9] since this outstanding author resorts to dramatic solutions that were pioneering in the Spanish *zarzuela*, which, although of great merit in themselves, are completely different from this play. The superiority of *Charm Is Beauty, and Charm without Witchcraft* over all the other works by Salazar has not gone unnoticed by several critics unaware of the problem of co-authorship: Mesonero Romanos—"very well arranged scenes and simple and harmonious versification, which make it greatly superior to all the others by this author" (47:xv); O'Connor—"his Celestina play will stand out all the more boldly in stark contrast to his previous dramatic productions" ("Language, Irony, and Death," 69); Suárez Radillo—"a much higher level of maturity" (89). This dramatic quality is due to the fact that Sor Juana "perfected with graceful artistry" the unfinished manuscript by Salazar, as is noted in the prologue by Castorena y Ursúa, already cited, which Sor Juana herself humorously signaled in *The Trials of a Noble House* with the assertion that "if it lacked a plan, it had plot lines."

An Examination of the Measurement of Style in The Second Celestina. The utilization of computerized measurement of style has allowed us to carry out tests to quantify multiple parameters that are grouped together under the concept described as style. This methodology has been utilized to untangle problems of dubious authorship in Shakespeare, Carlyle, Aristotle, Herodotus, Saint Paul, and Dostoyevsky. Schmidhuber conducted a computer-aided study of this play with findings that prove Sor Juana's authorship according to five parameters: word frequency counts, word lengths, initial letter frequencies, sentence length frequencies, and chi square test for heterogeneity. This research proved that the ending proposed as the one by Sor Juana exhibits great parallels with *The Trials of a Noble House*, with a degree of significant correlation higher than 95 percent (Schmidhuber, "Measurement of Style"). Moreover, the results show several parameters, such as sentence length and verbal segment length, from the ending by Sor Juana that are comparatively different from the *loa* and *Choosing the Enemy*, both works by Salazar y Torres. Consequently, the linguistic evidence brought to light the multiple parallelisms that exist throughout the whole text of the play, whose parameters are similar to the style of Sor Juana. In summary, the analysis of the measurement of style proved that the final one thousand lines of the play being studied are stylistically similar to *The Trials of a Noble House* in the same way as the ending attributed to Sor Juana and the three early acts of The Second Celestina.

On the other hand, indications of dissimilarity between the *loa* and the rest of *The Second Celestina* were found, thus indicating a different author. The first act shows a slight incongruity with the second act and with the first half of the third act, especially in the use of sentences of more than sixty words, a length also characteristic of Sor Juana's ending and of *The Trials of a Noble House*. It is clear that according to the evidence of statistical dissimilarity, Salazar did not write the first part of the play in its entirety. In conclusion, the parallels shown by the stylistic analysis between the ending and the first act with *The Trials of a Noble House* allow us to assign to Sor Juana the co-authorship for the play in its entirety.

The adjudication of Sor Juana's co-authorship of *The Second Celestina* has been accepted by Paz in his prologue to the edition of the play ("Chance or Justice"), which was reprinted in *ABC de Madrid*, and in a critical note *"The Second Celestina* and Its Critics." Additionally, it has been accepted by Luis Leal, Georgina Sabat-Rivers, Carlos Miguel Suárez Radillo, Lee Alton Daniel, and Thomas Austin O'Connor—this last critic is a specialist on Salazar y Torres.[10]

Use of Archaisms and Americanisms. The use of *A Dios*, the early form of saying *Adiós*, is employed in the octosyllabic lines by Sor Juana in "Prologue for the Reader": "And *a Dios*, as this is nothing more than / a sample of my wares: / if you do not like the piece / do not unwrap the package" ([26] 1:4); she also uses it throughout all of *The Second Celestina* ([27], 73, 84, 85, 124, 134, 158 and 191). In the edition by Vera Tassis [Salazar, *Apollo's Lyre*] this early form is modernized. The ending by Sor Juana uses the hypothetical future subjunctive form *estuvied* (if you were), the archaic form of *estuviera* ([27], 217).

Another archaism is the use of the pronoun placed after the verb in the infinitive: ataja*llos*, reduci*llos*, and resisti*llo*, instead of ataja*rlos* (to cut them off), reduci*rlos* (to reduce them), and resisti*rlo* (to resist him) ([27], 173, 175); as also happens in "yo no puedo cree*llo*" (I can't believe it), instead of creer*lo*, in *The Trials of a Noble House* ([26] 4:120). These forms "were fashionable in the sixteenth century, primarily among Andalusians, Murcians, Toledans, and people of the court who, in the time of Charles V, adopted the linguistic style of Toledo; afterwards they declined" (Lapesa, 250).[11] Similarly, the orthography of *Ruyseñor* ([27] 144) and the preference for the *x* in *xilguero* (from the Latin *silguero*), [which] is today *jilguero* [linnet]. All of these archaisms of common usage in America are corrected in the version by Vera Tassis (258), according to the peninsular usage of the time, which must have been the same for Salazar y Torres. The same thing happens in the editio princeps of 1692 of Sor Juana: the orthographic differences that call to mind the original manuscript are retained, though they were later corrected by editors: *páxaro, dixe, debaxo* ([26] 1:441).

The term *marchante* ([27], 161) is an Americanism that means a person who customarily shops in the same store, as it still means in Mexico today, compared with the homonymic Gallicism meaning "seller" or "trader." This term is not used in Spain.

Leísmo and Laísmo. *Leísmo* [use of the Spanish pronoun *le*] in Sor Juana has been shown by Méndez Plancarte, following the path of Pedro Henríquez Ureña: "'Sor Juana uses the accusative *lo* and the dative *le*, as has always been done in America,' sacrificárse*lo*, instead of the peninsular sacrificárse*le*, and *le* dije, instead of *la* dije" ([26] 1:368). For example, in *The Trials of a Noble House*: *le* responde, in the edition of 1692, and *la* responde in the one of 1693, perhaps corrected by the editors, as Salceda suggests ([26] 4:xlvii, [26] 4:547). When we analyze *The Second Celestina* we find that in the first act there is a mixture of usages, while in the second act and the ending only the American usage of the dative occurs (see table 7).

In his edition Vera Tassis corrects the American uses of the accusative *lo* and the dative *le*, according to the peninsular use of *le* as accusative and *la* as dative. This evidence is some of the most conclusive for demonstrating Sor Juana's co-authorship.

Onomasticon and Toponymy. In *The Second Celestina* there are proper names and places that also appear in other works by Sor Juana;

Table 7. Use of *Leísmo* and *Laísmo*

Mixture of *Leísmo* and *Laísmo* *The Second Celestina*	*Laísmo* *Charm Is Beauty*
I was going to talk to *her* through the window bars (51).	I was going to talk to *her* through the window bars (235).
All that they asked of *her* (133).	All that they asked of *her* (256).
My concern having become apparent to *her* (141).	My concern having become apparent to *her* (258).
[Que iba a hablarla por la reja (51).	[Que iba a hablarla por la reja (235).
Todo lo que le pidieren (133).	Todo lo que la pidieren (256).
Habiéndole dado cuenta de mi cuidado.]	Habiéndola dado cuenta de mi cuidado.]

Note: Numbers refer to pages in [27] for *The Second Celestina*, and to pages in Salazar, *Apollo's Lyre*, for *Charm Is Beauty*.

especially well-known are Betis, Etna, and Mongibelo. This last name is also mentioned in the satirical epigram penned by Sigüenza y Góngora that was given to her in a gloss that won the literary competition of 1683: "It is a gloss of Mongivelo" (271). Some of the names shared between works are shown in table 8.

Similarities of Words or Ideas with Sor Juana's Theater. The coincidences of some speeches with familiar poems by the nun are more than significant:

> I bring a concern with me,
> and it is so elusive,
> that, although I know how to feel it so intensely,
> I myself don't feel it. (*Sacred Ballad*, 56, [26] 1:166)

> You must be the relief
> for a care, for a pain
> I don't know how to explain,
> even though I know how to suffer it. (*The Second Celestina*, [27], 67)

> Divided into two parts
> My soul is in confusion . . . (*Décima* 99, [26] 1:234)

> What will I do, honor, now my affront
> is divided into two parts
> it is getting worse instead of better? (*The Second Celestina*, [27], 202)

Table 8. Sor Juana's Repetition of Proper Names

The Second Celestina [27]	Other Works
Athens, 112	Athens, 24 references; in the two plays, *The Trials of a Noble House* and *Love Is Indeed a Labyrinth* [26]: 211, 215, 216, 220, 224, 226, 227, 233, 255, 298, 308, 323, 324, 335, 344, 346
Betis, 45	
Cadiz, 90, 102	
Cynthia, 45	
	Betis, [26] 3:154, 3:174
Diana, 80	
	Cadiz, [26] 2:213
Etna, 108	
	Cynthia, [26] 1:179, 1:183, 2:105, 3:311, 3:312
Mars, 54	
Mongibelo, 108	Diana, [26] 2:68, 2:175, 4:182, 4:257, 4:365, 4:379, 4:380, 4:406
Seville, 52, 57, 58, 80, 89, 102, 110	
	Etna, [26] 1:132, 2:303, 3:407, 4:106
Venus, 54	
	Mars, 28 references; in the two plays: 4:117, 4:182
	Mongibelo, [26] 1:19, 1:132, 1:199, 3:432
	Seville, [26] 3:141, 3:154, 3:161, 4:410
	Venus, 34 references, especially [26] 4:23, 4:117, 4:177, 4:179, 4:182, 4:204, 4:273

Could this be then
the first time, if you look at it,
that the sacristans
set the offenders free? (*The Trials of a Noble House*, [26] 4:45)

And let the listener beware,
that this play has been
the first in which the old man
has hidden himself. (*The Second Celestina*, [27], 161)

I beg of you
that you examine with your heart
the *fierceness of love*. (*The Trials of a Noble House*, [26] 4:162)

The *fierceness*
of love, I say again,
I despised . . . (*The Second Celestina*, [27], 108)

An example of similar dramatic denouements is in *The Trials of a Noble House*, when Acevedo, the supposed author of the play, decides to commit suicide upon seeing himself about to be ridiculed by being booed in public; this also happens to Tacón when Celestina accuses him of failing to honor a marriage agreement:

> I'm going off there to hang myself!
> (*The Trials of a Noble House*, [26] 122)
> I'm going to hurl myself over a balcony.
> *The Second Celestina*, [27], 221)

Salceda has noted the possible influence of *Disdain in Exchange for Disdain* (1654), by Moreto, in which a humorous effect is also sought when the comic foil Polilla says to his master: "A reason to hang yourself? / well if not, nothing can hang you" ([26] 4:558).

The contrast between Sor Juana's style [and that of Salazar] stands out clearly when her work is compared with the *loa* that precedes the play, which was written entirely by Salazar y Torres. Equally noteworthy is the disparity between the style of *The Second Celestina* and other plays by Salazar: *The Glory Is the Crown, and Charms of the Sea and of Love*, 1674; *The Finest Flower of Sicily, Saint Rosolea*, 1674; *The Olympic Games*, 1673; *Thetis and Peleus*, 1671; and *One Also Loves in the Abyss*, 1670 (O'Connor, "On Dating the *Comedias*," 80). In *The Second Celestina* there exists a subtle difference between the opening speeches by don Juan and the closing ones by the same character:

> Beautiful deity of these forests
> lovely rival of Cynthia,
> who among beasts and men
> strikes down both the bright and the dull. (Act I, [27], 45)

> If my pain is more specific
> than that one, it will not come from love,
> and this other one will, since it has sprung
> from two women who have now
> departed from this place. (Act III, [27], 201)

The extremely cultured language of some of the first speeches is toned down throughout the play, approaching everyday language, with dialogues similar to those found in *The Trials of a Noble House*.

Proof of Sor Juana's Authorship

For each of the working hypotheses the corresponding proofs were given in the foregoing sections in terms of documentary and factual evidence, ideological and thematic evidence, and linguistic and statistical evidence.

Hypothesis 1 is that Sor Juana wrote the last one thousand lines of *The Second Celestina*, and Hypothesis two is that Sor Juana *perfected* the play in its entirety, not including the *loa*. The two hypotheses are proven entirely by the evidence given in the foregoing sections, without any information being found that would cast doubt on the co-authorship of Sor Juana. What has been proven: after more than three centuries of darkness and oblivion, this play can now being included in the dramatic production of Sor Juana Inés de la Cruz.

The Other Ending for the Play by Salazar y Torres

The play *Charm Is Beauty, and Charm without Witchcraft* is not like *The Second Celestina* until halfway through the third act,[12] where Vera Tassis includes a note assuring us that he himself finished the play: "Don Agustín left the play in this state, and from here whoever brings his works to light will finish it" (Salazar, *Apollo's Lyre*, 231). Additionally, in the last speech in the ending, the editor refers to himself as the co-author, with no small degree of petulance, in the words of Celestina:

Celestina: And here, ladies and gentlemen,
Celestina ends her entanglement.
Don Juan de Vera begs your
pardon for the impudence
of finishing a Play
by such a superior genius,
but it was motivated
by a sovereign decree,
and to confirm,
The Best Friend, The Dead Friend. (*Apollo's Lyre*, 279)

The last line not only pays homage to the dramatic superiority of Salazar y Torres but also alludes to another work written in collaboration, *The Best Friend, The Dead Friend*, by Francisco de Rojas

Zorrilla, Luis Belmonte, and Calderón de la Barca.[13] The third act, by Calderón, ends with the same line as in the ending by Vera Tassis:

Lidoro: Don Juan, enter the city
and make known to all
that it is God who rewards piety,
and the best friend, the dead friend. ([4] 488)

Thus Vera Tassis, also the editor of the works of Calderón, included 601 lines of é-o assonance in order to be able to end the piece by Salazar with this reference.

The dual title of *Charm Is Beauty, and Charm without Witchcraft* is included by Vera Tassis in the last lines of the play and in all of the editions with the ending by Vera Tassis.[14] It should be noted that the title is close to other Calderonian titles: *Charm without Enchantment, The Weapons of Beauty,* and *Love, the Greatest Charm.* The title *The Second Celestina* is the only one for the version with the ending by Sor Juana in all of the volumes found, and the title is incorporated into the last speech of the play: "And here ends, ladies and gentlemen, / *The Second Celestina.*" The staging of this play in the Coliseum of Mexico City in 1679 was done with the triple title of *Charm Is Beauty, Charm without Witchcraft, and The Second Celestina* (María y Campos, 98) and must have been staged with the ending by Sor Juana. During the editing of the play with Sor Juana's ending at the close of the seventeenth century, the title was shortened to *The Second Celestina,* as much with the intent of differentiating it from the edition by Vera Tassis, which had already been published at that time, as from another play of the same title by Calderón—today lost.[15] It is not until 1859 that Mesonero Romanos combines the two titles into a single edition of the play (with the ending by Vera Tassis) in the *Biblioteca de autores españoles* (Rivadeneyra).[16] It is not gratuitous to think that Vera Tassis knew the anonymous ending written in 1676 (the one by Sor Juana) but decided to write another ending so as to include his collaboration in the edition of the works by Salazar that he himself was completing.

There are great similarities between the endings by both authors; the first line has the same meaning in the two versions:

Ana: We escaped a real shock. (Vera Tassis, *Apollo's Lyre,* 261)
Ana: We got out of a jam. (Sor Juana, [27], 171)

And after two dialogues similarities are found again:

Beatriz: And don Diego de Guevara
          with good sophistry
          tried to prove his *skill*
          at courting *two*.
Ana: The answer was precise, since a *lover*,
          if he sees himself *proven*,
          in the art of ingenuity
          excuses his crudeness. (Vera Tassis, *Apollo's Lyre*, 261)
Ana: With good sophistry
          he tried to say that it is a rare
          skill to serve *two* women.
Beatriz: A lover proven
          late, or never, has used
          the best excuse. (Sor Juana, [27], 172)

Other examples of similarities are the arrival of the police at the end
of the act and Celestina's vengeance upon Tacón by demanding that
he marry, using the same constables the servant had called for:

Celestina: And so now I plan to
            take revenge
            on Tacón. Sir, I beg you,
            now execute justice for me
            upon this vile cheat,
            because he should honor his *word* . . .
            Of *marrying*, . . .
            which you have given me a thousand times,
            and you have feigned these entanglements,
            to avoid honoring her. (Vera Tassis, *Apollo's Lyre*, 278)
Celestina: Nothing hidden shall remain
            thus I plan to take revenge,
            gentlemen, upon this rascal.
            He has given me his word
            that he'll marry, and because he didn't
            want to do it, he feigned
            all of this . . . (Sor Juana, [27], 220)

The response by the police is similar in the two versions:

Constable 1: If this is so,
              marry then,
              or you will go with me to prison.
                  (Vera Tassis, *Apollo's Lyre*, 278)

Officer 2:   Marry then, or from here
                you will be taken prisoner to jail. (Sor Juana, [27], 221)

Another similarity is in the dialogue between don Diego and don
Juan:

So if carefully *your life*
I defended, it was, I suspect,
keeping your life safe then
in order to take it from you later on.
Vera Tassis, *Apollo's Lyre*, 275)

And if then *your life*
I defended, it was taking care
to keep your life safe then
in order to take it from you later on. (Sor Juana, [27], 185)

The number of similarities compels one to think that Vera Tassis
was familiar with the ending by Sor Juana but that he created another ending for his edition of the works of Salazar y Torres.[17]

In the National Library in Madrid there exist two adaptations of
The Second Celestina: (1) *The Second Celestina, Witch of Triana*
(anonymous, dated 1818); and (2) *The Second Celestina*, a work by
Dionisio Solís.[18] The theatrical success of the latter adaptation was
great: thirty-nine performances between 1819 and 1841 (Castanien,
560). The version by Sor Juana—not the one by Vera Tassis—served
as the basis for these adaptations, proven by the continued use of
the title and the last episode of the women in disguise, although the
similarity varies with the wedding; in the first only Beatriz and Diego, and Ana and Juan, marry, whereas in the second the marriage of
Tacón and Antonia is added. In spite of these variations, the character Inés remains a spinster, as in the ending by Sor Juana. These
reworkings of *The Celestina* are not surprising, since the theme and
the characters of this work remained present throughout the Golden
Age.[19]

Dramatic Elements of The Second Celestina

The Plot

The Second Celestina takes place in Seville, and there is mention of
Flanders, Cadiz, and the Indies. It consists of three acts, and in the
individual edition (*suelta*) of the play [7] they are not divided into

scenes. The structure presented here divides the play according to scenes of dramatic unity, not by entrances and exits by the characters. The plot line of the play is included, as is a proposal for the division into scenes:

Act I, Scene 1. Along a stream of the Betis (Guadalquivir River) don Juan meets doña Beatriz on a hunt, but she leaves without telling him her name.

Act I, Scene 2. Don Juan explains to Muñoz and Tacón[20] his reasons for having fled to Flanders: a street duel and to protect doña Ana. Muñoz suggests that his master visit Celestina, a woman versed in the art of love, so that she can reveal to him the mystery of the huntress.

Act I, Scene 3. Celestina's house. Doña Ana asks Celestina if don Juan, her lover, will return. The old woman promises her news about the object of her affection. Don Juan, in turn, asks Celestina to help him find the huntress. As they leave the house there is a fight in the street, and don Juan saves don Diego without learning the identity of his rival in the duel.

Act I, Scene 4. The house of don Luis, father of doña Ana. Don Luis welcomes his niece, doña Beatriz, and exits. Celestina informs doña Ana that she will soon see don Juan, since she has identified him as the nobleman who had visited her. In the absence of doña Ana, don Juan arrives, and doña Beatriz refuses to speak with him again.

Act II, Scene 1. Don Luis's house. Doña Ana's father mentions his suspicion that someone is prowling outside his house (unaware that it is don Diego), and he exits. Doña Beatriz confesses to doña Ana she has come to Seville in search of her love, since her father wants to marry her to someone else in Cadiz. She tells about her encounter with a nobleman along the Betis. Antonia reports that Celestina is hidden in her room. Tacón announces the arrival of don Juan. Doña Ana, grateful, gives Tacón a jewel as a reward (the jewel had been given to the lady by doña Beatriz's father).

Act II, Scene 2. Don Juan causes an argument when he does not accept doña Ana's explanations. Doña Beatriz reveals to her cousin that the nobleman she encountered is don Juan. Doña Ana accuses him of infidelity. Tacón attacks don Juan, and Celestina and the servants enter. Don Luis enters. Celestina saves the moment by accusing Tacón of theft, and don Luis makes Tacón return the jewel. Don Luis exits (*Dramatic climax*).

Act II, Scene 3. Don Diego arrives with the intention of seeing doña Ana, and he also encounters doña Beatriz.

Act II, Scene 4. When don Luis arrives, doña Ana and doña Beatriz hide don Diego and implore Celestina to get rid of him. Celestina deceives don Luis by pretending to show the image of the man he had seen in his house (don Diego) in a mirror. Don Luis sees the reflection of don Diego as he is leaving the house, but he interprets it as an act of magic.

Act III, Scene 1. Celestina's house. Don Luis visits Celestina in order to solicit her help in discovering who was prowling around his house. When Tacón arrives, Celestina hides don Luis. Tacón tries to take the jewel from Celestina, and when the old woman cries out, don Luis comes to her aid. She now tells a lie by stating that Tacón had stolen 100 coins (that doña Ana had given to the page) from her. Don Luis forces Tacón to return them to Celestina. The old woman tells don Luis that it is don Diego who has been prowling around his house.

Act III, Scene 2. (Ending written entirely by Sor Juana) Don Luis' house. Doña Ana and doña Beatriz talk about their loves. Muñoz enters and states that Tacón has gone for the police and that don Luis visited Celestina.

Act III, Scene 3. Outside of Celestina's house. Don Diego finds Muñoz. Don Juan arrives. The two noblemen label each other enemies, challenge one another to a duel, and exit. Doña Ana and doña Beatriz arrive, disguised, and they go to Celestina's house to find out what happened to don Luis. Muñoz tells them about the duel between don Juan and don Diego. Celestina promises to help the women.

Act III, Scene 4. Somewhere near Seville. Don Diego and don Juan challenge each other. The ladies arrive and prevent it. The women depart because they know don Luis is coming in pursuit of them. Don Luis, who had been informed by Antonia, appears. Don Luis attempts to challenge don Diego, but don Juan stops it. Don Luis realizes that the two noblemen were fighting over doña Ana, for which he also challenges don Juan. The three stop fighting.

Act III, Scene 5. Celestina's house. Doña Ana and doña Beatriz go with Celestina to ask for help. The police arrive. Don Luis enters, followed by don Diego and don Juan. The entanglements are resolved and the charms by Celestina are explained. Celestina falsely accuses Tacón of breaching a promise of marriage. The questions of honor reach their conclusion with a triple wedding: Doña Beatriz and don Diego, doña Ana and don Juan, and Antonia with Muñoz.

The Structure

The structure of *The Second Celestina* shows a balance between each of the three acts, with a similar number of scenes, four, four, and five, respectively. The dramatic climax occurs in scene two of the second act, when don Luis bursts into the scene in Celestina's house and Celestina saves the moment with a clever ruse. In spite of the fact that it is a collaboration by Salazar y Torres and Sor Juana, the work possesses great linguistic, thematic, and dramatic unity. One can speculate that this unity is the result of the *perfecting* done by Sor Juana.

Figure 3 presents the structure of *The Second Celestina* and a brief description of its dramatic action. The structure of *The Second Celestina* shows bilateral symmetry (see fig. 4) similar to that which Williamsen has noted in the other two plays by Sor Juana.[21]

Final Commentary

Analyzing *The Second Celestina* with the use of the four semiotic codes mentioned in the Second Critical Act, we find interesting results that facilitate a present-day understanding of this play.

Psychological Code

Within the limits of time and space, one can claim that the psychological needs of the characters pertain to the same scale of human needs as those of the audience. The reactions of the characters to the vicissitudes in the play fit within the deportment of a woman today. There is no obstacle that prevents the effective decodification of this code.

Ideological Code

The theme of two women's desire to marry the man they love continues to be contemporary. Perhaps today it is more credible with

1. Doña Beatriz tells doña Ana about her search for don Diego and her encounter with a nobleman along the Betis. Don Juan's arrival is announced. *Act Two*	2. Don Juan does not accept doña Ana's explanations. Doña Beatriz reveals that the nobleman is don Juan. Tacón attacks don Juan. Don Luis enters. Celestina saves the moment. *(Dramatic climax)*	3. Don Diego arrives with the intention of seeing doña Ana, and he also finds doña Beatriz.	4. When don Luis arrives, don Diego is hidden by doña Ana and doña Beatriz, and he is saved with the help of Celestina.
4. Another meeting between doña Beatriz and don Juan.	→		*Act Three* 1. Don Luis visit Celestina to solicit her help.
3. Doña Ana asks for Celestina's help. Don Juan asks her to help find the huntress. Intervention by Don Juan, who saves don Diego, unaware that it is his rival.	↑	↓	2. Doña Ana and doña Beatriz talk about their loves.
			3. Don Diego and don Juan challenge one another to a duel. Doña Ana and doña Beatriz go to Celestina's house.
2. Don Juan fled to Flanders because of a duel with a stranger (don Diego).		↓	4. Another duel between don Diego and don Juan. Don Luis arrives, and everyone stops.
1. Beginning of the entanglement. Don Juan meets a lady (doña Beatriz). *Act One*	↑		5. End of the entanglement: The Police and don Luis intervene. Triple wedding *(Denouement)*.

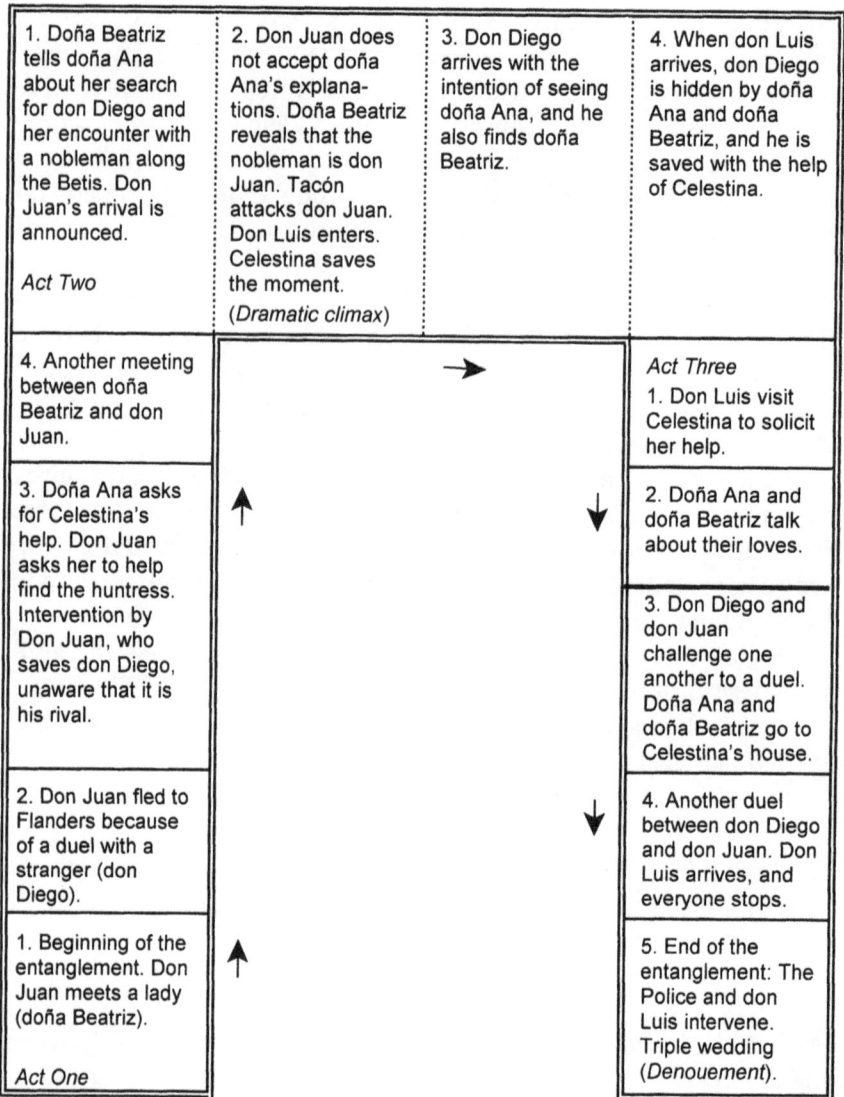

Figure 3. Structure and Dramatic Action of *The Second Celestina*

Diego sought and concealed

1. Doña Beatriz tells doña Ana of her search for don Diego and her meeting with a nobleman. *Act Two*	2. Don Juan's arrival announced.	3. Doña Ana reveals that the nobleman from the Betis is don Juan. (*Dramatic Climax*)	4. Encounter between don Diego and doña Ana and doña Beatriz.	5. When don Luis arrives, don Diego is hidden by doña Ana and doña Beatriz.

6. Another meeting between doña Beatriz and don Juan.	↑	Rival noblemen and their ladies	↑ *Act Three* 1. Conflict between Celestina and Tacón, don Luis protects her.
5. Intervention by don Juan, who saves a stranger (don Diego), unaware that it is his rival.			(Ending by Sor Juana) 2. Doña Ana and doña Beatriz told of the intervention by the father and the Police.
4. Don Juan solicits Celestina's help to find the huntress (doña Beatriz).	←	Rivalry between the noblemen →	3. Rivals find themselves outside of Celestina's house and challenge one another to a duel.
3. Doña Ana asks Celestina for help.	←	Helpful Celestina →	4. Doña Ana and Doña Beatriz ask Celestina for help.
2. Don Juan fled because of a duel with a stranger (don Diego).	←	Dual between the noblemen →	5. Another duel between don Diego and don Juan.
1. Beginning of the entanglement. Don Juan meets lady (doña Beatriz). *Act One*	← ↑	Separation/ rendezvous (Juan and Beatriz) →	6. End of entanglement: Police and don Luis intervene. Triple wedding (*Denouement*). ↓

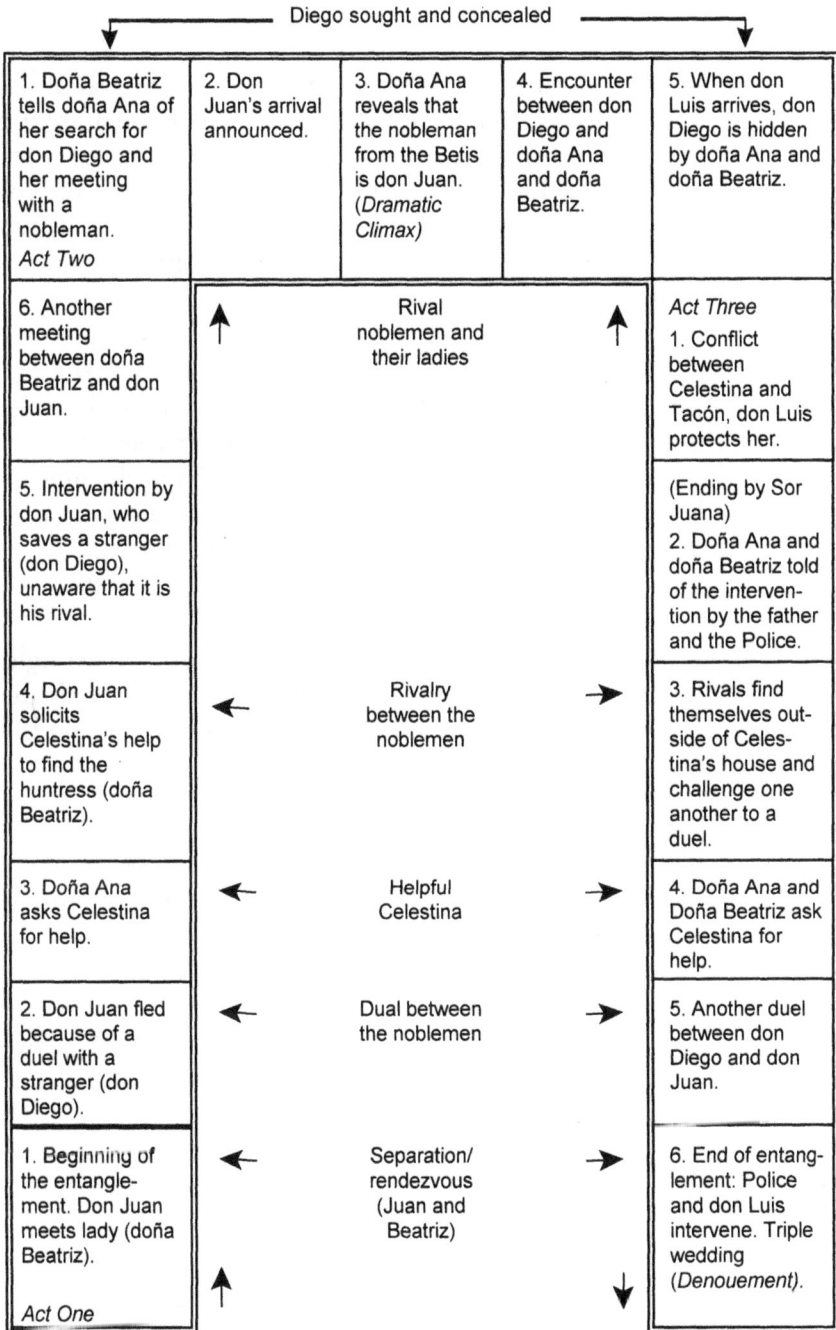

Figure 4. Structure of *The Second Celestina* (structural format proposed by Williamson in "Bilateral Symmetry")

regard to modern-day thinking, which stems from the vision of the woman as an active factor in her social nucleus, since the dramatic tension of the play springs from the conflict between women, men, and society. Moreover, the character of Celestina belongs to the literary and dramatic ancestry of *Don Quixote* and of *Don Juan*, which renders this character more attractive and makes the play hold a special interest for today's audience.

Aesthetic-Theatrical Code

The audience's understanding of Sor Juana's cosmos can be complicated by the abstract means through which the characters are presented, distancing them from the real world. This obstacle is diminished by the utilization of irony, giving the play a greater possibility for comprehension from a current perspective.

Linguistic Code

The refined language that the characters of higher station use might seem artificial for today's audience. This is not the case with the language of the servants, which must have been as effective on the stage in seventeenth century as it is today.

In conclusion, none of the four codes presents insurmountable obstacles for the contemporary audience's ability to enjoy this play once again on the stage, after more than three centuries of obscurity.

Fifth Critical Act

The Trials of a Noble House

Introduction

Ever since the derogatory opinion by Menéndez Pelayo, which describes *The Trials of a Noble House* as "an interesting and gallant imitation of the 'cloak and dagger' plays by Calderón" (*History of Spanish-American Poetry*, 76), critics have underrated this play in comparison with the poetic work by Sor Juana. Even when editing it, Jiménez Rueda renders a judgment of doubtful critical value: "The characters intervene casually in the event, without any more purpose than can be found in a contredanse step. The author is so removed from the theater, that she forgets to indicate changes of scene. Few pages have stage directions. The agile intelligence and the subtle spirit forget the minutiae of theater people, to amuse them by creating a skit that charms by its delightful baroqueness, very much in the seventeenth-century Mexican style" (xxvi).

This is the only critical appraisal contained in the prologue of this edition, which does not include the *loa*, the *sainetes*, or the remarks pertaining to the drama. It does, however, dedicate more than twenty pages to the life of Sor Juana and to presenting the Calderonian similarities to *The Divine Narcissus*, an *auto* not included in this edition. In some cases a selective viewpoint makes one lose sight of the overall appraisal, as when the importance of the drama is reduced to its thematic contents with opinions that claim that this play and *Love Is Indeed a Labyrinth* "are two pretexts for the author to continue her work on the 'philosophy of love'" (Salceda, "Introducción," [26] 4:xxii) or to refer to the plays only for their biographical correspondences between Sor Juana and the character Leonor. In contrast to this critical carelessness, there are brilliant studies on this play by Rodolfo Usigli (*Mexico in Its Theater*, 49-53), Alberto G. Salceda ("Introducción," [26] 4:525-70), Lee Alton Daniel ("A Terra Incognita," 87-106), and Stephanie Merrim ("*Mores Geometricae*," 103-6).[1] Usigli is a notable exception in seeking the theatrical perspective, perhaps because of his own status as a dramatist. This Mexican writer was the first to point out the influence of Lope de Vega on the theater of Sor Juana, noting the similarity of *The Trials of a Noble House* to *The Discreet Lady in Love*, although his appraisal favors the Mexican piece:

> *In both, an intrigue of human design—as soon as it is conceived of and connected to the movement of reality by the characters—begins to be controlled by greater powers. Continuously manifested in both is the intervention of adversity and confusion, wisely sought and brilliantly found by the authors. Sor Juana's Castaño is much more appealing to me than Lope de Vega's Hernando, even though the two servants disguise themselves as women. Moreover the axiomatic paradox is more brilliant in* The Trials of a Noble House, *and the subtleties of wit more—may I say ingenious?—and spontaneous. (*Mexico in Its Theater, *52)*

Usigli also points out "the gift for conversation present in all of the dramatic work by Sor Juana" (54).

The title of the play is a variation on *The Trials through Chance*, by Calderón, but the similarities do not end there, as James A. Castañeda has demonstrated (111) by the following similarities:

- Gallant A courts Lady A, who is named Leonor in both works.

- Gallant B, who is named Juan in both works, courts Lady B, who is the sister of Gallant C.

- In turn, Gallant C courts Lady A . . .

- In both works the father of Lady A is present.

- In both works there is a servant named Hernando.

This piece by Calderón was, coincidentally, the first one performed in New Spain about which we have any notice, in November 1679, that is to say, three and a half years before the performance of Sor Juana's play (Hesse, 14-15).[2] Although *The Trials of a Noble House* has enough similarities to the play by Calderón to indicate a direct influence, there is no possibility of considering it a reworking. A fundamental disparity is the fact that the play by Sor Juana has a conceptualization different from the code of honor, which prevents it from belonging to the subgenre of "cloak and dagger" plays, in which the viewpoint of the gallant and the dictates of his honor predominate. In this play by Sor Juana, the viewpoint that predominates is that of the noblewomen, who struggle until they get the love they desire, unlike those possessing only the virtuous traits traditionally attributed to their sex: audacity and an amorous, absolute, and passionate dedication, from a passive perspective. Sor Juana's female protagonists exceed the males in those traits characteristic of the gallant of the Golden Age theater: valor and boldness, generosity and constancy, and the capacity for suffering and idealism.[3] This role reversal forces us to come up with another name for this type of play, perhaps the *falda y empeño* (petticoat and perseverance) play;[4] this dramatic subgenre may be considered a parodic version of the "cloak and dagger" plays. Joseph A. Feustle has proposed ideas along this line, inviting a new reading of the play that no longer allows us to label it Calderonian (143-49). An example of the ironic and parodic viewpoint is in this dialogue:

Celia: Lady, nothing surprises me;
     in love it is not new
     to dress up truth
     in the colors of a lie.
     Nor who will be startled
     if what it is causes
     the temerity of women to be understood,
     nor the resolution of lovers,
     nor of the treacherous servants,
     since all of this happens in the world,
     and perhaps at home
     there are some Calderonian imitations. ([26] 4:30)

The ironic tone of the character lends to the above and to many other dialogues a distancing from the plot, to the point that the trials of love are reduced to human foolishness. Another example of irony is in the play on words in the last two lines of the previous speech: "perhaps at home / there are some Calderonian imitations" (a syncope of *calderonadas*), an ironic expression in a play whose title is, in itself, a parody of Calderon's work.

The festival for *The Trials of a Noble House* has an opening *loa*, three *canciones*, two *sainetes*, and a final *sarao* as well as its three acts. This baroque and mannerist banquet, in the comical vein, is a theatrical celebration like few others in the Spanish language, linking fraternally the theatricality of the carnival with the laudatory nature of the occasion.

Study of The Trials of a Noble House

Loa

The opening *loa* presents an axiomatic conflict between four values, Merit, Diligence, Fortune, and Chance, who have been called by the character/chorus Music to compete in a contest to determine "Which is the greatest of joys?" ([26] 4:3). The speeches by Music were sung by one voice or possibly a chorus. Merit and Diligence are human virtues, and Fortune and Chance are random events and external to persons. Figure 5 shows the allegorical characters divided into two groups.

The meter in this first part is varied: octosyllabic *décimas* rhyming in -ó with intercalated tercets in the style of the *villancico*; an *ovillejo* [three octosyllabic lines, each followed by a line of *pie quebrado* in consonant rhyme]; a *redondilla* with echo verses; ú-a *romance*; Espinelan *décimas* with simple *seguidillas* [alternating verses of five and seven syllables with second and fourth in assonance]; and assonant quartets rhyming in -é and í-a with refrains. The theme is presented through the baroque polarity of free will/ destiny, but this time the conflict is not resolved in a Calderonian manner, with its preference for freedom, but rather by the participation of Joy, who is summoned by the character Merit and invoked by all of the characters:

Merit:	Enough then, this question
	has been reduced to obstinacy;
	and since everything is being shouted out
	and nothing resolved,
	it's better to change the intent.
Fortune:	How?
Merit:	By invoking Joy;
	the one who is coming to this home today
	who is held to be more divine

	Ally ⇨ ⇦ Ally	
Antagonist ⇧	Merit	Fortune
Antagonist ⇩	Diligence	Chance

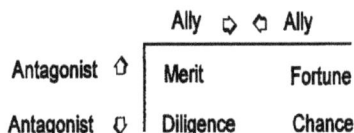

Figure 5. Allegorical Characters in *The Trials of a Noble House*

> than human, as a deity
> she will know how to say for herself
> To which of the four of us
> she should be attributed. ([26] 4:16)

After the invocation, Joy appears behind some curtains with a crown and scepter. First she denies the preeminence of the four partici-pants in the competition, and then she suggests that she herself is the winner, since she personifies the joy of paying homage to "Most High Mary . . . Invincible Cerda . . . beautiful Anteros" (son of the viceroys, who is described with the name of the corresponding god of requited love). The competitors rapidly accept their defeat and pay homage to the three guests, while Music sings a chorus: "Wel-come; / welcome" ([26] 4:23).

The meter in the second part has rhyming hendecasyllable lines; a simple quatrain; hexasyllabic and heptasyllabic *romancillos* and í-a ballad meter; and *romancillos* of í-a heptasyllabic verse with refrains.

In the arguments between Merit and Fortune, several historical personages are cited who were favored by fortune even though they did not deserve it. The conquest of Persia by Alexander the Great, the victory of the Mongol aggressor over the Turkish sultan, and the daring of Caesar in crossing the Rubicon and defeating Pompey are mentioned as victories over the courageous personages who did not achieve equal fame. Next, Fortune herself mentions personages who were helped by Chance: Theseus received the thread from Ariadne in order to escape the Labyrinth on Crete; the Greeks were favored by good fortune in the fall of Troy; and Ulysses received the arms of Achil-les, in spite of the protests by Ajax of Telamon. Theseus, the future protagonist of *Love Is Indeed a Labyrinth*, appears among the char-acters mentioned. The erudition of Sor Juana is manifested by estab-lishing two triads of those favored/disfavored by Fortune, and another two of those who are fortunate/unfortunate according to Chance.

The *loa* presents two irregularities that merit analysis. At the beginning of the *loa*, when Music issues a call for the competition, Merit and Diligence appear on one side, and Fortune and Chance on the other, each with a speech of two lines; then Music returns with its declaration and is interrupted by Merit, who makes a long speech, and then Diligence speaks in support of Merit. Salceda has suspected the omission of two lines in Diligence's part in order to complete the symmetry of the characters, but it could also be an irony that supports the idea that Diligence has lost its haste. The second irregularity occurs at the end of the *loa*, when there is a mention in the last ten lines of the entrance of Francisco Aguiar y Seijas into Mexico City as the new archbishop. There is no doubt that this was a circumstantial addition at the "last moment," as Salceda has noted ([26] 4:xx), since the time of his entry into the city was not known in advance, and the *loa* seems to end with the exclamation by Joy that it has won the competition that took place in the *Loa*:

Music: Welcome
          most sacred Joy,
          Joy always
          is very welcome!
Joy: And may it be so in your House,
          so that it may live forever,
          as does Nobility,
          a bond with Joy! ([26] 4:25)

A chorused refrain was possibly taken from the character Music, so as to be able to incorporate the greeting for the archbishop:

Fortune: And because it is good
             that we be grateful,
             everyone repeat with me:
Everyone: How grandly his Most High
             Lordship has *entered* the city,
             so with his ceremonious *entry*,
             the good fortune of his *entry*
             was the *entry* of our joy!
Music: The good fortune of his *entry*,
             was the *entry* of our joy! ([26] 4:25)

I doubt that this *décima* is an original work by Sor Juana. My thinking is based on the following six points:

- The change of meter without any reason, from an assonant *romancillo* of í-a rhyme to an octosyllabic *décima* with the same assonance.

- The error committed when Fortune, who has lost the contest, is the character who offers the welcome for the archbishop; besides, Providence, not Fortune, is the one who mediates in the naming of a prelate.

- The change in the gender of the entire chorus, from masculine in line 312 ("which of us four [masculine]") to feminine at the end of line 527 ("we [feminine] are grateful"). Also, in the editions of 1692 and 1693 the chorus is identified as "They [masculine] and Music" (lines 207-09), which confirms the masculine presence in at least one of the four contestants, thus making it impossible to use the feminine form.

- The lesser quality of the poetry due to the six repetitions of the same word in the last six lines: *entered* (once) and *entry* (five times).

- The contradiction "Que con bien . . . haya entrado" in the form of the subjunctive, which expresses the desire before the event, as opposed to the information in the following line, which signals the entry as a *celebration*, using the form of the preterit indicative, stating that the action *was*.

- The play on words that closes the *décima* ("The good fortune of his *entry*, / was the *entry* of our joy!") does not have the adroitness that Sor Juana demonstrated with the use of this rhetorical balance.

Regarding the possibility of staging this *loa*, it is necessary to point out that the psychological code indicates a visual presentation of a palace event that holds no meaning for a contemporary audience. The ideological code loses currency by presenting an axiomatic conflict removed from the present-day scale of values, in which diligence surpasses merit, fortune, chance, and above all, joy. Considering the aesthetic-theatrical code, the *loa* demonstrates that it is difficult to decode for today's audience. The same thing happens regarding the linguistic code, because of its markedly cultured dialogue. The four codes indicate a low plausibility for staging the *loa* and nullify any possibility that it was staged in independent form.

By staging the *loa* together with the play, the audience perceives a change in the humanization of the characters: from allegorical entities in the *loa*, who are composites approaching the Platonic world of ideas, one moves to the play with characters who possess their own psychology and move in a more real world. When the genre changes from *loa* to play, and by incrementing the degree of humanization of the characters, the theatrical discourse offers a greater verisimilar resemblance to the real world of the spectator, and therefore the *loa* lends a greater credibility to the play.

Lyrics for the Song "Divine Phoenix, Allow . . ."

The words for this song must have been sung by a female voice because of the need to distance it from any connotation of courtly love. There is no mention in the edition nor in history as to who composed the music that accompanied the festival, but it is quite possible that it was Joseph de Agurto y Loaysa, since this musician composed the musical score for the *Villancicos of the Assumption,* 1679; the *Villancicos of Saint Peter the Apostle,* 1683; and the *Villancicos of the Assumption,* 1685. The festival of Saint Peter the Apostle was on June 29; thus there could have been another collaboration between Sor Juana and this musician on October 4 for the performance of The Trials of a Noble House.

The words, in á-e ballad meter, describe the vicereine, the Countess de Paredes, as "divine Lysi" (an Arcadian name referring to Luisa) and expound on the theme of the festival as a propitiatory sacrifice before the divinity:

> It is not a proud sacrifice
> that comes to your altars;
> that even were it unworthy, the effect
> of being able to sacrifice oneself . . .
> Spiritual victims are
> those who lie before your throne,
> who are wounded by desire's
> incorporeal blades. ([26] 4:26)

This courtly address refers to the origins of the theater and the ceremonial poems of the cult of Dionysus called dithyrambs. There exists an etymological interpretation of tragedy, τραγῳδία, as a caprine song, referring to the sacrifice of a goat in honor of the god. But modern criticism has denied this, determining that it refers to the actors' costumes, which imitated the appearance of this animal representative of Dionysus, or to the fact that a goat was awarded as a prize.[5] Sor Juana makes use of the first interpretation in this song and imagines the theater as an altar and the characters as spiritual victims. At the end, doubts are raised about the acceptance of the sacrifice, but the tension is resolved by the pleasure of disdain:

> They do not fear your scowl; because
> when you become indignant,
> what better joy, than
> to have earned a rebuff?
> Secure, at last, from the pain,
> love works; because it knows
> that for the one who seeks punishment,
> it is a punishment not to punish him. ([26] 4:26)

Salceda has found similarities between these lyrics and Ballad 19, also dedicated to the Countess de Paredes, in whose lines 45-56 friendship is compared with the "divine altars," where ". . . only in the soul / in religious fires, / burns the pure sacrifice / of adoration and silence" ([26] 4:530).

Act I

The editio princeps of this play (1682 [9]) is not divided into scenes and *cuadros* (any change of time or place), but rather into acts, through which we can speculate that the author must have written it this way. When he published the play, Méndez Plancarte divided Act I into three *cuadros* and eight scenes; the first three due to changes of location (don Pedro's house, Leonor's house, don Pedro's house) and the second eight due to the exit or entry of characters. Upon studying this play, Vern G. Williamsen correctly changed the format of the first act, noting its true dramatic structure of six scenes ("Bilateral Symmetry," 218-19). The final three scenes, when joined together by temporal immediacy and dramatic causality, well may have formed a longer scene. Nevertheless, it is possible that Sor Juana had in mind the bilateral symmetry of this play, which verifies six scenes in the first act, as well as in the third. In any case, the division of the first act into four scenes facilitates an understanding of the plot.

Scene 1. In an expository dialogue, doña Ana and her servant, Celia, tell about the kidnapping of doña Leonor by don Pedro, doña Ana's brother. He does this to prevent her from running away with don Carlos to avoid a marriage arranged by her father, don Rodrigo.

Scene 2. The authorities leave Leonor at doña Ana's house. Don Carlos, in turn, has escaped from the authorities and seeks refuge in doña Ana's house, as this lady is in love with him. The gallant hides in another room of the house.

Scene 3. Don Rodrigo, Leonor's father, finds out from his servant, Hernando, that his daughter has run away from home.

Scene 4. Don Juan, another of doña Ana's lovers, surreptitiously enters a dark room and mistakes Leonor for his beloved. Don Carlos and doña Ana come in. Celia appears with a light and all the characters are disclosed, without being able to explain their presence. When don Pedro arrives, they all hide in different rooms, while the siblings talk about the manner by which don Pedro will be able to win doña Leonor's love.

The action takes place in the city of Toledo, and there are also references to Madrid. The time is not specified, but the plot invites one to think that it takes place at the close of the seventeenth century.

Several of doña Leonor's dialogues have been interpreted as biographical, especially the monologue in the first act, "I was born beautiful . . .":

Leonor: I was inclined toward my studies
           since my early years
           with such ardent efforts,
           with such anxious determination,
           that I reduced to a brief time
           what normally was a great labor.
           I was industrious and turned time
           into intense work,
           so that in a brief time
           I was the admirable object
           of everyone's attention,
           in such a way that they came
           to venerate as innate
           the laurels acquired through effort.
           I was the glory of my country

the venerated object
by all of that adoration
which formed the common applause . . .
Among this applause I
was foundering in the attention
among such a throng,
without finding a sure mark,
I didn't aim at loving anyone,
seeing myself loved by so many. ([26] 4:36-38)

The similarities to Sor Juana's biography are undeniable, as Méndez Plancarte ([26] 4:534-35), Paz (*The Traps of Faith*, 139-40), and Sabat-Rivers ("Introducción," [25], 16-17) have pointed out. Some of her traits exceed those in the verisimilar biography of her character, since aside from her beauty and intelligence, Leonor does not have Sor Juana's talent nor the recognition of her "talent for language."

Lyrics for the Song "Most Beautiful Mary . . ."

This heptasyllabic *romancillo* with á-e assonance is dedicated to "Most Beautiful Mary,"[6] who is identified at the end as "divine Lysi," an Arcadian epithet for the Countess de Paredes, María Luisa Manrique de Lara, about whom a poetic portrayal is written in which she is transfigured through courtly flattery borrowed from the cult of hyperdulia. The á-e assonant rhyme is the same as the versification of the first song. This song must have been sung by a female voice in order to prevent it from being confused with a courtly song. The last eight lines are a petition for forgiveness for not having mentioned, pleading ignorance, the physical beauty of the vicereine:

Finally, divine Lysi,
forgive me if, through ignorance,
upon a sea of imperfections
I embarked in a fragile boat.
And so for your applause
there are never competent voices,
since you praise yourself, as one of a kind
it is right that you praise yourself. ([26] 4:64)

Since there was no break or intermission in the baroque performance, the song and the first *sainete,* which followed it, served as the necessary break before the second act and functioned as dramatic elements to introduce the theme.

The First Palace *Sainete*

In the first palace *sainete* there is a return to eminently dramatic space-time parameters similar to those presented in the *loa*. Dramatic conflict is created through a poetry contest that will determine who it is that most deserves the ladies' disdain. The character Mayor of Terrero[7] issues an invitation to the "courtly entities," who personify the courtly amatory relations, and according to the opening stage directions it should be sung ([26] 4:65). The "metaphysical" courtly entities respond, one by one, to the invitation: Love, Respect, Deference, Courtesy, and Hope. Love and Hope come disguised, the others without disguise; all identify themselves and solicit the prize as the one who is most scorned by ladies. The Mayor disqualifies all of the contestants because disdain is given without being deserved:

Alcalde: And since all of the entities
            have finished,
            without anyone
            taking the prize,
            know that among Ladies,
            even disdain,
            although perhaps received,
            is not deserved. ([26] 4:72)

Each of the five amatory courtly entities sings a quatrain accepting its defeat, and the *sainete* ends without the expected dramatic conclusion of selecting a winner. There is little variation in the meter compared with the *loa*: there is *romance* meter with -ó and é-o assonance and with intercalated refrains in the form of simple *seguidillas*. At the end the Mayor announces the defeat of all in a song:

Alcalde: So know, that in the Palace,
            those of you present,
            scorn itself
            is impossible. ([26] 4:74)

This *sainete* presents an aspect that warrants clarification. In the edition of 1692 [2], Courtesy makes a speech as a female character in line 77: "I, My Lord, of all ladies, alone / am the one who deserves the prize" (4:544); in the editio princeps of 1682 it reads: "of all ladies, only." Salceda changes the gender in order to justify the masculine characters: "My Lord, of all, I, the only lady / am the one who deserves the prize" ([26] 4:69). It seems to me that the editio princeps is the correct one because the palace entities must have been portrayed by actresses, or more likely by ladies at court, and thus the gender must be feminine.

The *loa* thematically relates the lovers with Fortune, Diligence, Merit, and Chance. The first *sainete* presents the confusion of feelings that the characters of the play have between the first and second acts: Love, Deference, Respect, Courtesy, and eternal Hope. A shadow of feminine disdain is cast over these feelings, which is the dramatic motive for the lyrics and the first *sainete*. Consequently, these additional pieces bear structural and thematic relations to the entire play. Nevertheless, on more than one occasion they have been analyzed as individual works, to their critical detriment: "Is it a comic version of the doctrine of perfect love as one of unrequitable? If so, it is rather insipid" (Paz, *The Traps of Faith*, 434). And even more to the point: "This first *sainete* may hold some interest to the social historian, but it is too contrived and abstract to be considered good theatre" (Flynn, 54). Upon studying the first *sainete* one may observe that it has genius, and although it lacks an independent dramatic worth, its quality resides in presenting the themes of the work with an ironic counterpoint, which permits the observation of the courting by the characters from a different viewpoint. Additionally, the allegorical characters, because of their sketchiness and single passion, allow the audience to view the protagonists of the following act of the play as more fully humanized.

Act II

The second act preserves the unities of time and action. It takes place early the next morning.

Scene 1. Don Carlos speaks with his servant, Castaño, about his love for Leonor and his desire to get her out of the house. Celia arrives and asks the nobleman to go out to the garden because don Pedro is going to leave and should not see him.

Scene 2. Doña Ana wants to distance doña Leonor from her love for don Carlos. Don Pedro arrives and he speaks of love to doña Leonor; he sings a song to entertain doña Leonor. In a parallel manner, Celia has guided don Carlos and Castaño to a barred window so that they may listen to the song, and there the nobleman discovers his be-loved Leonor. They hear a song about "Which is the greatest pain / among love's pains?" ([26] 4:91). In a reasoned exchange (similar to the first *sainete*) the chorus mentions favor, lack of sleep, impatience, worry, and not enjoying the beloved. The characters respond with their amatory preferences: Don Pedro indicates the absence of the beloved, and Ana, jealousy; Leonor asserts that it is love not recipro-cated; Castaño indicates that it is love without money, and Celia claims it is the proximity of gallants who fail to woo her. Doña Ana interrupts the song upon seeing doña Leonor engrossed. Doña Ana asks Celia to create an amatory trick against doña Leonor.

Scene 3. Celia tries to make don Carlos believe that doña Leonor has accepted don Pedro's love, but the nobleman insists upon removing Leonor from the house. From a window don Carlos sees when don Rodrigo asks don Juan's help in convincing don Pedro. Don Carlos is seen in the distance by these noblemen, and don Juan feels jealous about doña Ana. Celia and Castaño vainly attempt to lead don Carlos away, don Rodrigo approaches them, and don Carlos decides to hide him-self (at the window) in order to save doña Ana's honor in the pres-ence of her brother. Don Pedro enters and don Rodrigo accepts him as a son-in-law, although doña Leonor opposes it. From the window, don Carlos has witnessed the scene without being discovered. In a soliloquy, don Pedro entertains the hope that Leonor will accept him.

Scene 4. Castaño suggests to don Carlos that he take doña Ana, who is wealthy, unlike doña Leonor, but the nobleman insists on remov-ing his lady from her house.

In the song in scene 3 there are two choruses (Chorus I and II) and five voices (Voice I, II, III, IV, and V), with a musical accompani-ment of stanzas sung by the entire company. This lyrical scene has been identified by Williamsen as the dramatic climax and structural axis for the bilateral symmetry of the play (219-20).

The treatment of love mentioned in the first *sainete* made an impression on the characters. Thus the two ladies and their three suitors attempt to search for *love* through gallant *attentions*, having the false *respect* for their elders, such as don Rodrigo (line 739), and they try to continue with more *courtesies*, but the act ends with only don Pedro's *hope* of being accepted and with don Carlos's of recovering his beloved, without their loves having been reciprocated. The courtly entities of the first *sainete* act as an ironic counterpoint to the events in the second act; love, deference, and courtesies are transformed by the trials of this house. Only hope is true, but it does not correspond to merit nor diligence in the opening *loa*, rather to fortune and chance, without having achieved the joy of love up to this point.

The servants are more perspicacious in understanding the entanglements of the house, and thus they have a point of view constantly charged with irony. Castaño exceeds his condition of being a servant: it is he and not don Carlos who slept among doña Leonor's clothes ([26] 4:11-12) and who disguises himself in them. This comic foil shows cynicism in the dialogues with his master ("Since you have lost Leonor, they all seem like 'leonors' to you" ([26] 4:76); he dares to ironically criticize his master's lady ("Well, if she is the Sun, how could / she not shine?" ([26] 4:79); and he even knows Latin phrases: "So, if he caught her / they would come back to you (*volaverunt*)," and "much worse than possessed by the devil, / part of the family forever (*in aeternum*)" (4:114). Celia, in turn, is a practical and intelligent woman, though she shows cynicism and less virtue in her dialogues:

Celia: My Lady, nothing surprises me;
        it is nothing new that in love
        truth is dressed up
        in the clothes of a lie. ([26] 4:30)

The two servants give us a candid vision of the amorous entanglements; while their masters pretend to love the servants' mistresses, the latter make use of their amatory weapons such as tyranny, aloofness, and disdain. The wisdom of the servants is the counterpoint to the foolishness of their masters.

A speech by don Carlos can be described as [an imitation of] "Foolish Women"[8] because it has stylistic and thematic similarities to the well-known verses by Sor Juana, as has been noted by Ezequiel A. Chávez (93). This famous poem could well have been composed by 1683 because it is parodied in the following speech:

Carlos: But they are the vain ideas
            of arrogant youths:

who in seeing them as courtly
later judge them as loose;
 and their wicked ways
contained in their own evil,
if young men do not consider them discourteous,
they do not consider them honorable;
 and for such abnormal thinking
and still not worthy of disdain,
they never do more good
than when they mistreat them,
 so for the one who prides himself
on the slightest presumption,
attention harms him
and it is because he does not deserve it. ([26] 4:76-77)

In a speech by don Pedro there is another similarity with "Foolish Men": "in order to see me in it / I would sooner blemish the mirror" ([26] 4:111), with its counterpart: "he clouds the mirror himself / and regrets it isn't clean" (*Castalian Flood*, [25], 182).

There exist in the second act several metatheatrical elements that can be identified according to Hornby's ideas (32): the piece does not reflect life, but rather itself; the theater within the theater, as when several characters observe the action of other characters, for example, in the scene at the window, or when a group of musicians sings a song about love and the characters interrupt the song with their opinions; the characters' dramatic self-awareness, exemplified in a speech by Celia in an aside directed to the audience that refers to the "stage machinery" ([26] 4:97); or as the last three lines by Castaño that close the act: "Come on, stop complaining / the act will be too long / if we stop here any longer" (4:116).

Lyrics for the Song "Tender, Adored Adonis . . ."

This song was in honor of José, first-born son of the viceroys, Tomás Antonio de la Cerda and his wife, María Luisa Manrique de Lara, Counts de Paredes and Marquises de la Laguna. This child was born in Mexico on July 5, 1683; thus, on the night of the performance he was three months old less a day. The little one is compared to a *pimpollo*, that is, to a young tree or rose bud about to open, as a metaphor for a youth of beauty and grace; to Cupid, the god of love; to a rising star; to an amorous bond between two hearts, comparable to Mars and Venus. The song ends with a rationalization:

Youth accepts
then the petitions
that aspire to your courtliness,
it is not right that they become frustrated. ([26] 4:117)

Thus the child's young age is not a reason for the good wishes not to be fulfilled throughout his life.

The meter is in heptasyllabic *romancillo* rhyming in ú-e. The title "Tender, adored Adonis," does not correspond to the first line ("Tender, beautiful young tree"), which turns out to be more acceptable. With these lyrics, the festival changes the space-time coordinates of the day of the performance by an allusion to a real person. Thus the fictional characters of the preceding act open the way for a female singer—a supposition based on the cradle-song tone—without completely destroying the perception of a fictional cosmos. All of this is accomplished in a performance that has been erasing the boundary between what is real and what is fiction.

The Second *Sainete*

Critics have paid more attention to this fragment than to the rest of Sor Juana's plays because of its metatheatricality and because it contains historical references that allowed Salceda to fix the date of the performance and Schmidhuber to suspect the existence of a lost play and subsequently to find it (*The Second Celestina*).

In this *sainete* various historical personages have been identified:

- Fernando Deza, the owner of the house where the festival took place.

- Attribution of the play to Acevedo (lines 70 and 105), a possible reference to Francisco de Acevedo, who was the judge of a literary contest in 1693 in which Sor Juana was the winner (Sigüenza, 313-15, 318; Méndez Plancarte, [26] 1:390; Salceda, [26] 4:xxvii).

- Another personage, Arias, may be identified as the lawyer Francisco Arias Maldonado, one of the winners of the literary contest of 1683.

- Andrés Muñíz, another of the personages in the *sainete*, is mentioned coincidentally in the will of Sor Juana's mother (Salceda, [26] 4:555), which makes one believe that it is a reference to the official by that name.

- A mention of the prison in Cavite (line 6), in the Philippines.[9]

- The reference to a "Celestina" as a work in collaboration by the "author" of *The Trials of a Noble House* and by another genius (Agustín de Salazar y Torres). The existence of said collaboration has been proven by Schmidhuber with the discovery of *The Second Celestina*.

The reference to the dual authorship of a "Celestina" was analyzed in the Fourth Critical Act, but it is worth mentioning that the two last lines contain a pun referring to a machine and a genius:

Muñoz: But the *Celestina* which caused you
so much laughter, was mestiza
and finished in fragments,
and if it lacked a plan, it had plot lines,
and with a diverse spirit
it was formed from a machine and a genius. ([26] 4:119-20)

The final line may be interpreted humorously in light of the biography of Luis Sandoval y Zapata, a contemporary of Sor Juana and member of one of the most illustrious families of New Spain, as well as a notable poet and author of *Panegyric about Patience* (1645). Beristáin tells the same joke about him: "He was the owner of a plantation or sugar mill; and alluding to this and to his talent, and also to his genius and prodigious nature, he told a clever story: 'From two great machines, which God had given him, one had made him wealthy and the other had reduced him, along with his family, to great poverty'" (3:115). Thus Sor Juana used palace humor to create laughter by recalling an anecdote known to some of the audience and to joke about the collaboration of the genius of Salazar y Torres and a machine or lesser genius, i.e., she herself.

There are several riddles in the second *sainete* that deserve commentary, for example, the confusion on the part of the character Arias concerning the author of the play: first, he claims to know who it is (lines 32-35), then he contradicts himself (lines 71 and 76) by saying he does not know, only to later affirm that he knows (lines 168-69). This incongruity has been understood by Salceda as an error in the order of the characters (4:555), with the need to change some of the speeches in the *sainete* after line 40, which is almost impossible to do. In order to explain this puzzle, it is worth noting that Arias does not know the name of the author, only that he is "a student / who is a beginner at writing plays" (lines 32-33); and Muñiz reports, concerning the authorship by Acevedo, that "It has been said" (line 73); but no one affirms this categorically, rather, only as palace gossip. The references to Acevedo might seem to us like a misplaced joke, especially in a play with subtle ironies and during a celebration of viceregal friendship: acts "longer than a whole play" (line 4); "such a long play and without plot" (line 30); "a student who is a beginner at writing plays" (lines 32-33); "a ridiculous work" (line 82); since "they hissed at the play I wrote" (line 105); the confession by the author that her head is "empty" (line 129); the author's promise, "I give you my word / that I will not write another" play (lines 152-53); and her refusal to rewrite it, preferring to "die from the hisses" (lines 170-174).

Sigüenza y Góngora's book, *Parthenic Triumph*, notes several poetry contests that took place at the University of Mexico in celebration of the Immaculate Conception in 1689. In the fourth poetry contest the following won with ballads of sixteen stanzas: first place, *Juan Sáenz del Cauri* (the anagram for Juana Inés de la Cruz); second place, Juan de Guevara (later, co-author of *Love Is Indeed a Labyrinth*); and third place, don Francisco de Azevedo, who had won the grand prize but ceded it to Sor Juana, since he was the judge of the contest (318). Sigüenza y Góngora won first place in the sonnet category, and the lawyer Francisco Arias Maldonado won third. As an illustration I include in table 9 the epigrams of Sor Juana, Francisco de Azevedo and Francisco Arias Maldonado.

We must understand the humor of the second *sainete* to be in a joking tone, which we could classify as "belonging to the university," since the poetry contest took place at the university, where Azevedo was a professor and Arias was possibly a student. The edition mentions the date, "Today, the 15th of July of the year 1683" (Sigüenza, 327), that is to say, this event was on the minds of everyone, even of the viceroys, who had observed the poetry contest. The atmosphere for the contest seems to have been filled with jokes, since each winner received an award in kind and a humorous epigram written by Sigüenza y Góngora.

Francisco de Acevedo (or Azevedo) is not mentioned as a dramatist by Beristáin; he is remembered as "one of the most reputable professors of humanities in Mexico at the close of the seventeenth

Table 9. Prizes and Epigrams of the Winners of the Poetry Contest of 1683

Sor Juana	Azevedo	Arias
"She was awarded two silver trays with which she can adorn her dresser, and this epigram was sent to her with them."	"The prize he won was a beautiful silver tray in the shape of a hazelnut."	"An elegant silver box for powders and some silk hosiery."
What does it matter if you hide, Sáenz, your name in this situation, if there's a spirit in your verse is it necessary to discover your name? But because you don't merit any complaint, since it cost you a lot of effort, they award you as if for two, don't you see, well, they've given you two trays.	If your muse is a bird, and you win the prize as one sees, Azevedo my friend, upon my word your muse is not confined. Besides, notice that the tray which they give to you to influence you, although you see it as modest and as a hazelnut, it is not obsolescent.	Take this prize and box upon your return; and if you're not surly, it's possible, don Francisco, for a prize to be returned. If your silk doesn't get tangled up, in order that you may put the finishing touches on it, let the prize be given to your effort.

Source: Sigüenza y Góngora, 315, 320, 325.

century, chosen by the city council to design and write the *Triumphal Arch* for the entry into the city by Count Galve in 1689, which he himself published" (1:8); previously he had published a poetic eulogy for the canonization of Saint Francis de Borja in 1672. Monterde names the only play by Acevedo that we know of, *Herald of God*, which was performed in the Coliseum of Plays on October 4, 1684.[10] The lawyer Francisco Arias Maldonado is cited by Beristáin under the name of Brother Francisco (Agapito) de las Llagas, who received lesser degrees in theology and canon law in the capital of New Spain—perhaps during the time of the poetry contest—and who won literary awards in Puebla and in Valladolid. He subsequently assumed the habit of Saint Francis. His book of poetry, *Soliloquies of a Repentant Soul*, was published in 1754 (Beristáin, 170). Arias must have been very young during the contest of 1683, but not Azevedo, who seems to have been an older man.

Another riddle in the second *sainete* is the reason for the booing. With regard to this, there is a quote from Góngora in line 101, "so many hisses, so many cat-calls," and an allusion to la Nava de Zuheros (line 103), both references to a ballad by Góngora:

So many hisses, so many cat-calls
the lowlands of Zuheros heard,
well protected in its valleys,
poorly protected from its echoes! (Góngora, 188)

The same opening line is found in another ballad by Góngora entitled "On the Birth of Our Lord Christ" (Góngora, 222). We can interpret it as a reference that functioned as a private joke on the night of the premiere of the play, with regard to the poetry contest of 1683, since Sor Juana won with a gloss of a ballad by Góngora.[11] Oddly, the physical impossibility for Muñiz to hiss is mentioned, although it may be explained as a reference to the sibilant pronunciation of the "s" by peninsular Spaniards: "They appear to be recently arrived / Spaniards / because the whole theater / is filled with hisses" ([26] 4:123). The *sainete* ends with music, when the hissers sing some verses that claim Acevedo's head is empty (lines 128-34). Metrically, the *sainete* utilizes *silvas pareadas* (*silbas?*) and, at the end, *seguidillas* of varied assonance [of course, *silva* and *silba* are pronounced the same in Spanish].

The theatrical self-awareness of the characters, which makes it possible for them to be judges of their own play, has been indicated as a forerunner of Pirandello's methods since Monterde first made the suggestion.[12] If the historicity of the characters is accepted, all metatheatricality is discarded, since, in their condition as persons, the actors are making a joke. We cannot show metatheatricality in the two songs included in the festival because they are performances that took place in time and space during the event. But if we reject the real existence of the characters, and accept them as fictional entities, metatheatricality is present in several forms: the self-awareness of the characters; the possibility of communication between the characters and the audience; the literary references to Calderón, Moreto, and Rojas, and the allusion to the *Celestina* by the characters; and the mention of the process of writing and performing a dramatic work. On the night of the festival's performance, the audience must have thought that the second *sainete* belonged more to the real world than to the fictitious one; today, although we have partly lost the historical reference, this *sainete* is surprising for its elaborate metatheatricality.

There is great staging possibility for the second *sainete*, and it could well be staged today as an interlude for any classic Spanish

work that might be performed, changing the names of the characters for the authors of the new dramaturgy and including Sor Juana
among the established authors:

> Well I would like, friend, to be a barber
> and shave off whole lines,
> lines so ragged
> that it's certain they were well shorn.
> Would it not have been better, friend, in my opinion,
> that if you wanted to put on a festival for his Excellency,
> to choose, without anguish,
> one by Calderón, *Sor Juana*[13] or Rojas,
> that by hearing their names,
> by my faith, there would not be
> any hissing: I sure wouldn't hiss them? ([26] 4:119)

These lines from the second *sainete* are an example of the use of
metatheater and irony to create laughter.

Act III

The last act of the play begins without any transition. The second
sainete has the rapid pace of a modern farce ending in chaos on the
stage, this time amidst songs and hisses. The tempo of the third act
is slower; thus the scenic tumult is again contained by a change of
the time-space coordinates and a change of tone. In this act the scenic action is linked with the second act, without any temporal or
spatial changes.

Scene 1. Doña Leonor recapitulates the events in a dialogue with
Celia, then goes to her room. Don Carlos is with Castaño in a room,
and he asks him to take a letter to doña Leonor; meanwhile don Juan
is in the garden with a key that Celia gave him.

Scene 2. Castaño dresses as a woman in order to avoid being caught
by the authorities (monologue) and he runs into don Pedro, who
mistakes him for doña Leonor. His wooing leads Castaño to feign
accepting a marriage proposal, but a fight between don Juan and don
Carlos interrupts the amorous scene. Doña Ana tries to separate the
two men. Castaño decides to blow out the candle to prevent an inci-
dent. Don Carlos takes doña Leonor from the house, thinking that
she is doña Ana, whom he wishes to save from her brother's wrath.
Doña Ana meets don Juan, whom she mistakes for don Carlos, and

she leads him to her room. Meanwhile, don Pedro locks Castaño in another room, still mistaking him for doña Leonor.

Scene 3. In front of don Pedro's house. Don Rodrigo arrives to make sure that the wedding of his daughter, Leonor, takes place. Don Carlos and doña Leonor, who has her face covered, return to the house and meet don Rodrigo, to whom don Carlos hands over the supposed doña Ana, who is none other than his own daughter.

Scene 4. Inside don Pedro's house. While doña Ana observes the scene, don Rodrigo tries to convince don Pedro to accept the relationship between doña Ana, his sister, and don Carlos. Doña Leonor also observes the scene. Don Carlos appears and a fight ensues. Celia and Castaño—still disguised as a woman—and doña Ana and don Juan, who declare themselves lovers, enter in order to break it up. Castaño's identity is discovered and the identity of doña Leonor is established again. Three marriages close the play, doña Ana and don Juan, doña Leonor and don Carlos, and Celia and Castaño, leaving don Pedro as the "deceiver deceived."

The dramatic action is based on the technique of the foreshadowing scene in which the discovery of the false identities is expected, especially don Rodrigo's discovery that the lady he looks after is none other than his daughter, Leonor. In the first and second acts doña Ana is the protagonist, but in the last act the chaos generated by the false identities and the darkness makes her unable to follow the sequence of events that could have led her to fulfill her affections. In a parallel manner, doña Leonor acquires greater scenic importance, as much by her presence as by that of Castaño, who is disguised as a woman using doña Leonor's identity. The third act ironically presents the efforts to achieve the the third step in love—marriage. Nevertheless, "this restoration of the social order in marriages . . ." has a different impact on each character, as Raquel Chang-Rodríguez has correctly noted: "Happiness and love (Carlos and Leonor); love, lack of love, and appearance (Juan and Ana); solitude and feigning (don Pedro) are the three possible alternatives. Circles that seem to close themselves when chosen, yet continue infinitely: they reveal the loss of the center dictated by classical aesthetics and the appearance of concentric circles that underscore the baroque conception of art and of life" (416).

Love is perceived as a game of ironies, and Ezequiel A. Chávez was the first to notice it: "Was not Sor Juana joking about this, about the entanglements of that viceregal court that she knew so well? Was there not in her jovial laughter a kind of distant pardon, without rancor nor melancholic nostalgia? . . . The fact that there are no traces, not even the slightest, of bitterness in her charming and joyful play, nor of a sadness inappropriate in tone or out of place, does this not evince the moral balance of Sor Juana Inés?" (98). On the one hand, the amorous adventures are presented from a point of view that distances them from any credible sentiment, and on the other, there is no concession to moral lesson or social reprimand.

In this act there exists another biographical similarity when doña Leonor mentions the convent:

Leonor: I intend, friend, for you,
                 since I have confided my woes in you,
                 to let me leave
                 from here, because when my father
                 returns, let him not find me
                 and force me to marry;
                 I will go away from here
                 to seek in a cell
                 a corner to bury myself in,
                 where I can cry over my tragedies
                 and where I can suffer my misfortunes
                 in the life remaining to me,
                 that perhaps hidden there
                 my beloved will know nothing of me. ([26] 4:128)

A valuable critical recognition of these biographical references, which borders on conjecture, is that of José Juan Arrom, who has identified autobiographical elements in the female protagonists: *Ana* is Ju-*ana*, "she herself," and *Leonor* is "*le-honor*," the "woman that Juana de Asbaje would have hoped to be" ("Cambiantes imagenes," 9-11). The first is the weaver of desires and the second is the intellectual. The irony resides in the fact that *Le-honor* is, in turn, ridiculed by Castaño, who is disguised in women's clothing.

The metatheatricality of the third act is even greater than that of the preceding two. The ladies observe the action of the men, that is, characters observe other characters in the same manner that the audience does. Castaño is conscious of the audience in the scene where he dresses up in women's clothing, and he even mentions the viceroy:

Castaño: Attention, my ladies,
         this is a part of the play;
         don't think that they're tricks
         hatched here in my imagination,
         because I don't want to deceive you,
         much less His Excellency. ([26] 4:138)

The end of the monologue, "I'm afraid that someone will fall in love with me," is a premonition of what will happen in his encounter with don Pedro. Castaño's asides following this monologue are not an exteriorization of the character's thoughts; rather they are ironic commentaries for the audience, aware that laughter will follow. When don Pedro says he will die with joy over his marriage to Castaño, disguised as Leonor, the comic foil gains a self-awareness and exclaims: "Well my Lord, don't die, / for Heaven's sake, not until / you leave me a child / who will inherit your estate" ([26] 4:143). Castaño's metatheatricality runs to the end of the play, when he utters the customary petition for the audience's pardon:

Castaño: And here, most high Lords,
         and here, discreet Assembly,
         The Trials of a Noble House
         concludes. Forgive its errors. ([26] 4:174)

The *Sarao* of Four Nations

The *sarao* is a nocturnal gathering of persons of station for the purpose of entertaining themselves with dance and music. Its etymology derives from the Latin *serum* (afternoon); the French word *soirée* is still used. The complete title is "*Sarao* Of Four Nations, Who Are the Spanish, Africans, Italians and Mexicans." It consists of three choruses and a musical group, in addition to four dancing groups personifying the nationalities mentioned in the title. The dramatic structure is complex: at the beginning a group of Spaniards comes on stage, accompanied by three opening choruses who have a debate about whether love or obligation is superior, until there is a mention of the first of the three individuals being celebrated, the "Most High Cerda" and "his divine consort," who are accompanied by "handsome Joseph" ([26] 4:176-77). Next appears the group of Negroes and

Choruses I and II, again naming the three individuals being celebrated; the Italians enter in honor of the Countess de Paredes, who belonged to the Gonzaga family and the duchy of Mantua, while Chorus I sings another praise of the celebrated persons; and at the end the Mexicans enter while Chorus II sings a song with a pre-mestizo theme: "If America, once / barbarous and heathen, / tried to make the sun / its deity." At the end, after mentioning for the fourth time the celebrated persons: "To these three deities, / happily bow / proud America / your arrogant head" (4:180), the Nations come together and play the "Reina" and sing, with the help of Chorus III, the solution to the debate, in which Love triumphs. Afterwards, again mentioning the celebrated persons, they dance two dances, the Turdión and the Jácara. The Turdión, a Gallicism for *tordion*, from *tordre* (to twist), is a type of very graceful dance from the Spanish school; the Jácara comes from the Arabic *yakkara* (to make someone furious, to irritate someone); it is a joyous, special dance for an ending, before the petition for forgiveness:

Chorus III: Your good will makes up for
the brevity of the festivity:
its size excuses
the lack of proportion of the object,
and in being yours
it assures success,
since, it never could be lacking,
if it is seen as yours. ([26] 4:184)

The meter is varied. *Villancicos* and a *romancillo* in hexasyllabic -é assonance are sung when the Spaniards enter; then, when the Negroes enter it is *romances* of -á and -é hendecasyllabic assonance; with the Italians it is dodecasyllabic octaves in -á assonance; and lastly, with the Mexicans, it is a hexasyllabic quatrain in -í assonance. The final song and the two dances are *romances* with é-a, é-e, and é-o assonance, respectively. The theme of bullfighting,[14] a much appreciated spectacle in colonial Mexico, is mentioned at the beginning of the *sarao*, when Choruses I and II support Obligation:

Chorus I: Your opponent is Obligation,
who aspires to win the laurel,
because it is he who, you must understand,
is right,

Chorus II: and so, he defends it
with skill and courage;
and upon entering
shows signs of *attacking.* ([26] 4:175)

In spite of the complex structure of the *sarao*, Schilling considered it almost nonexistent, and he adds: "it may be considered as a good lyrical piece of this kind for elegantly concluding a theatrical performance" (246). On the other hand, Daniel has argued intelligently that if there is no physical dramatic conflict, there is indeed a mental one, showing the audience in colonial Mexico the conflict that relates to Spain: Obedience or Love. The *sarao* affirms the supremacy of Love, given the supposed quality of the viceroy and his family (Daniel, «A Terra Incognita,» 125-28). Conflict is also signaled by the four nations, with a separation between Spaniards and Mexicans, as two distinct peoples, together with the Italians and the Negroes.

Included among Sor Juana's poetry is another celebration for the Count and Countess de Paredes and their son, which took place in the Saint Jerome convent between 1683 and 1686, undoubtedly in the presence of Sor Juana. Méndez Plancarte suggests July 5, 1684 ([26] 1:470). On that occasion there was no play, only an Introduction, four dances—Turdión, Españoleta, Panamá, and Jácara—and to conclude, a song in honor of the vicereine ([26] 1:177-87). This is a festival that does not belong to the dramatic genre, since it is a panegyric in honor of the viceroys, the Counts de Paredes and their small son. It does not show any ideological or circumstantial conflict, and there are no characters, only lyric voices.

Dramatic Elements

The Trials of a Noble House is Sor Juana's most elaborate play and the one in which she most demonstrates her style and dramatic freedom, perhaps because she had more time for its creation. It is necessary to note that the three acts each have four scenes, if they are divided into dramatic units and not merely into changes that mark the entrance and exit of characters. Its debt to the Calderonian theater is balanced with elements taken from Lope de Vega, and especially by the ironical and parodical vision that is omnipresent in the piece. The structure possesses a balance interesting as much for the dramatic action, which focuses on the climax of the second scene in Act II, as for the length of the performance, which has its midpoint in this same scene. The structure of the festival is shown in figure 6.

Final Commentary

In spite of being a counterpart to the «cloak and dagger» plays by means of dramatic anecdote, *The Trials of a Noble House* has a greater freedom in the dramatic presentations of the characters and an irony unknown in its period of Spanish theater, only comparable perhaps, borders and styles aside, to the humor of Molière, who was almost a contemporary of Sor Juana. Following is an analysis using the four semiotic codes.

Aesthetic-Theatrical Code

In its capacity as courtly theater, the baroque or mannerist festival belongs to another period of history. Nevertheless, the play, with its two *sainetes* and its *sarao*, does not present any obstacle to its being appropriately decoded today, primarily because of its play on ironies and by its concern with the search for woman's liberation. There is no doubt that a modern audience can find satisfaction watching a performance of this work—the most staged among Sor Juana's works—perhaps as much as a baroque audience would have found.

Psychological Code

While the male characters could seem parodical to a modern audience, the characters achieve some degree of humanization, which brings them closer to the spectators.

Ideological Code

The theme of love, which is central to this work, continues to prevail, and the baroque vicissitudes of the characters' mistaken identities, the confusion in the darkened scenes, the comic foil in women's clothing, and the conventional denouement lend to this piece a distancing that colors it with greater ironies than the baroque audience would be able to decode.

Linguistic Code

The cultured language of some of the speeches increases the distance necessary to decode the play as scenic metaphor and not as

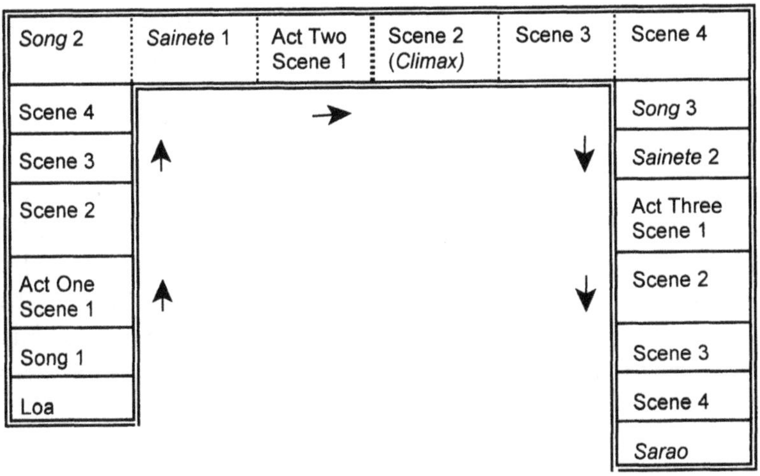

Song 2	Sainete 1	Act Two Scene 1	Scene 2 (Climax)	Scene 3	Scene 4
Scene 4		→			Song 3
Scene 3	↑			↓	Sainete 2
Scene 2					Act Three Scene 1
Act One Scene 1	↑			↓	Scene 2
Song 1					Scene 3
Loa					Scene 4
					Sarao

Figure 6. The Structure of the Festival of *The Trials of a Noble House*

metonymy. The popular speech of the world of the servants retains its wit and freshness on the modern stage. In contrast, the speeches in the *loa* and the first *sainete,* as well as part of the *sarao,* are difficult to interpret appropriately owing to their decidedly cultured lexicon.

The importance of *The Trials of a Noble House* in terms of a staged spectacle is greater than critics have previously noted, because it is the only New World baroque/mannerist festival that has been preserved completely.[15] The editors from that period rarely incorporated into their books or *sueltas* the structure of the spectacle as it was carried out, which means that today we rely on totally edited examples or on descriptive manuscripts of these celebrations. That is, the editors never included with the edition of the *play* its *loa,* its *interludes,* its *dances,* its final *sarao* or *mojiganga* (masquerade). Concerning this deficiency, Javier Huerta Calvo has commented that "because of it, some modern editors have attempted to make up for this lack by publishing the play and the interludes of an author. In any case, it would be a hypothetical reconstruction that does not conform, *sensu stricto,* with reality" (116).[16] Consequently, upon publication in its entirety, the festival of *The Trials of a Noble House* has a dual value: as a piece representative of Mexican baroque/mannerism, and as the best paradigm of a theatrical festival in the Spanish language, only comparable to the festival of *The Fate and the*

Affection of Leonido and Marfisa, performed on March 3, 1680, which includes a *loa* and a play by Calderón as well as an interlude, a dance, and a *sainete* by other authors.

Sor Juana's play has been performed in modern times on several occasions, and among them should be noted the production by Luis G. Basurto, in 1979. After a long time in Mexico it went on tour in Spain and was successful with both the public and the critics (Rabell, *Decade of Theater*, 109). Recently it was performed by the theater group Tecnológico de Monterrey, under the direction of Rubén González Garza (1992). Unfortunately, the complete festival has not been performed again, but some of its elements could be adapted, such as the two *sainetes* and the *sarao*, to frame the contemporary staging of this play with baroque elements that can be appreciated by today's audience.

As a final commentary it is worth noting that along with the intrinsic value of *The Trials of a Noble House* one must also consider the additional value that this is the work of a genius who shares with us her concept of woman by presenting to us, for the first time in the history of the theater in the Spanish language, a theatrical cosmos from the liberalizing perspective of the female characters.

Sixth Critical Act

Love Is Indeed a Labyrinth

Introduction

The very title of the play in the editio princeps relates that the "first and third acts are by Mother Juana; and the second by the lawyer, don Juan de Guevara, a famous intellectual from Mexico City" ([26] 4:207). Daniel has concluded that the need for co-authorship and the simplicity of the festival (a *loa* and three acts) were due to the haste of the celebration ("A Terra Incognita," 107), a supposition that seems plausible to me, especially when comparing this play with the ten dramatic elements found in *The Trials of a Noble House*. During his years of literary activity Guevara must have been much older than Sor Juana, since in 1689 he was around sixty years old; he died on April 11, 1692 (Robles, 3:82, cited in [26] 3:587). Méndez Plancarte includes him in his edition of *Poets of New Spain* (xxxii-xxxiii, 86). The following biography of the co-author was quoted by Beristáin (1819):

> Guevara (D. Juan), a native of Mexico City, presbyter, chaplain, and confessor for the convent of nuns dedicated to Saint Ines, in the same city. He was outstanding in the humanities, and because of this he was elected secretary of the poetry competition held before His Excellency, the Duke of Albuquerque, viceroy of New Spain, in honor of the Immaculate Conception of the Virgin Mary and held at the royal university of Mexico City in the year 1654. His taste in poetry was that of his century, as may be seen in A Patchwork of Gongorine Poetry, more appreciable then than those of the Iliad, and which won for him a poetry award in a public competition to commemorate the dedication of the chapel of the Jesús hospital, founded by Hernán Cortés . . . [Author of] The Most

Splendid Entry into Mexico City by the Viceroy, the Duke of Albuquerque, *1653. (Beristáin, 2:63)*

Following the assertion by Francisco Fernández del Castillo, several
critics have stated that Juan de Guevara was Sor Juana's cousin, but
there is no certainty regarding this assertion (Paz, *The Traps of Faith*,
167, 438).

The theme of the Cretan labyrinth and the loves of Theseus was
staged on other occasions. Barrera y Leirado cites three plays with
the title of *Labyrinth of Crete:* one by Lope de Vega (published in
1621), another by Juan Baustista Diamante (published in 1674), and
a later one by the Portuguese Antonio José de Silva (1736) (*Catalog*
558). Daniel cites two works by Calderón inspired by this myth, the
second act of the play *The Three Greatest Wonders* and the sacramental *auto, The Labyrinth of the World*, from 1677 ("A Terra Incognita," 109). There is no information that proves Sor Juana was
inspired by any of these works. It is more feasible that she followed
the original sources, that is, Sor Juana learned the details of the Greek
legend of the Cretan labyrinth through Publio Ovidio Nason's *Metamorphosis* (42 B.C.-A.D. 18), the very book in which the legend of
Echo and Narcissus is also included and which provided the story
for *The Divine Narcissus*.[1] Later, we shall examine the correspondence between the closing three lines of *Love Is Indeed a Labyrinth*
and the desires expressed by Jason in *Metamorphosis*.

Study of Love Is Indeed a Labyrinth

The *Loa* Celebrating the Birthday of His Excellency, the Count of Galve

This *loa* is the longest one Sor Juana wrote, consisting of 624 lines
(Daniel, "A Terra Incognita," 157), and thematically it is one of the
more complex. Salceda divides it into five scenes with changes according to the entrances of characters or changes in poetic tone; nevertheless, the dramatic structure possesses only a single scene. It
begins with the singing of some quatrains but without the musicians being visible to the audience, then a curtain opens up to show
Age as a "very valiant" lady ([26] 4:185) who invokes the four seasons of the year: Winter, Summer, Fall, and Spring. Two choruses
intensify the clamor by rhetorically asking who has invoked the seasons, and Age responds haughtily:

Age: Who, with so much majesty,
        can bring you together
        except Age, as the Lady of
        Time. ([26] 4:187)

Four actors appear representing the four seasons; of these, at least
one must have been male because the dialogue so indicates: "And
given that you four / are the integral parts" ([26] 4:188, lines 63-64).[2]
The theme of the *loa* is twofold; on the one hand is the concept of
time and its measurability, and on the other is the honor paid to the
guests of the festival, especially the viceroy, Gaspar de Silva y
Mendoza, Count Galve, whose birthday it was, and his wife, Elvira
de Toledo. The thematic duality of the *loa* presents a philosophical
conflict: infinite time versus finite time, as these two fragments
demonstrate:

Age: All of which when well considered
        caused, although time may be
        indivisible, human
        discourse to subdivide it . . .
        that although years are time
        time is more than years. ([26] 4:189)

The conflict is resolved by the desire to transubstantiate age into
eternity, in the presence of the viceroy. Several systems for measuring time are mentioned: hours, days, months, and years, thanks to
other forms now forgotten such as the signaling numbers by finger
position on both hands.[3] Once the conflict of finite time/infinite
time is resolved by the desire to perpetuate the viceroy's time, the
festival continues with the entrance by Music, who had opened the
loa but who had remained offstage.

    The *loa* closes with the recognition of the impossibility of giv-
ing eternal life to the viceroy, but perhaps the gods can indeed give
him the years alloted to his subjects: "*All:* Let the gods / take our
years, and / double yours!" ([26] 4:207). Salceda notes the parallel-
ism of this petition with the one included in Ovid's *Metamorphosis*
when Jason begs Medea: "Take away my years, and add them to
those of my father" ([26] 4:578).

    Janus—to whom the ancients dedicated January–is employed in
this *loa* as a metaphor for the viceroy; the abundant mythological
references included belong as much to fiction as to history, and they

are intertwined with facts and temporal references. The following points contain historical reference:

- The viceroy's birthday (January 11, 1689).

- The recent arrival on November 18, 1688: "what can be done for him / His Excellency being so recently arrived" ([26] 4:xxi, [26] 4:193).

- The choice of the festival by the viceroy in order to celebrate his birthday: "because already / a more sovereign concern / has directed the Play" ([26] 4:194).

- The presence of those who were former viceroys of New Spain, the Counts de la Monclova and their three offspring, Joaquín, Antonio, and Josefa ([26] 4:204).

- The lack of time to prepare the festival (less than two months): "And being such an arduous task / wishing to make a festival / worthy of such a lofty Prince, / how can it be so hurried?" ([26] 4:193).

- The hand game of numbers which tells that 1688 is a leap year, the year of naming the viceroy to his post and of his arrival in Mexico

- The mention of women in the audience attending the premiere: "the beautiful women, among whom / I do not know which one most astonishes me, / I don't know what about them astonishes me the most, whether their delightful beauties or their beautiful discretions" ([26] 4:205).

The mixture of fiction and reality again is an effect of metatheater, since it fictionalizes reality and invests the imaginary with greater verisimilitude.

One cannot deny that the theme of the infiniteness of time and its human measures evinces a certain irony when one thinks about the temporal limitations under which the festival was celebrated. Perhaps this is the reason why the *loa* elaborates upon the concept of time, since there does not seem to be any other reason that justifies it. The investiture of the viceroy was on November 20, 1688, and the public arrival was on December 4 of the same year, and also on that day a *loa* by Alonso Ramírez de Vargas was performed, published that year with the title *Historical and Political Tale about a Prince Concerning the Fable of Cadmus* (Eguiara, 1:295-96). If the selection of the theme of play was done by Count Galve, as the *loa* seems to indicate, the decision could not have been made until after the first days of December; thus the play must have been written in less than one month. Would the play be finished for the celebration of his feast day? Oddly, the editio princeps bears the following information: "*Loa* for the birthday celebration of His Most High Excellency, Count Galve, *which appears* to have preceded the play that follows" (italics mine), although in the later editions the verb was changed to the preterit: "*Loa* that preceded . . ." In spite of the fact that Salceda thinks the editors of 1693 must have had some motive for this change, there is no evidence that this play accompanied the *loa* for the performance that took place in the viceroyal palace on January 11 ([26] 4:xxi). The *Diary of Notable Events* mentions a play at the palace on January 11, and later a *loa*: "Sunday, the 23rd . . . there was a *loa* at the palace of the viceroy, Count Galve, and another at the palace of the Count of Monclova" (Robles 3:6-7); thus both could have been performed on different occasions.

In the *loa* for *Love Is Indeed a Labyrinth*, Sor Juana experiments with the musical theories of Athanasius Kircher.[4] The characters EDAD (age), Invierno (winter), Estío (summer), Otoño (fall), Verano (spring), and Música (music) utilize a combination stratagem that lists the order of all of the dialogues by the characters representing the four seasons (EDAD, I, E, O, V, and M) since their entrance, as table 10 demonstrates. This internal structure, learned by Sor Juana through her studies of music, separates the speeches into seven homogeneous segments in which the characters of Music and Age serve as the axes. In Sor Juana's structure we can prove the use of Kircher's combination theories according to their explanation in his *Musurgia Universalis* (Rome, 1650), a book of music theory that defines music as an art of mathematical combinations (*Musurgia Combinatoria*). The following combination of the letters A, R, and O is an example presented by this German musicologist: ORA, OAR, ROA, RAO, AOR, ARO. With three letters, six combinations are achieved (2:3). With the name *María*, which has five letters, there are 120 possibilities. Table 11 shows another Kircherian paradigm with 24 combinations based on four letters (2:5).

As for Sor Juana's interest in music, it is necessary to recall that one of her lost works is the musical study titled "The Conch Shell,"

Table 10. Kircher's Strategy Applied to *Love Is Indeed a Labyrinth*

1	2	3	4	5	6	7
IEVO	M	VOEI	I	M	IV M	EDAD
IVOE	V M	EDAD	TODOS	EDAD M	O M	TODOS
TODOS	O M	OIEV	V	EDAD M	IEVO M	M
EDAD	E M	EDAD	TODOS	EDAD M	I M	
IEOV	I M	EIVO	E	EDAD M	E M	
EDAD		EDAD	TODOS	EDAD M	V M	
IVEI[a]		VIOE	O		O M	
		EDAD	TODOS			

[a] In order to preserve the combinations it should be IVEO, removing the repetition of Invierno [winter] and substituting Otoño [fall]. Note that the dialogue by Age ("I get out of every difficult spot") is added in order to introduce the information about the celebration "of giving years" to the viceroy ([26] 4:194), since it breaks with the structure inspired in the mathematical combinations that must have been written in advance.

as the author herself tells us in Ballad 21, "After Considering My Love" ([26] 1:64), and as Diego Calleja notes in his biography of Sor Juana [3]. Kircher also uses the figure of the conch shell in order to explain musical harmony; perhaps Sor Juana's lost manuscript is an elaboration of this Kircherian concept.[5]

The versification of the *loa* is carefully done in spite of the hurried circumstances of the festival. It begins with quatrains sung in heptasyllabic *romance* of á-o assonance; when Age enters, it changes to octosyllabic and hexasyllabic *romance*; the appearance of the four seasons is followed by rhyming couplets of varied assonant rhyme, then by a long *romance* of á-o assonance. Beginning with "Claro Silva, excelso Jano" ([26] 4:195) there are *décimas* rhyming in abbccddeed, which are intercalated in the sung quatrains. Later, Sor Juana again uses the echo effect with echoed *ovillejos*. The *loa* closes in ó-e assonant *romance* of octosyllabic verse intercalated with tercets in *arte menor* of five, seven, and five syllables, with ó-e assonance in the pentasyllabic lines. These and other echo effects in Sor Juana's poetry have been studied with considerable skill by Daniel in "The Use of the Echo" (71-78).

Act I

As with all of Sor Juana's plays, in the editio princeps of 1692 [2] the first act is not divided into scenes. In the edition by Salceda [26] it has ten scenes. Nevertheless, if we pay attention to the internal struc-

Table 11. Kircherian Paradigm Based on Twenty-four
Combinations of Four Letters

N	A₁	M₁	E₁	N₁
1	AMEN	MAEN	EAMN	NAME
2	AMNE	MANE	EANM	NAEM
3	AEMN	MEAN	EMAN	NMAE
4	AENM	MENA	EMNA	NMEA
5	ANEM	MNAE	ENAM	NEMA
6	ANME	MNEA	ENMA	NEAM

ture instead of the entrances by characters and the meter, it becomes necessary to reduce the number of scenes to four.

Scene 1. Chorus 1, out of the audience's sight and accompanied by music, introduces Ariadne and Phaedra, princesses, who enter accompanied by Laura and Cintia, their respective servants. Chorus 2 sings about the misfortunes of Theseus from off stage. Chorus 1 sings with optimism about victory and beauty, while Chorus 2 sings with pessimism about ill fortune and death. Laura reports, in a lengthy speech, the history of the labyrinth and the Minotaur, the strife between Athens and Crete, and the fact that Theseus is going to be sacrificed. The two sisters are moved by the misfortune of the Athenian prince.

Scene 2. King Minos, their father, rushes in, accompanied by Bacchus and Lidoro, princes, and Racimo and Tebandro, footman and captain, respectively. The king recalls the death of his son Androgeus at the hands of the Athenians, and his vengeance by demanding from the conquered people six maidens and as many young men selected at random to be sacrificed to the Minotaur, who is enclosed in the labyrinth. In an intercalated parallel subscene, Lidoro declares his love to Phaedra, but the love is unrequited. The scene again turns to King Minos, who summons Theseus, accompanied by the Athenian ambassador, Licas, and by Atún, Theseus's servant and comic foil. From different places, Ariadne and Phaedra, feeling moved, observe the meeting between the prisoner Theseus and the king. Theseus has a long speech in which he asks that he be the last human to be sacrificed so that the feud may end, since he too is a prince, as was the son of Minos; Phaedra comments on the scene from afar. The king does not heed the petition and, in spite of the desperation of the sisters, orders Tebandro to kill Theseus, then they exit.

Scene 3. Theseus has remained alone, and Phaedra manages to move close in order to speak with him; Ariadne and Cintia watch the meeting. In a parallel scene, Atún speaks to Laura of his love for her, and she rejects him with dignity.

Scene 4. Following the advice of Atún to court Phaedra, the prince speaks about his misfortune to Phaedra, who tacitly accepts him. In a parallel scene, Atún speaks of love to Laura, who arrogantly scorns him. A jealous Ariadne, who has observed all that has happened, decides to save Theseus from the labyrinth with a thread; similarly, a jealous Bacchus listens to the conversation between Ariadne and Cintia. When the lady and her servant exit, Racimo suggests to Bacchus that he court Phaedra to avenge Ariadne's scorn; the lady appears and accepts his wooing. Lidoro, as the jealous lover, watches the scene and manages to overhear that Phaedra does not love him. Lidoro draws his sword and challenges Bacchus, but the King enters and the duelers sheathe their swords, while Phaedra lies about the nature of the altercation. The four noble characters have several asides in which they summarize their dominant passion, while Racimo ridicules the nobles.

Act II

As we have stated before, this play was published for the first time in the editio princeps of 1692 with the authorship ascribed to Sor Juana (first and third acts) and Juan de Guevara (second act), and it has been accepted thus by critics without any subsequent examination. Sor Juana's ability for writing verse was much greater than Guevara's, and her experience as dramatist was also greater, since by 1688 she had written two plays and several other pieces for the stage. *The Divine Narcissus*, published in 1690, could have been written in this period. In Guevara's case, he was writing dramatic art for the first time; previously he had written only poetry, and because of the scant amount of poetic production that he left, it cannot be compared with that of the best poets of his generation.

Salceda's edition [26], the only one that until today has broken the act into scenes, divides the play into fourteen scenes. Nevertheless, for a greater understanding of the climax and dramatic tension, I suggest the following organization:

Scene 1. In the palace, Tebandro tries to dissuade the King from following through with his revenge and to save prince Theseus. Atún watches from the distance. The Captain announces that Ariadne and Phaedra will have a big celebration in the Castle of Diana.

Scene 2. Theseus comes out of the labyrinth, where he has remained hidden since killing the Minotaur, and Atún tells him about the upcoming "*sarao*." The Prince confesses his love for Phaedra and his gratitude toward Ariadne for having saved him from death in the labyrinth. Laura arrives with a sash, which Phaedra sends to Theseus; after the servant exits, Cintia enters with a feather from Ariadne for the gallant. Everyone exits and Racimo enters to tell the audience that Bacchus will also attend the masquerade.

Scene 3. Music is heard in the palace ballroom. The King and all the characters enter, including the servants, all with "masks and hats with feathers." Theseus (with the sash) dances with Phaedra, and Bacchus with Ariadne. Lidoro dances with Laura, believing her to be Phaedra, and Cintia with Atún, who drops the feather he was carrying. Bacchus recognizes it as Ariadne's, but he confuses Atún with Lidoro. Phaedra recognizes Theseus by the sash he is wearing and arranges to meet that night. Ariadne confuses Bacchus with Theseus because of the feather he is wearing, and she arranges a meeting with him for that evening, but the gallant believes that the person being invited for that evening is Lidoro. The three suitors discuss a verse sung by Music:

Music: In matters I do not believe in
 I feign belief sometimes,
 just to see if I get some hope
 from the force of desire. ([26] 4:270)

The King interrupts the soiree to go off and rest. Before leaving the noble women and men he has an aside. Atún notes that he has lost his feather, and Racimo unmasks himself.

Scene 4. From the shadows Phaedra and Ariadne enter, each through her own door, and they give a soliloquy in sonnet meter, the first on hope and the second on the anguish of love. Theseus's soliloquy follows, while he waits for Phaedra. Ariadne discovers the identity of Theseus, but the gallant confuses her with Phaedra, while she, jealous, finds the two of them talking, until Theseus calls her Phaedra and Ariadne discovers the error of mistaken identity. On an order from her mistress, Laura takes Bacchus to meet Ariadne, but the nobleman confuses Ariadne with Phaedra, and he speaks to her about the feather he supposes to belong to Phaedra. Cintia explains Ariadne's error to her. Theseus and Bacchus fight. When Lidoro enters with his sword unsheathed, Theseus and Atún flee to the labyrinth. Laura and Cintia enter holding lights, Bacchus and Lidoro are surprised to find themselves fighting each other and, jealous, they resolve the identity of the other suitor. The last scene invites one to pursue the future vicissitudes of love through eighteen auspicious asides; the last one is shared by the the noblewomen:

Phaedra: (But, will he know my anguish . . .
Ariadne: (But, will he know my suffering . . .
Phaedra: Sensing that in my confusion,
       Love Is Indeed a Labyrinth?). ([26] 4:301)

So read the last four lines of the second act in the editio princeps, but in Salceda's edition the last two lines are spoken by "The two noblewomen"; nevertheless, I believe that the editio princeps is the correct one, with the last speech by Phaedra, who is the one Theseus loves.

Act III

Scene 1. Racimo explains to the audience that he is taking a letter of challenge to Lidoro from Bacchus, his master. Similarly, Atún reports that he is looking for Phaedra in order to give her a message from Theseus. Now the servants become confused, and Racimo gives the letter to Atún, thinking that he is Lidoro's servant. Theseus reads the letter—written in prose—and since it is addressed to a prince he believes it to be for him, and he accepts the challenge. Atún picks up the letter that his master dropped when he left in anger, but because he cannot read, he believes it is a love letter from Phaedra for Lidoro.

Scene 2. In the palace, the King tells Bacchus that upon learning of the supposed death of Theseus, the Athenians have organized an armada, which is sailing toward Crete; this will prevent Bacchus from answering the challenge.

Scene 3. In the garden outside the palace Theseus waits in vain for Bacchus. Lidoro arrives hurriedly, since he finally has just received the letter of challenge, which he is holding in his hand. The two suitors fight, thinking they are fighting with Bacchus. Lidoro falls mortally wounded and Theseus flees.

Scene 4. Bacchus goes out to the garden to lessen his boredom of being with the King. Tebandro finds him there, along with the dying Lidoro. A guard picks up the letter of challenge, which Lidoro dropped, and with which they are able to incriminate Bacchus. Tebandro believes in Bacchus's innocence, allowing him to escape, but his position as a captain compels him to inform the King. In a soliloquy, Bacchus decides to flee because no one will believe in his innocence. Similarly, Atún tells Ariadne about what has transpired; the noblewoman asks the servant to arrange a meeting with his master on the balcony that overlooks the garden. Ariadne gives a soliliquy in the form of an amorous sonnet and exits. Theseus asks Phaedra to accompany him to Athens; the lady accepts the invitation; Theseus will go to the port in search of a ship that will take them to his homeland, while the lady awaits him at the entrance to the garden.

Scene 5. In the garden, at night. Bacchus, disguised, finds Ariadne, who is waiting for Theseus on her balcony, and he pretends to be the supposed suitor. Believing him to be Theseus, Ariadne agrees to go to Crete with him and tells him she is coming down from her balcony. Phaedra is at the gate and she goes off with Bacchus, who believes her to be Ariadne. Similarly, Theseus leaves with Ariadne, believing her to be the sister. Trying to find his master in the dark, Atún causes the mistaken identities to be discovered. Bacchus and Theseus, jealous of one another, fight. Tebandro and some soldiers stop the fight, and because of the shouting the King enters. Upon seeing his daughters he feels betrayed, and he condemns the two couples to death: "Let them die, and let my honor live, / they have tried to offend it!" ([26] 4:346). Two soldiers and the two female servants arrive with the news that the palace is being occupied by Athenians. Ambassador Licas, now acting as a general, appears with the Athenian soldiers. At the point when they are about to execute King Minos, Theseus stops them by announcing that he is alive. The prince refuses the kingdom of Crete, asking only for himself Phaedra's hand in marriage. Ariadne, feeling rejected, accuses Theseus of Lidoro's death, but the King pardons the crime, giving Ariadne's hand to Bacchus. The servants also wed: Racimo marries Cintia, and Bacchus marries Laura.

The Dramatic Structure

In spite of its dual authorship, the play has a perfect structural balance, with parallelisms in the number of scenes in the three acts. The first act has its climax with the technique of the foreshadowing scene, when Phaedra meets Theseus while Ariadne watches from afar. In the second act the climax occurs in Scene 3, where the soiree is more lyrical and visual than dramatic, and with the couples Phaedra-Theseus and Ariadne-Bacchus giving us an indication of the denouement of the play. In the third act the climax is in the scene where Phaedra agrees to escape to Athens with Theseus, and the denouement occurs in Scene 5 with the multiple marriages. Figure 7 shows the play's dramatic structure. The dramatic factor that permits this denouement is the opportune appearance of the Athenian army, which prevents the death of the protagonists and turns around the dramatic action that would necessarily lead to tragedy. This solution recalls the ending of *Life Is a Dream*, with the liberation of Segismundo by the people who wish to crown him king.

The customary petition for forgiveness at the end of the play is spoken by Tebandro:

Tebandro: And a full pardon
             is beseeched of you by the pen that,
             contrary to the genius which inspires it,
             wrote to serve you,
             without knowing what it was writing. ([26] 4:352)

These last lines do not reveal the dual authorship; rather they only mention a pen, perhaps referring to the harmonious collaboration.

Could Sor Juana Have Collaborated on Act II?

The beginning of the second act is surprising for its perfect organizational and dramatic unity, although there are some subtle stylistic differences. This situation is contrary to what happens in innumerable Golden Age plays that were written by two or more geniuses; in them the change of author is more conspicuous. In the following

Act Two Scene 1	Scene 2	Scene 3 (*Visual Climax*)	Scene 4
Scene 4		→	Act Three Scene 1
Scene 3 (*Climax*)	↑	↓	Scene 2
Scene 2			Scene 3
Act One Scene 1	↑	↓	Scene 4 (*Final Climax*)
Loa			Scene 5 (*Denouement*)

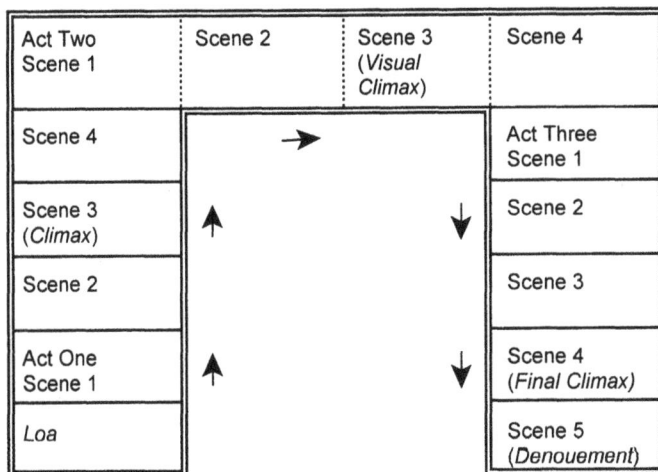

Figure 7. Dramatic Structure of *Love Is Indeed a Labyrinth*

passages I attempt to prove the research hypothesis claiming that Sor Juana wrote some sections of the second act of *Love Is Indeed a Labyrinth*, a possibility never before examined (see table 12). There are six reasons.

1. The dialogue between the King and Tebandro, in the rhyming *silvas* in the cultured style, shows a lyrical change from the preceding act, but with the entrance by Atún the festive dialogue similar to that of the first act returns (lines 47 to 52):

Atún: Sticking my head out, I infer
           I'm a tuna, and I want to be a turtle.[6]
King: Death to Theseus!
Atún: What a horrendous blunder!
           There's no doubt that he'll be tough to kill.
King: I cannot calm my ire;
           I'm all anger and fury.
Atún: O Burning rage!
Tebandro: Let your Majesty try to relax.
Atún: Let it be, and let him be more than consumed,
           for with this imprudent king,
           I will learn the secrets of the one consumed. ([26] 4:256-57)

Table 12. Lines Attributed to Sor Juana from the Second Act of
Love Is Indeed a Labyrinth

Scene Number	Line Number	Characters
1	47 to 52	Atún and the King
2	67 to 78	Atún
3	157 to 328	Theseus, Atún, Cintia, and Laura
4	631 to 668	Atún and Racimo
	Total: 224 lines	

Note: The line numbers are from the edition by Méndez Plancarte [26], corresponding to scenes 1, 2, 3, and 4.

I suggest that these lines were written by Sor Juana. Later, the cultured tone reappears in line 57 with the closure by Tebandro and the King: "The Princesses, my Lord, have prepared / a great celebration for Your Majesty" ([26] 4:257), which well could have followed originally line 42: "Tebandro, how / happy I would be, if I could alleviate / this fierce battle of my anger!" ([26] 4:256).

2. Scene two begins with Atún's dialogue in line 64, although it belongs metrically to the *silvas pareadas* of Scene 1, and after only three lines the meter changes to á-e *romance*, without any dramatic justification; this meter is maintained through the following 158 lines. I conclude that in this scene change there is also a change of author. Lines 67 to 78 may be the work of Sor Juana (almost all of Scene 2):

Atún: Let's get out to see the day,
         for there is a large Labyrinth,
         and I am in it;
         May it please God that this end well.
         Let's get out to see the day;
         for in this horrible prison
         where darkness reigns,
         light is unknown.
         Certainly, I am ready
         almost, almost to help
         my master in order
         almost, almost to
         help solve his problems. ([26] 4:258)

Salceda has found similarities between some of these lines and those of the *Villancicos of the Assumption*, 1677: "Dancing joyfully I'm almost, almost about to tell her / in front of everyone" ([26] 2:247).

3. Starting from line 79 the poetry loses its popular vitality, which is especially noticeable in the speeches by the comic foil. The long expository speech by Theseus and the subsequent dialogues are undoubtedly by Guevara, until line 156; the following fragment proves that they cannot be by Sor Juana:

Atún: Because the King
          was advised by Tebandro
          that Ariadne and Phaedra wanted to give him a celebration
          to lighten his sorrows,
          and they, courtly goddesses, had prepared
          a banquet such as is the custom,
          with courtly decorations. ([26] 4:260)

Starting from line 157 there is a change in tone, once again from cultured to popular, with abundant breaks in the verse halfway through the line while moving from one speaker to another. Atún also speaks Latin in the second act, as does Castaño in *The Trials of a Noble House*; the Latin phrase "Being the *tu autem* / from which you exit . . ." ([26] 4:261) is the same as the one used by Sor Juana in the *Villancicos of the Assumption*:

          The sonorous fugue, which resounds magnificently
          written in Latin and sung in the vernacular,
          from the voices which angelically resound
          come glorious triumph, it is only the *tu autem*. ([26] 2:247)

The expression *tu autem* is the phrase with which the breviaries conclude: "Tu autem, Domine, miserere nobis . . ." ([26] 2:475), and it means something that is considered essential and important for some purpose.[7]

The popular tone of Atún's dialogues, which are the center of dramatic focus in many scenes, recall the dialogues of Tacón:

Laura: I am looking for Theseus
          but, if I don't deceive myself,
          the one I'm looking at is Atún.
          —Ce [Hey],[8] handsome!
Atún: This kitchen talk refinement
          doubtless contains a fishhook,
          to catch me. ([26] 4:261)

The last expression was used by Sor Juana in the first act ("fregatriz desdén," [26] 4:244); it is difficult to believe that Guevara would repeat it. The same may be said for the metatheatrical irony in the words of Atún:

Atún: What am I seeing?
        That's the second part
        of the romantic play
        where there are pairs of beauties. ([26] 4:265)

The self-referentiality of theatrical consciousness and the irony of there being two noblewomen (and two authors for the play) are clever devices by the dramatist that are not expected from a novice at stage-craft. In addition to this, Sor Juana used linguistic artifices on multiple occasions based on proper names, as in the two plays on words in the second act that change nouns into verbs: "You call these things foolish / pretending, somehow, / to turn me into a prince from a foot-man" ([26] 4:244); and: "My gosh, he is handsome: / once again he makes a minotaur of us" ([26] 4:270). Word games not far removed from Atún's speech in the first act: "She is Prince Phaedra / and you [are] Princess Theseus" ([26] 4:239), or in the third act: "What trouble can befall me / since he Lidores me" ([26] 4:304), and many others by Sor Juana.

4. Starting from line 329, with the change to assonant *romance* rhyming in á-o, the act seems to be entirely the work of Guevara, because of its prolix stage directions and the lack of changes of speeches from one character to another in the middle of a line.

5. Atún's new intervention, from line 631 until line 668, is another subscene that demonstrates the dramatic art of Sor Juana. There is subsequently another intervention by Tacón that does not appear to be by Sor Juana—when the comic foil and Theseus enter the labyrinth ([26] 4:296)—because this shows little dramatic inventiveness for an exit that should be extraordinary.

6. The second act has two sonnets in succession, spoken by Phaedra and Ariadne ([26] 4:283), and both are unquestionably the work of Guevara, as is the rest of the act. The moralizing commentaries of the scene with the *sarao* ([26] 4:277-79) show an ethical interest never utilized by Sor Juana in her plays.

Regarding the second act of *Love Is Indeed a Labyrinth*, Paz has stated that "it is not inferior to the two written by Sor Juana; apart from the verbal merit of the whole, it has theatrical moments that Moreto would have applauded" (*The Traps of Faith*, 438). Méndez

Plancarte ([26] 1:xxxiii) and Daniel ("A Terra Incognita," 108) note a similar perception. On the other hand, Karl Vossler denies that it has any kind of style (*Investigaciones linguisticas*, 64). For his part, Gerard Flynn sees the play as having great thematic inconsistency because it is unable to unify the theme of labyrinthine love with the style of the "cloak and dagger" plays (51). My opinion is that in spite of the dual authorship, the play possesses structural, linguistic, and thematic unity, especially through a language with sufficient homogeneity and dramatic efficiency, and through the psychological continuity of the characters, above all, of the noblewomen and Atún. Coincidentally, the majority of the passages in the second act in which the comic foil is present are those designated in this study as the ones by Sor Juana. It is worth noting that the name of one of the comic foils, Racimo, comes from *It Cannot Be*, by Moreto, which had been staged on November 6, 1678, in New Spain; the comic foil Tarugo uses it to conceal his identity. Similarly, Tacón, in *The Second Celestina*, corresponds to the name of the comic foil in *The Look-Alike at Court*, also by Moreto.

Dramatic Elements in Love Is Indeed a Labyrinth

Through the use of an imaginary space and the kind of amatory relationships, this play presents characters who have been subjected to a process of emotional simplification and to an imaginary time not very distant from that in the pastoral world: Crete is Arcadia. Instead of the audience imagining, in an amatory game, that the lovers are shepherds, in this play the public can imagine that they are heroes in a world close to the one re-created in a children's story. The continual anachronisms force the spectator/reader to recall that the stage presents the Hispanic world with *alcázares* (citadels) instead of palaces, with words that did not exist in the Greek world, such as *zahorí* (clairvoyant) and *mondongo* (tripe), and with relationships between masters and servants that are characteristic of Golden Age plays and not Greek mythology.

Irony is omnipresent in the play. The irony is born of the similarity between the action in the world of the noblemen and the same events in the microcosm of the servants. This occurs by sometimes having a more dignified servant, as in the first act, when Laura scorns Atún's flattery while both noblewomen swoon with love at the first sight of Theseus. The very title of the play contains irony, for love is a greater labyrinth than the one on Crete, because in it there is no life-saving thread from Ariadne, but rather mistaken identities, which are dramatic metaphors for the fears and discord found in all human relationships until genuine love is reached.

Love Is Indeed a Labyrinth is a play in which many elements are arranged in pairs, in opposing correspondences (see table 13), so much in vogue during the baroque; this is what lends variety and dramatic tension to the piece. In the last scene paired loves multiply, and at the exit of the love's labyrinth, there is not only one couple, but four.

On the other hand, *Love Is Indeed a Labyrinth* loses thematic dimension by reducing the heroic archetypes to mere amatory relationships; the tragic depth of the Greek characters does not continue in Sor Juana's plays. There exists a different point of view and concept of life. It is not a "cloak and dagger" play, as critics since Menéndez Pelayo have considered it. Rather, it belongs to another genre in spite of the masked men and challenges to fight; its true genre is the love play, a nomenclature proposed by Francisco Ruiz Ramón for this type of play by Lope de Vega: "In all of them we witness, led along the most diverse paths, the triumph of love, which overcomes all obstacles, leaps over all barriers, ridicules all norms, invalidates all rules, frees all individual potential—intelligence, will, instinct, ingenuity, fantasy—and exalts the totality of living. The protagonist of all of these pieces is neither the woman nor the man, rather the couple" (Ruiz Ramón, 173-74). These considerations may be applied without hesitation to this play by Sor Juana, because neither Theseus nor the Cretan sisters are the protagonists; rather, they represent the apotheosizing celebration of love.

The play presents the rivalry between two states, Athens and Crete, and the effort by the Greeks to free themselves from Cretan domination, which ends with the taking of the palace at Minos and the marriage of Phaedra and Theseus. The theme of liberty is present in the first act, with a few mentions of democracy, in spite of the fact that this concept still had not been shaped by history:

Theseus: Let this truth be proven,
              by saying that the first
              to impose on the world
              dominion, were deeds;
              since all men

Table 13. Opposing Correspondences of *Love Is Indeed a Labyrinth*

Mythic Crete, with ancient and pagan elements, taken from Greek mythology	Anachronistic Crete with Spanish elements: Alcázar, Infantas [princesses], the concept of honor and style
The Cretan labyrinth that leads to the Minotaur	The labyrinth of the play that leads to love
The microcosm of the masters	The microcosm of the servants
Phaedra loves Theseus	Ariadne loves Theseus
Foolishness and confused identities. Darkness	Intelligence and clear identities. Light
Shared authorship: Sor Juana	Shared authorship: Guevara

> were equal, there was no means
> to introduce the inequality that we see,
> like that between king and vassal,
> like that between nobleman and commoner . . .
> From which I infer, that only
> effort was able
> to differentiate among men,
> who were born equal,
> with such a great distinction
> to make some men, being all the equal,
> serve as slaves
> and others command as masters. ([26] 4:225)

Paz described this speech as unusual, "because it is not easy to explain how such principles could be discussed openly at the viceroyal palace without a scandal" (*The Traps of Faith*, 439). Nowadays it is ironic to find the thematic solution of the *loa*—infinite time/measurable time and the desire to extend time for the viceroy's life—in the same play with a speech that evinces the desire for equality and freedom. The polarity of intelligence/foolishness is also ironic because the servants, not the masters, are the knowers of the true nature of the events, and thus, while the masters become lost in the amatory labyrinth, the servants find love without so much confusion and excessive subtlety. The distribution of intelligence does not seem homogeneous; the servants—especially Laura and Atún—have been favored in the play.

The classical allusions only invite the audience/reader to enter this game that masks love with the attractions of courtship and courtly flirtations, without pretending to emphasize the true sorrows from love that the same characters suffered in the Greek mythological stories, as when Theseus, in love with Ariadne, flees Crete with her but then abandons her in Naxos because he has fallen in love with Phaedra (a tragic ending staged by Corneille in *Ariadne,* 1672); or when Phaedra, in love with Hippolytus, Theseus's son, suffers disgrace from an unrequited love which leads to her death, as happens in Racine's *Phèdre,* 1677. The epic element is also absent from this play by Sor Juana in spite of Theseus's struggle against the Minotaur, since this deed happens between the first and second acts and is only briefly mentioned (lines 110 and 111). The very advance of the Athenian ships, to avenge the supposed death of their Prince Theseus, and to thereby free Athens of Cretan domination and the unjust sacrifice of its youth, is reduced to being the dramatic motive causing this theatrical chess game to leave the labyrinth of the complications of courtship, with Ariadne's ball of thread that leads to love.

Calderón wrote about twenty mythological dramas, outstanding among them *Child of the Sun, Phaëton or Not Even Love Can Escape from Love; The Statue of Prometheus;* and *The Beast, the Bolt, and the Stone.* Their author "dresses these myths in the latest fashion of the seventeenth century and with marvelous fantasy, theatrical mastery and lyrical enthusiasm throws himself into weaving and unweaving flamboyant adventures of a complex intrigue, but this modern version of the myths does not mean, in any regard, a dramatic in-depth examination of them" (Ruiz Ramón, 253). In this play Sor Juana continues the dramatic example set by Calderón, but she adds a greater irony by underscoring with ironic foolishness the mistaken identities and by allowing the observation of the world of the masters through the clarifying eyes of the servants. Sor Juana's play shows the influence of Moreto and perhaps of Rojas Zorrilla because of the importance of the servants in the plot and because of their intelligence and astuteness.

Final Commentary

Love Is Indeed a Labyrinth is a play that needs critical reassessment, for it has enough dramatic elements to be considered one play that unites two dramatic subgenres, that of the mythological plays of the late Calderonian period (after 1650, according to the chronology of Calderón's work by Ruiz Ramón) and the subgenre of the love play. Paz and Daniel have been pioneers in proposing a change in the critical awareness of Sor Juana's third play. This latter critic of Sor Juana thinks that: "The play has sufficient intrinsic value just as it was written" ("A Terra Incognita," 108). Another reaffirming opinion is by Margaret Sayers Peden, who in an illuminating study, analyzes the play from four perspectives: metatheatricality, the author's comments about her time, the changes from the original myth, and the curious and ambiguous focus on the character of Ariadne. Peden has noted that the character of Ariadne conveys Sor Juana's sentiments through autobiographical connotations: "I propose that there *was* an identification on the part of Sor Juana with the character of Ariadna. Was this identification conscious? . . . Ariadna plays a role that is important to Sor Juana. And what is that role? That of a woman who gives love that is not returned, that of a woman rejected, a woman resigned to self-abnegation" (46). Again Sor Juana plays with the female characters and lets the depths of her sentiments shine through, as she does with Beatriz in *The Second Celestina* and with Leonor in *The Trials of a Noble House*. Peden notes that at the ending of the play there are changes with regard to the original plot of the myth; if the death of Lidoro and the return of Licas are part of the original plot, that is not the case for the psychological reactions by Ariadne. This distortion is due to the fact that Sor Juana altered the character in order to have the opportunity to present her sentiments.[9]

Love Is Indeed a Labyrinth has the same difficulties with staging and comprehension as some of the Shakespearean plays, such as *Cymbeline*, *Twelfth Night*, and especially *Much Ado About Nothing*, because their theatrical codes are similar. Although the ideological code of Sor Juana's plays is not shared by today's audience, so removed from baroque fictions about love, the reality represented can be decodified through other connotations, which distance reality and permit one to enter into other amatory forms, such as courtliness, fineness, and aloofness, which possess in this play a greater appreciation than the fulfillment of sexual love, contrary to what happens today. Consequently contemporary reading/staging acquires ironic and parodic connotations that were not present in the first staging of this play nor in its original reading, but they allow the play to be accepted today with pleasure by an audience that is disposed to laughing at the foolishness love causes, as happens in the Shakespearean plays just mentioned. Thus, the inherent difficulties in this code do not turn out to be an impediment, but rather a positive addition to this play, since the entanglements acquire greater credibility in the idyllic and mythological world of classical Crete than in a Spanish or New World staging, as happens in the first two plays by Sor Juana.

The linguistic code is complicated by a cultured dialogue of difficult comprehension in a modern setting, especially in the speeches by the male characters. This does not happen in the speeches by the comic foil and the servants, which are facilitated by the use of a popular vocabulary filled with humor and word games that today can be decodified effectively.

The aesthetic-theatrical code facilitates an understanding of the play, since modern lighting and sound engineering allow scenes called for in the play to be presented with special effects, such as the entrance to the labyrinth on Crete and the palace of King Minos. With regard to this code it is worth comparing the play with the Italian theater of Carlo Goldoni (1707-1798), who has had so many successes in the modern European theater since the stagings done in the fifties by Giorgio Strehler (b. 1921), especially *The Lovers, The Holiday Trilogy,* and *Quarrels in Chioggia.* What kind of a show would we see if Strehler or another director of his caliber would put on this play by Sor Juana?

A consideration of the psychological code applied to this play is necessary in order to conclude. From the modern humanist-feminist perspective, this play is not the most proficient at presenting the free will of women and the use of their intelligence in order to achieve their desires, at least not with the care taken in Sor Juana's other two plays. Nevertheless, if we consider the ironic and parodic contents, the characters of this play can be justified by being understood within a ludic world, with different rules from the actual world of human relationships, but retaining, as in children's literature, a candor and pristine sensibility, which would make the audience accept what would otherwise seem antiquated and absurd. As proof of the currency of this fourth code, it is necessary to cite *Leonce y Lena*, by the German George Büchner (1813-1837), which is a satirical play that had no impact on Romanticism and which has been one of the theatrical successes of the twentieth century, and whose characters are not very far removed, from today's perspective, from the world of Sor Juana's play about love.

Seventh Critical Act

Posthumous Reputation of Sor Juana's Theater

As a colophon, we include in this study of Sor Juana's plays a brief commentary about the theatrical achievements of this playwright. Two kinds of dramatic authors exist in the history of the theater: those who initiate a style and become a school, like Lope or Moratín, in their respective periods, and those who take a dramatic model to its maximum height, like Calderón de la Barca and Sor Juana. Sor Juana's plays closely follow the aesthetics of the Calderonian cycle, although not so much Calderón as Moreto, and they may be compared, without exaggerating their merit, to the most successful plays from the end of the seventeenth century. As regards dramaturgy, Sor Juana's plays contribute unique thematic achievements to the Golden Age theater; what Stephanie Merrim has described as "womanscript" (94) and what is an innovative perspective for having been written from the point of view of the female characters and not from the patriarchal vision of the male characters, as happens in the majority of the secular Golden Age plays, with the only exceptions being some pieces by Tirso de Molina, Rojas Zorrilla, and Moreto.[1] For the first time in the history of the theater in the Spanish language a female dramatist presents on the stage her perception of women (with a production of fifty-two dramatic pieces).

The differences among the three plays are slight, yet significant. From the dramatic simplicity of the first play, the author moves toward greater complexity. Greater feminist interest is shown in *The Second Celestina* and *The Trials of a Noble House* than in *Love Is Indeed a Labyrinth*, perhaps because the mythological plot prevented it. The use of dramatic language is one of her more significant dramatic accomplishments because of its effectiveness on the stage, distinguishing noble characters with a elegant lexicon from the servants and comic foils with a popular speech filled with color and humor, what Usigli described as "its facility for conversation" (*Mexico in Its Theater*, 52). Critics have considered *The Trials of a Noble House* Sor Juana's most important play. But this study proposes the same level of quality among the three plays; on the one hand, by presenting new aspects of the play recently discovered and, on the other, by proposing that its author collaborated not only in the first and third acts of *Love Is Indeed a Labyrinth* but also in some parts of the second act, especially in the dialogues by the comic foil. This study proposes that the festival of *The Trials of a Noble House* is one of the best remaining examples of a baroque theatrical festival, either in the New World theater or in the Spanish.

Concerning Sor Juana's dramatic originality, the theatrical contributions are found especially in the subgenres of the *loa* and *villancico*. Daniel has claimed that Sor Juana takes the *loa* to its highest degree of evolution, compared to the *loas* by Calderón and other baroque authors, because she makes it independent, without its being a dramatic appendix to a longer piece ("Sor Juana's Pentad," 78). With regard to Sor Juana's *villancicos*, Méndez Plancarte considers them outstanding among the works by this author, owing to their very polished expression of her piety, and because they are the most significant result of centuries of evolution in the lyric and drama of peninsular Spain and New Spain ([26] 2:xlvi). In the opinion of Darío Puccini, "It is safe to say that the rigorous structure of the whole trend of *villancicos* is due to Sor Juana" (223-27).

The three *autos* are paradigms of their specific genres, given their demonstrated quality: as sacramental *auto*, *The Divine Narcissus*; as hagiographic *auto*, *Martyr of the Sacrament, Saint Hermenegildo*; and as biblical *auto*, *The Scepter of Joseph*. Usigli notes two tendencies in Sor Juana's *autos*: the mystical and the nationalistic, the first linked to the disciples of peninsular mysticism, and the second defined as "a constant sympathy for the Indian, a protest against his social backwardness, against his vulnerability as to human value in the operative plan of the conquest" (*Mexico in Its Theater*, 53).

Metatheatricality is ubiquitous in the dramatic works of Sor Juana, and the variety of degrees presented makes it so that the events transpiring on stage are understood with a multiple perception that allows at least three levels of comprehension: the literal level provided by the plot and by the cosmos to which the noble men and women belong; the metatheatrical level, which determines the comprehension of the commonplace world of the servants and comic foils; and the ironic level, which presents the characteristic view of the author. One of the most important contributions of Sor Juana's dramaturgy is the capacity for metatheatrical self-consciousness of some of the characters, which allows them to recognize themselves as entities belonging to an intrinsically theatrical cosmos.

Critics have found an abundance of mannerist elements in her theater, but they have not noticed some elements that in the later theater would be accepted with great success, such as the social free will of women. This was the theme staged more than a century later in *When a Girl Says Yes,* by Moratín (a piece that also utilizes the stage trick of blackout, as does *The Trials of a Noble House*). The principles suggested by Luzán in his *Poetica* (1737) for the Neoclassic theater, in spite of the fact that they discount the baroque theater in general, allow one to say that Sor Juana's plays belong as much to the end of the baroque/mannerist period as to the beginning of the new Neoclassical aesthetic, because of their greater subjection to the three unities of space, time, and action, and because they present thinking beings who resolve their conflicts more by intelligence than by excessive action. Nevertheless, there is a discrepancy with the principle of "verisimilitude" because, according to Luzán, "the improbable is not believable, and the unbelievable does not persuade or move" (107). These premonitory elements in Sor Juana's plays could seem without grounds because they contradict the traditional notion of presumed decadence at the close of the baroque/mannerist period, but they do have grounds if the plays by Sor Juana and Moreto are compared to those by the great European dramatists of the Enlightenment, such as Carlo Goldoni (1707-1798) in Italy and Alain René Lesage (1668-1747) and Beaumarchais (1732-1799) in France. It was not in vain that these three dramatists borrowed plots and characters from Spanish Golden Age pieces. In the same manner in which the works by Leandro Fernández de Moratín contain dramatic elements foreshadowed in the plays by Moreto, *The Trials of a Noble House* also prefigures Moratín's drama.

As the author of this book, I have included my discovery of unknown texts by Sor Juana: *The Second Celestina* and a *Declaration of Faith Signed with Her Blood.* Additionally, I have pointed out as innovative critical contributions: (1) the proposition that Sor Juana had a greater collaboration in *Love Is Indeed a Labyrinth* than had previously been acknowledged, especially in the speeches by the comic foil in the second act; (2) a critical assessment of *The Trials of a Noble House* that includes the ten parts of the baroque (and mannerist) festival, not just the three acts of the play, as well as an explication of the second *sainete* that sheds new light on its enigmas; (3) a first study of Sor Juana's dramatic theory in writing plays; and (4) a reevaluation of all of her dramatic work, including the *loas* and *villancicos*.[2]

At the beginning of this study I presented some documents showing that Sor Juana encountered obstacles to her being a playwright, obstacles that must have been greater than the ones we know about in order to pursue her vocation as a poet. The silence to which Sor Juana's contemporaries condemned her contributions, without any written censure or praise, makes one think that the author did not develop all of her qualities as a dramatist, since she only sporadically wrote commissioned dramatic works. These adverse circumstances make Sor Juana, as a dramatist, suffer from a lack of willingness to become a woman of letters, that virtue that Rodolfo Usigli described as "volition," of wanting to be a dramatist (*Teatro completo*, 3:497).[3] It is worth reflecting on the reason that Sor Juana's dramatic art did not leave us a work comparable to *First Dream*. Sor Juana's position toward her theater was, above all, that it was the contribution of one night of a festival, to celebrate a royal birth or birthday, or the celebration of a feast day, but it never became her life's project, as was the case with her poetry, and this despite her religious vocation and her being a woman. When Sor Juana concludes her dramatic works with the customary petition for forgiveness by those present, she has more in mind the *machine* than the *genius*:

> Finally, divine Lysi,
> forgive me if, through ignorance,
> upon a sea of imperfections
> I embarked in a fragile boat. ([26] 4:64)

Thus when she closes her third acts with the petition for forgiveness, she stresses the commissioned nature of the work and her unfamiliarity with the dramatic art:

> And a full pardon
> is beseeched of you by the pen that,

> contrary to the genius which inspires it,
> wrote to serve you,
> without knowing what it was writing. ([26] 4:352)

This and other self-deprecating remarks acquire a more human perspective when they are understood as baroque expressions of false humility that should not be interpreted as judgments about her own ability, but rather as expressions of a feeling of less artistic compromise for the theater than for her poetic work. Besides, Sor Juana combined the paradox of knowing herself to be a genius and of not wanting to make a boast of it because she was a nun. The best example of this ambivalence is in the unfinished poem that was found after her death, "When, divine Numina . . ." in "recognition of the inimitable Writers of Europe who made their works greater with their eulogies":

> So much praise for me?
> So much encomium for me?
> Was distance able
> to add so much to my portrait?
> Of what stature do you make me?
> What colossus have you wrought,
> since the loftiness of the original
> does not recognize the lowliness?
> I am not the one you think I am,
> rather, over there you have given me
> another being through your writing
> and another breath through your lips,
> and different from myself
> among your writings I go,
> not as I am, but
> as you tried to imagine it. ([26] 1:158-59)

Through the perspective generated by these considerations we can better understand the humane Sor Juana, a magnanimous image that we could find at odds with the literary and dramatic concept with which we have sought to classify this Mexican author.

Undoubtedly, Sor Juana was the most important author of the baroque in New Spain and at the close of the Spanish baroque. If we compare her to the dramatists and poets with whom she was historically contemporary, she is comparable only to Calderón. It is true that the dramatic work of Sor Juana is not as abundant as that

of Calderón, nor of Lope; but it is also true that there were less prolific playwrights, such as Ruiz de Alarcón, Moreto, and Rojas Zorrilla,
with twenty-five, thirty-two, and thirty-five original plays, respectively (MacCurdy, 578, 329, 516). The dramatic versatility of Sor
Juana is another reason why we can describe her as a genius, without diminishing this term, owing to the variety of dramatic genres
of very high caliber she cultivated: the play, which we have labeled
falda y empeño; the *loa*, which she conceived of as an independent
dramatic genre; the *auto*, with its three subgenres (sacramental,
hagiographic, and biblical); and the dramatic *villancicos*, which con-
stitute the highest expression of this genre in the Spanish language.
Never before had there been a female dramatist of Sor Juana's merit,
either in Spain or its colonies, and many generations had to pass
before we would find female dramatists of the same stature in the
Spanish language. I hope that the present study can make a contribution so that "the last of the forgotten"—as I described in the First
Critical Act, the meager appreciation that across the years has been
afforded the theater of Sor Juana in books and on the stage—can
receive critical acclaim and the revitalizing applause of audiences.

For all of Sor Juana's merits as a dramatist and poet, and for her
pioneering importance in the struggle for the rights of women as
thinking beings, I propose that this author be included in Golden
Age Spanish literature. We would have to reconsider the date for the
end of the baroque, which is usually fixed at the death of Calderón
in 1681, and accept the year of Sor Juana's death, 1695, to be able
thereby to include a *female genius* of equal stature among so many
illustrious men.

This study of the three plays by Sor Juana grew out of my admiration for Sor Juana's dramatic art, and as a joyful celebration of my
discovery of *The Second Celestina*. I also desired to contribute, as
critic and dramatist, to the baroque and postmodern festival for the
Third Centennial of the Death of Sor Juana, 1695-1995.

Notes

First Critical Act

1. For a study of the baroque and mannerism in Sor Juana, see Alessandra Luiselli, *The Mannerist Dream of Sor Juana Inés de la Cruz*, 37-116.

2. There are two other works by Sor Juana that have dramatic traits through incorporating dialogical elements, such as the lyrics for *St. Bernard* (1690), especially lyrics VIII, IX, XVIII, XXI and XXII; additionally, lyrics I for the *Presentation of Our Lady* ([26] 2:182-206, [26] 2:217-18).

3. Published without the author's name but attributed to Sor Juana by Méndez Plancarte. For the editions of the *Villancicos* I follow the criteria of Méndez Plancarte in *Obras completas* [26] 2:355-523.

4. Francisco de las Eras (or Heras) was the secretary of the Marquis de la Laguna from 1680 to 1686. According to the *Diario* of Antonio de Robles (2:450), he left for Spain on March 28, 1686, perhaps taking with him the manuscript of *The Second Celestina*, since he had the original. Sor Juana dedicated an epistolary ballad to this personage to commemorate the New Year, possibly 1681. Later he was the governor of Madrid. Alatorre suggested the possibility that the anonymous author of the prologue of *Castalian Flood* was Francisco de las Eras ("Reading the *Fama*," 466).

5. Guillermo Schmidhuber has been conducting research on some of the missing originals by Sor Juana, especially "Moral Balance" and the correspondence between Sor Juana and Father Diego Calleja, her first biographer. In the near future he will present his findings.

6. 1691 ed.

7. Examples of works co-authored by three writers: *To Sicken with the Cure*, by Calderón, Cáncer, and Vélez de Guevara; *La Baltasara*, by Rojas Zorrilla, Antonio Coello, and Vélez de Guevara; and *The Priest of Madrilejos' Suit Against the Devil*, by Vélez de Guevara, Rojas Zorrilla, and Mira de Amescua (Barrera y Leirado, 469, 530, 709). The edition of Calderón's works by Juan Eugenio Hartzenbusch cites eleven plays written in collaboration.

If this authorial collaboration seems strange to us, we should remember the collective creation that is occurring today in Spanish America.

8. Father Diego Calleja "was born in Alcalá on November 7, 1638, and entered the Jesuit Order on February 25, 1663; he preached for several years in the province of Toledo. He also led the Congregation of the Immaculate Conception in Madrid. In 1725 he was assigned to the residence in Navalcarnero. During his youth, Calleja made a name for himself with his sacred dramas in Spanish, some of which appeared with his name, while others were anonymous" (Sommoervogel, *Bibliotéque de la Compagnie de Jesús [Bibliotheca of the Society of Jesus]* [Brussels and Paris, 1891], trans. Les Essif, 2:559). When Calleja wrote the biography of Sor Juana he was 62 years old, and he lived to be older than 87. The exact date of his death is unknown. His original works consists of three pieces: (1) *The Spanish Phoenix, Saint Francis of Borgia*, performed at the imperial College to celebrate the canonization of the saint, on the afternoon of August 11, 1671 (Part 43, 1678; Valencia: Viuda de Joseph Ortega, 1762); (2) *Return Courtesy for Impoliteness* (Part 23, 1665; Part 41, 1675; Madrid: Antonio Sanz, 1743; Barcelona: Suriá y Largada, n.d.); and (3) *Saint Francis Xavier, the Sun of the Orient, by a Genius of This Court* (n.d.). He wrote three plays in collaboration with Manuel de León Marchante, published in *The Complete Posthumous Works of Master Don Manuel de León Marchante* (Madrid: Gabriel del Barrio, 1722), and in separate editions. The titles are *The Two Stars of France* (Part 17, 1662; Madrid: Antonio Sanz, 1748); *The Virgin of Salceda* (Parte 24, 1666; Madrid: Antonio de Sanz, n.d.); and *The Two Finest Brothers, Saints Justo and Pastor*. As editor he compiled the elegies written by the Jesuits on the death of Queen Mariana de Habsburgo: *Llantos imperiales de Melpomene regia. Llora la muerte de la ínclita reina señora doña Mariana de Austria . . . por las voces y por las plumas de los padres de la Compañía de Jesús y las refiere don Jorge de Pinto, Clérigo* [pseudonym], *presbítero natural de Madrid. Madrid: A. de Zagral, 1696 y dedica al rey nuestro señor don Carlos II*. Additionally, there was a moral work entitled *Talentos logrados en el buen uso de los cinco sentidos, por el padre Diego Calleja de la Compañía de Jesús, y los dedica a don Felipe de Arco Aguero, secretario del rey nuestro señor y tesorero propietario general del Consejo de la Cámara de Castilla* (Madrid: Juan García Infançón, 1700).

9. Olavarría y Ferrari writes, in five thick volumes, the best study on the Mexican theater before Usigli's *Mexico in Its Theater*, but he only includes four and one-half lines about Sor Juana, and these in the chapter titled "1700-1753," erroneously noting "Joseph's Scepter" (Olavarría, 1:26).

10. One is obliged to recall Sor Juana's contemporary female dramatists, among them Sister Marcela de San Félix, the daughter of Lope de Vega and Micaela de Luján; Sister Marcela was the author of several dialogues,

including the *Appetite's Death*. Also in Spain, Sister María de San Alberto wrote brief works that were performed in her convent; in addition, there was the Portuguese nun, Sister María del Cielo. Another was Angela de Acevedo, the author of three plays: *The Man Pretending to Be Dead; Margarita of the Tajo, Giving Fame to Santarem;* and *Joy and Sadness of the Game, Devotion to the Virgin;* Leonor de la Cueva y Silva, the author of *Fortitude in Absence,* who was the daughter of Francisco de la Cueva y Silva, a poet and dramatist who was a contemporary of Lope; Ana Caro Mallén de Soto, the author of *Valor, Insult, and Woman* and *Count Partinuplés;* and María de Zayas y Sotomayor, the author of *Betrayal in Friendship* (Barrera, 4, 72, 121, 508). Early in the seventeenth century we have also a Feliciana Enríquez de Guzmán, the author of *Tragicomedy about the Gardens and Fields of Sheba,* although she was not a religious and she married on two occasions (Serrano, 356-88). There are others as well. It is necessary to mention that the proportion of dramatist nuns to dramatist married women is about even; in general their production was very scant and not of the quality of Sor Juana's work. When he published the anthology *Dramatists after Lope de Vega,* Mesonero Romanos only included two female dramatists: Sor Juana, with her *Trials of a Noble House,* and Ana Caro, with her *Count Partinuplés,* both of whom were called the "tenth muse," the latter by the editor of *Part Four of the Selected Plays,* published in 1653. Even in other languages it is difficult to find a female dramatist of Sor Juana's stature prior to the nineteenth century, except for the extraordinary case of Hroswitha or Hrotsvitha (935-1001?), the Saxon noblewoman who lived in the Gandersheim abbey of the Benedictine order as a volunteer who never took holy orders. She wrote six dramatic pieces: *Abraham, Calimachus, Dulcitius, Gallicanus, Pafnutius,* and *Sapientia,* dealing with the triumph of virginity over the temptation of the flesh and Christian marriage. The editio princeps of her works appeared five centuries later in Nuremburg, in 1501. Today there is renewed literary and theatrical interest in the work of Hroswitha, as in that of Sor Juana.

11. Father Antonio Núñez de Miranda was born in Fresnillo, Zacatecas, on November 4, 1618. He studied philosophy in the capital of New Spain and was a teacher of Latin, philosophy, and moral theology. He eventually became rector of the Jesuits' most important provincial school, and he worked for the Holy Inquisition as a qualificator for thirty years. He was the spiritual advisor for two archbishops and three viceroys, and the author of numerous ascetic books aimed principally at nuns and women who were seeking the way of perfection. When the young Juana Ramírez lived in the viceregal court, this priest suggested to her that she join the Discalced Carmelite order (August 14, 1667), which the postulant left after three months (November 18, 1667) in order to later join, on his advice, the

Hieronymite order (February 24, 1669), in which she would remain twenty-six years until her death. Nevertheless, this relationship of spiritual advisor was severed for some years for motives not totally clear, but it was renewed—or imposed by a higher authority—during her last two years.

12. Theatrical performance was regulated on several occasions by secular authorities. Two regulations are noteworthy. The first theater regulation in the history of Spain is in the canon of the Third Council of Toledo, during the Visigothic era, which denounces jumping, dancing, and lewd songs; later, in the *Siete partidas* of King Alfonso the Learned, performance of religious dramas is accepted only in large cities and without any profit, but "mockery plays," as the medieval farces were described, were not approved (Partida 1, law 34, title VI, cited by Fernando Lázaro Carreter, 23-24). Also noteworthy is the prohibition against *autos* in 1765 by Charles III.

13. The adjective *Athenagoric* was not written by Sor Juana; instead, Fernández de Santa Cruz added it to the title of Sor Juana's essay as homage to her intellect. Ezequiel A. Chávez suggested the erroneous etymology: "from the Greek words *Athena, Minerva,* and from the suffix *ica,* meaning belonging to, worthy of" (300). All subsequent critics have accepted this explanation in spite of the fact that the adjective should have been *atenaica* or *ateniense.* I am suggesting a new interpretation: *Athenagoric* meaning "worthy of Athenagoras," relating to the famous Greek philosopher and apologist of the second century who, already converted to Christianity, dedicated his work, *Súplica en favor de los cristianos,* to Mark Anthony.

14. We rely on the writings of Sor Juana and the exiguous information preserved by her contemporaries in order to reconstruct those years. From this period are the *Villancicos of Santa Catarina* (1691) [22] and the *Villancicos of San Pedro* (1691 and 1692) [23], [24] and the ballad "When, divine Numina . . ." [26], which was found unfinished after the poet's death. Several prose documents pertain to this period of crisis: *Vow to the Immaculate Conception* (February 17, 1694) [3], [26], *Declaration of Faith Signed in Her Blood* (March 5, 1694) [3], and *Statutory Petition* [3], [26], without a date; and two documents by Sor Juana included in the *Book of Vows* in the convent of Saint Jerome: a renewal of the *Profession of Faith* signed in her blood [3], [26], and an autograph request that the day of her death be recorded in said book [3], [26]. For this reason, the discovery of the *Declaration* included in the present book is of such importance. For an article on the *Declaration,* see Schmidhuber, "Discovery and Significance."

15. *Perpetual enclosure* refers to the obligation that certain religious took not to leave the confines of the convent.

16. *The Declaration of Faith* was published in a book of meditation by Father Antonio Núñez de Miranda. *Mystical Testament of a Religious Soul Suffering from Love for Her Divine Spouse, Already Moribund, Prepared to*

Die to This World, She Makes Her Beloved, Voluntary Heir to all Her Goods. Set Down by M.R.P. Antonio Núñez, Prefect of the Congregación de la Purísima. This book by Father Núñez de Miranda is important in order to understand the paths of asceticism that Sor Juana was compelled to follow and that doubtless made more difficult her labors as a dramatist. It is advisable to recall that Sor Juana had made her legal will on February 23, 1669, one day before joining the convent of Saint Paula of Saint Jerome, of the Augustinian order, having Father Núñez as her witness (Ramírez España, 19); thus it is no mere coincidence that the *Declaration* is included in the *Testamento místico,* by Father Núñez de Miranda.

17. The *Declaration* affirms the authorship of Sor Juana, but it leaves the spaces corresponding to the name of the nun and the convent blank, so that the religious could personalize it. The information that follows could seem irrelevant to the topic of drama, but I consider it pertinent in order to explain this discovery of an unknown text by Sor Juana. An article on this topic appeared in *Hispania:* Schmidhuber, "Discovery and Significance." In spite of the brevity of Declaration No. 412 in the *Book of Vows* in comparison to the recently found *Declaration,* both possess similar phrases that invite one to suspect that the declaration written in the *Book of Vows* is a summary of the *Declaration* that I discovered, as can be proven by the following:

Declaration No. 412 (114 words)

And in the same manner I vow to believe any of its articles, if it is not in opposition to the Holy Faith.

In witness whereof I signed with my blood on February 8, 1694 . . . I wish that all of it would be shed in defense of this truth for His love and the love of His son.

Discovered Declaration (414 words)

I wish and declare that I shall live and die in this faith and belief, and let it be understood that it is not my will to do, say, or believe anything contrary to this truth . . .

for which I am prepared to give my life a thousand times over and for which I would shed all the blood in my veins and thus as I write with it these lines, so I desire that all of it be spilled . . .

The discovered *Declaration* has no information regarding the date, but it can be dated February 8, 1694. To confirm this idea it is necessary to compare the form in which Sor Juana records the date on several documents: in Vow 408 [26] ("I swear, affirm, promise and ratify it, on February 17, 1694); in Declaration 409 ("I sign it . . . on March 5, 1694); and in Declaration 412 ("In witness whereof I signed with my blood on February 8, 1694). The verb is conjugated in the present at the end of the first two documents, while in Declaration 412 the verb is in the preterit, which could well refer to a separate document, that is, to the *Declaration* recently discovered. In his biography of Sor Juana [3], Father Calleja also mentions two writings signed in her blood: "Two Declarations That She Wrote With Her Blood, Drawn Without Pain, Reviewed Everyday, With Affection." Declaration 409 is one, but the other is not found among the known works by Sor Juana; thus I believe that Calleja was referring to the text recently discovered. If we compare the newly discovered *Declaration* with Declaration 409, included in *Obras completas* [26], we find discrepancies. Declaration 409 is longer and has a different thematic structure:

Declaration 409 (569 words)	Discovered Declaration (414 words)
Name of the nun	Name of the nun
Paraphrase of the creed	Succinct paraphrase of the creed
Perpetual promise of obedience to the church	Provision for martyrdom written in her blood
Confession of sins without visible signs	Confession of sins with regret
Reiteration of the Marian vow	Irrevocalbe renewal of four religious vows
Signature in her blood	Signature

There is also disparity between the styles; No. 409 is more legalistic: "Whereby I am prepared to spill my blood and defend, at all costs, the Holy Faith that I profess, not just believing it and adoring in my heart"; whereas the discovered *Declaration* is more personal: "for which I am prepared to give my life a thousand times over and for which I would shed all the blood in my veins and thus as I write with it these lines, so I desire that all of it be spilled." The differences indicate two different documents, especially because No. 409 (March 5, 1694) does not include a renewal of the four religious vows, since such a renewal had just been made on February 8th of that year.

18. *Saint Catherine's Villanicos* [22] were sung in the Cathedral of Antequera, today Oaxaca, on the feast day of the saint, November 25, 1691. This same year, on May 1, Sor Juana wrote the *Reply to Sor Filotea*, as a reaction to the publication of the *Athenagoric Letter* by the then bishop of Puebla, Manuel Fernández de Santa Cruz, who hid behind the pseudonym of Sor Filotea in a letter included in the edition, the one which coincidentally is dated November 25, 1690.

Second Critical Act

1. O'Connor advances the supposition that the play was performed before Queen Mariana in 1676 with the ending by Vera Tassis ("Introducción," xxxviii). For my observations regarding this, see the Fourth Critical Act.

2. The names of the company at the Coliseum in 1673 are known. Mateo Jaramillo was the *author* or director of the company, and the roster of actors included the following: Isabel Gertrudis, Josefa y Micaela Ortiz, Antonia de Toledo, Francisco de Castro, José Martínez, Antonio, Ventura y Bartolmé Gómez, Diego Jaramillo, Felipe de Viaja, Lorenzo Vargas y Juan de Saldaña (Olavarría, 1:14). Could one of these actors have performed in the dramatic works of Sor Juana?

3. The Coliseum of Plays in Mexico City had, in 1683, the following roster of actors: Bernarda Pérez de Rivera, María y Ana de Villegas, María Ortiz Jaramillo, Ignacia de Cárdenas, Juan de Dios, Antonio Pinto, Diego de Sevilla, Juan Ferrete, Juan Ortiz de Torres y Antonio de Ventura Cerdán. In that year there was a meeting in the home of the presbyter, Antonio Acosta, administrator of the Royal Hospital for Citizens, where the Coliseum was located, because the *author* Ignacio Marqués had become destitute (Olavarría, 1:15). Some of these names make one think of relatives of those included in the roster of 1673, with the surnames Ortiz and Jaramilla now combined in the name of a possible daughter. It is not known if one of these actors could have taken part in the opening of *The Trials of a Noble House,* but these were some of the few theater professionals in Mexico City during that time.

4. He was also the author of two sacramental *autos: The Triumphs of Jesus Transubstantiated* and *Andromeda and Perseus* (could this be the sacramental *auto* by Calderón?) and of the play *What It Is to Be Predestined,* which was prohibited by the Holy Office (María y Campos, 95).

5. The *Diary of Notable Events* only notes: "In the vestibule there was a play by Cardinal Francisco Jiménez" (Robles, 2:241), which I identify as *The Famous Play: "The Great Cardinal of Spain, Francisco Ximénez de Cisneros" by a Master Playwright* (Valencia: Joseph y Thomas de Orga, 1777). Barrera y Leirado attributes it to Juan Bautista Diamante and Pedro Francisco Lanini y Sagredo (125).

6. According to the studies by Varey and Shergold, *It Is Impossible to Guard a Woman* was staged in Madrid on several occasions: May 23, 1680, April 12, 1682, October 26, 1684, January 15, 1690, and December 5, 1695 (174).

7. *Choosing the Enemy* was staged in Madrid in 1684 and three times in 1686; and *The Olympic Games* ten times: 1673, 1677, 1680, 1686 twice, 1688, 1694, 1695 twice, and 1698 (Varey and Shergold, 107, 140). There is no information about *Charm Is Beauty, and Charm without Witchcraft,* although O'Connor speculates that there was a performance before Queen Mariana in 1676 ("Introducción," xxxviii).

8. In Madrid there were four productions: 1660, 1682, 1690, and 1692 (Varey and Shergold, 107).

9. Salceda speculates there was a production of *In This Life All Is Truth and All Is Falsehood,* by Calderón, together with the *Loa to Celebrate the*

King's Birthday [II] by Sor Juana, but the chronicles of the era do not record its performance ("Cronología," 346).

10. María y Campos mistakenly writes Alfonso instead of Alonso (98).

11. The *Diary of Notable Events* notes with regard to the "Unusual masque": "On said day there left from the house of the writer D. Fernando Valenzuela a formal masque patronized by the Royal University to celebrate the marriage of the king; and there were in it many people mounted on horseback, some in the costume of different animals, such as eagles [and] lions, and others in native dress, such as of Turks, Indians, and Spaniards, and other people were upside down, with their feet pointing up and their heads pointing down, with their torches in their hands and all running before the balcony of the palace; and it lasted until after 11:00 at night" (Robles, 3:61). Valenzuela had been a minister of Queen Mariana (1676), and he had organized multiple performances for her; later he was expatriated to the Philippines and Mexico, where he died in 1692.

12. The "Index of Names" composed by Cristina Ramírez España ([26] 4:699-715), who is a descendant of Sor Juana, was of great use to me in preparing this study on citations.

13. The modern version by José Alemany Bolufer: "As a gift from the great god and eminent glory of this earth: she is the breaker of horses, she possesses good colts and she navigates happily by sea. Oh child of Chronos! You, king Neptune, elevated her to this glory, inventing the bit for horses" (Flickinger, 574).

14. The modern version by José Alemany Bolufer: "Venus, you were the judge of the combat that you attended" (Flickinger, 691).

15. The reference only makes mention of "Rojas," a proper name that, being placed seven lines below with the *Celestina*, allows us to speculate that in the mind of the author it could also have been the name of Fernando de Rojas.

16. The meter of *The Second Celestina* was analyzed by O'Connor ("Language, Irony and Death," 64), and the other two plays were studied by William C. Bryant ("Metrical Study," 45-47).

17. This model is an adaptation of the one proposed by Pavis, 406.

18. A magnificent exposition of New World baroque theater is found in Schilling, 141-50; for peninsular festivals see Díez Borque, 11-40, 71-95, with articles by José Antonio Maravall ("Theater, Festival, and Ideology in the Baroque"), Antonio Bonet Correa ("Ephemeral Architectures, Ornamentation and Masques"), and Díez Borque ("Relationships Between Theater and Festival in the Spanish Baroque").

Third Critical Act

1. The history of the Spanish and Spanish American theater does not have many works on dramatic theory, at least compared with those existing

in other languages. If we start with what was written prior to 1700, aside from the considerations by Lope de Vega and Tirso de Molina, one is only able to add the writings of Francisco Cascales (1564-1642), supporting the ideas of Aristotle and Terence; Bartolomé Leonardo de Argensola (1562-1631), with his inclination toward comedy more than tragedy and his appreciation of prose; and Cristóbal Suárez de Figueroa (1571-1645) who complained that "almost all of the plays performed in our theaters are done against reason, against nature, against art" (Guardia, 69). There is the case of a female poet, Feliciana Enríquez de Guzmán, who studied in Salamanca disguised as a man, as Sor Juana had dreamt of doing one day, and who left her written censure of poor plays, proposing as a model her *Tragicomedy about the Gardens and Fields of Sheba* (Serrano, 356-88); also, Juan Caramuel de Loblokowitz (1600-1682), from whom some innovative considerations on dramatic genres are preserved. The following authors have also left texts alluding to this topic: Torres Naharro, Juan de la Cueva, Alonso López Pinciano, and Juan Rufo, as pointed out by Sánchez Escribano and Porqueras Mayo in their work, *Spanish Dramatic Precepts* (Madrid: Gredos, 1965). From a subsequent period, the Enlightenment, the following are worthy of note: Benito Jerónimo Feijoo (1676-1764) and especially Ignacio de Luzán (1702-1754), with his *Poetics* (1737 and 1789). The best critical study is *A Vision of Dramatic Criticism*, by Alfredo de la Guardia, 67-73.

2. Corominas claims that it comes from the Portuguese words *meco* (libertine) and *trefe* (mischievous), although the Arabic origin has also been affirmed, *mogatref* meaning petulant (349), and even from a Mexican word, as is discussed at the end of this Critical Act. Coincidentally, Calderón named his comic foil Meco in his play *Friend, Lover and Loyal*.

3. The semantic difference between *being* and *entity* is that *being* signifies substance, and *entity*, action. A rational being means that reason is within that being; while a rational entity means that [reason] is its own work. God represents the being; man creates the entity that only exists in his mind (Roque Barcia, *Spanish Synonyms* [Buenos Aires: Editorial Sopena Argentina, 1954], 195-96). Thus the theater of Sor Juana does not propose verisimilar human beings, but rather metatheatrical entities, that is, entelechies.

4. It would be necessary to add the influence of León Marchante in the *villancicos* by Sor Juana, perhaps through Diego Calleja, her first biographer, and friend and collaborator of the Spanish dramatist and presbyter.

5. For the dramatic characteristics of Calderón, I have closely followed Hesse, 37-46, and Daniel, "A Terra Incognita," 104-5, 115-17. The characteristics of Sor Juana's theater are, according to Daniel: Calderonian theory and dramatic art, the use of Greco-Latin mythology, the use of echo verses, the technique of *Ad Spectatores* by which the characters acquire the condi-

tion of metatheatricality and literary eclecticism, as well as the conception of the *loa* as an independent genre (8).

6. The differences between soliloquy and monologue, dramatic elements that are often taken to be synonymous, is defined by Pavis, 462.

7. I use *j* to reflect Mexican usage.

Fourth Critical Act

1. Thomas Austin O'Connor has researched and written about Salazar y Torres more than any other critic, beginning with his doctoral dissertation, "Structure and Dramatic Techniques in the Works of Agustín de Salazar y Torres," 1971. He has subsequently written numerous articles. Those that contain a direct reference to *Charm Is Beauty* or to *The Second Celestina* are listed in the Bibliography. There is also a bibliographical study by José Simón Díaz that refers to this play (268).

2. The first two volumes do not have a date or place of publication. Volume R 12162 shows the seal of Pascual de Gayangos (1809-1897), a famous Spanish critic. I am grateful to Professor Sabat-Rivers for the information about the third volume. In the British Library there is an edition similar to the one in the Harrach collection (11728. f 33; the catalogue gives this information for the edition: *Madrid 1676?*), as well as a book the same as T 9222 (11728. I. 2. 16; the catalogue suggests the publication in *Seville 1700?*).

3. The program LitStats, developed by Stephen R. Reimer (Canada), was utilized for the creation of the study on the measurement of style. The principal sources consulted for the realization of this study were Ian Press, "Geir Khetsaa: Attributed to Dostoevsky: The Problem of Attributing to Dostoevsky Anonymous Articles in Time and Epoch," *Literary and Linguistic Computing* 3, no. 2 (1988):144-45 (the three basic methods proposed by Geir Khetsaa for his research into the authorship of several articles attributed to Dostoevsky are discussed here). Estelle Irizarry produced a similar study that served as my basis; see the introduction to Carlos de Sigüenza y Góngora and Alonso Ramírez's *The Misfortunes of Alonso Ramírez* (Puerto Rico: Editorial Cultura, 1990). Other books consulted were F.U. Yule, *The Statistical Study of Literary Vocabulary* (Cambridge: Cambridge Univ. Press, 1944); Alvar Ellegard, *A Statistical Method for Determining Authorship: The Junius Letters 1769-1772* (Goteborg: Bothenburg Studies in English 13, 1962); Susan Hockey, *A Guide to Computer Applications in the Humanities* (Baltimore: John Hopkins Univ. Press, 1980); A.Q. Morton, *Literary Detection* (New York: Scribner, 1978); and Evelyn Hatch and Hossein Farhady, *Research Design and Statistics for Applied Linguistics* (Cambridge: Newbury House, 1982). I am grateful to Professor Irizarry for her assistance

in carrying out this study on the measurement of style; I learned of the LitStat program and the article by Ian Press through her.

4. The performance of this play at Court on March 6, 1696, in Madrid (Varey and Shergold, 216), would seem to contradict the statement by Castorena y Ursúa that the work was being printed when he was preparing the edition of *Reputation and Posthumous Works* in 1700, but the edition had been out in Europe since the end of 1698, as demonstrated by the "Favorable Assessment" dated December 19 of the same year. The delay in publication was due to "the intention of reprinting the two earlier volumes at the same time . . . at last finishing it all," as Barrera y Leirado states (110). The editor's journey [to Spain] was in 1697, and one must note that his prologue mentions seven *post-scripta* (Alatorre, "Reading the *Fama*," 431), which leads me to think that the composition of the "Prologue to the Reader" could have been started earlier, perhaps partly before leaving Mexico. Almost at the end of the book Castorena y Ursúa adds a postscript written in Spain, in which he mentions his journey: "I brought from Mexico a very erudite book in a lavish style, entitled 'Mythological Exequies' . . . written by the lawyer don Lorenço Gonçález de la Sancha"; in it there is included the "Funeral Prayer" by Sigüenza y Góngora, which was never published (272). Thus, the form in which Castorena y Ursúa edits his book makes one think that the manuscript was incorporated at different moments and with different contents, as much in New Spain as in old Spain.

5. Méndez Plancarte sets the writing of the *loa* (I) in 1675; see his explanatory note in [26] 3:652.

6. Moreto no doubt admired the feminine mind, refined by the virtues of dignity and courtesy, in works such as *It Cannot Be*; and Rojas Zorrilla wrote the best pieces about determined women to be penned by a man, such as *Everybody's Due* and *Procne and Philomela*.

7. Both quotations refer to the *Quixote*, vol. 1, 2: "Injuries that he planned to redress, injustices to right." Here are four Cervantine allusions by Sor Juana. A reference to Clavileño: "Better a Clavileño / of sticks, that moves or stays still" ([26] 1:80) with regard to having sent a wooden horse as a gift to the young Joseph, son of the viceroys and Marquises of la Laguna; this adventure is from the *Quixote*, vol. 2, 40-41. Another reference recalls the adventure of Maese Pedro, narrated in vol. 2, 26-27: ". . . whoever wishes to see the Phoenix, / let him pay two coins, / Maese Pedro is showing him / in the Jaques inn" ([26] 1:147). This adventure is cited again by Sor Juana in *The Trials of a Noble House*: "I will advise Marsilio / that Melisendra is getting away from him" ([26] 4:150) with reference to the plot of the work about the retable represented in the *Quixote*, vol. 2, 26. In the same play there is another similarity to Cervantes when the comic foil, Tacón, exclaims: "Oh, you, whoever you were; / oh you, whoever you might

be . . . may you inspire a plot line for me / like one from Calderón / about how to get out of this jam!" ([26] 4:136), which seems to parody the invocations in the chivalric novels: "Oh, you, wise enchanter, whoever you may be, to whom being the chronicler of this strange tale must befall!, I implore you not to forget about . . ." *Quixote*, vol. 1, 2.

8. There is a speech that makes one think about the mature age of Inés: Antonia calls her "señora Inés" ([27], 92), but when Vera Tassis finishes the play he fails to notice this and marries the character to Muñoz, who had not shown any preference for doña Beatriz's servant; moreover, this page does have a great friendship with Celestina ([27], 74-76), leading one to think that he is a young man. In the ending by Vera Tassis, the disdained gallant's servant marries the servant of the lady who rejected him; however, in the ending by Sor Juana, Muñoz marries Antonia, whom Tacón had courted, portraying the gallants, don Juan as well as Tacón, as even more ridiculous.

9. The influence of Salazar on the poetic work of Sor Juana is studied by Georgina Sabat-Rivers in *The "Dream" of Sor Juana Inés de la Cruz* as well as in note 44 of her edition of *Castalian Flood* ([25], 51). Similar work is found in José María de Cossío, "Homage to Sor Juana Inés de la Cruz on the Third Centenary of Her Birth," *Boletín de la Real Academia Española* 32 (1952):27-72. See also Méndez Plancarte, [26] 2:35.

10. Leal (45); Sabat-Rivers ("The Problems of *The Second Celestina*"); O'Connor ("The Entanglements of a Play"); Daniel ("Encuentran *La Celestina*"); and Suárez Radillo (via correspondence with the author). Upon learning of Schmidhuber's discovery, Antonio Alatorre published an article, "The Theatrical Process of Sor Juana," *Proceso* 710 (1990):50-52, claiming that he had previously found the play and that he had also concluded that it belonged to Sor Juana. Subsequently, Schmidhuber proved in an article that the edition found and cited by Alatorre was not the original, but rather a highly altered later edition, and for this reason his "discovery" had not been published sooner; see "The Traps of Literary Research: The Discovery of *The Second Celestina*" *Proceso* 713 (1990):56-57. Surprisingly, Alatorre changed his mind and denied Sor Juana's co-authorship, although he adds that "of course, the fact remains that Sor Juana wrote an ending for *The Second Celestina*, but the one that Schmidhuber and I found 'by different paths' is definitely an anonymous work" ("*La segunda Celestina* de Agustín Salazar y Torres: Ejercicio de crítica," 46. In the same issue of *Vuelta*, Octavio Paz wrote a reply to Alatorre, "*The Second Celestina* and Its Critics," discrediting his critical solution: "Alatorre now rejects Sor Juana's authorship. A sudden change of mind that intrigues us: fifteen days before the text discovered by Schmidhuber came to light, and unaware of this circumstance, Alatorre declared in *Proceso* that he had found the ending for the

play written by Sor Juana and that he was prepared to publish it in a carefully annotated edition. Now, the text discovered by Alatorre is no different from the one published by Schmidhuber. We are dealing with individual finds of the same text . . . The opinions . . . , instead of clarifying the problem, are complicating it: they postulate the existence of not two, but three authors for *The Second Celestina*: Agustín Salazar y Torres, Sor Juana Inés de la Cruz and a third anonymous one. A solution, as mathematicians would say, not very elegant" (44). The note cited does not carry Paz's name, but Oscar Díaz Chávez, who saw the manuscripts, assured me that it was he, and Paz himself told me in a telephone conversation that he did not sign it in order to avoid increasing "the pack of intellectual hounds." For a collection of anecdotes about the discovery see Sarah Gorham, "The Celibate Matriarch."

11. The assimilations present in *The Poem of the Cid* continued to be used by some poets, such as Quevedo and Vélez de Guevara, because they facilitated the versification (Spaulding, 116). The significant thing in this case is Sor Juana's usage of them and Salazar y Torres's lack of preference for them; they are also in the corrections by Vera Tassis, which are similar to Sor Juana's writing, as in *encontrarlos* (273).

12. There are differences between the separate edition [*suelta*] of *The Second Celestina* [7] and the edition by Vera Tassis before the two texts diverge, especially in regard to the use of words. The first contains some errors of meter and punctuation, and a predominantly more popular vocabulary, while the second has abundant corrections of style that are evidence of Vera Tassis's preference for a more cultured language. In general, I prefer the version of the separate edition. If we compare the meter, the ending by Vera Tassis has 1075 lines in octosyllabic verse, rhyming in í-a and é-o, while the ending by Sor Juana has 1003 lines. For the metrical study of the ending by Vera Tassis see O'Connor, "Language, Irony, and Death," 64.

13. Varey and Shergold note a performance on May 28, 1684 (160).

14. The incongruity between the title *Charm Is Beauty* and the plot of the play is surprising, since the cause of the dramatic action is not the charm due to beauty (except in the unfruitful encounter between don Juan and doña Beatriz, which opens the piece), but rather the clever sophisms of the female protagonists. On the other hand, in the subtitle of the play, *Charm without Witchcraft*, there is indeed a correspondence because witchcraft is not present. This disparity between the title and the plot may be another proof of the *perfecting* by Sor Juana.

15. "The Celestina" is mentioned by Vera Tassis in the promised *Décima parte* [*Tenth Part*] of Calderón's plays, but it was never published (Barrera, 55). There also exists an interlude entitled *The Celestina*, by Juan Navarro

de Espinoza, included in *New Interludes by Divers Authors for Chaste Recreation* (Alcalá de Henares, 1643).

16. Vera Tassis also collaborated on finishing *The Greater Triumph of Consummated Love*, by Salazar, a play he oddly did not include in the edition of the complete works of this dramatist.

17. The research by Thomas Austin O'Connor is an example of erudition and critical fidelity toward an author, and it aided me in great measure in coming to understand Salazar y Torres. This critic claims that it was Sor Juana who was familiar with the ending by Vera Tassis, and from this she created her own ending ("The Entanglements of a Play"). This claim is based on the year of publication of the complete works of Salazar, *Apollo's Lyre*, with editions in 1681 and 1694, consisting of a volume of poetry and of drama, respectively. The second volume of the editio princeps is extremely rare (O'Connor, "A Bibliographical Note"). There are copies in the library of the British Museum and in the National Library in Madrid. Varey and Shergold also cite the editio princeps of the drama of 1681 (216). The existing copy in the Hispanic Society of New York has the cover of the second volume and the interior part of the first, that is, the cover refers to the drama, while the content is a repetition of the poetry belonging to the first volume. My opinion is that the limitation of the hiatus of five years between the death of Salazar and the edition of the play by Vera Tassis is not an argument that makes impossible the hypothesis of Sor Juana's co-authorship. The information that Salazar was writing this play at his death and that he only finished two and a half acts comes from the "Discourse on the Life and Writings of don Agustín de Salazar," the prologue written by Vera Tassis (Salazar, *Apollo's Lyre*, 231); unfortunately we do not have another source for corroboration. Salazar could well have left it unfinished months before because of his lengthy illness, and thus Sor Juana could have had more than five years to finish the play and her version even could have traveled to Spain.

18. The two reworkings are *The Second Celestina*: MS 16.080, *The Second Celestina, Witch of Triana* (dated 1818 and anonymous); and MS 18.075 (no date and with the initials D.S.). Donald G. Castanien has identified the author of the second work as Dionisio Solís (559).

19. *The Tragicomedy of Calisto y Melibea*, by Fernando de Rojas, has generated a Celestinesque lineage: *The Second Celestina* (1534), a novel of the same name as the play, by Feliciano de Silva; another imitation, *The Third Celestina*, by Gaspar Gómez de Toledo (1539); and many others. In the theater the original tragicomedy has also influenced the type of "Celestinesque play" of Gil Vicente, Juan del Encina (*Eglogue of Plácida and Victoriano*), Juan de la Cueva (*The Defamer*), Bartolomé Torres Naharro (*Himenea*), Lope de Vega (*The Sands of Seville, The Knight from Olmedo, Castrucho the Villain*, and *Fenisa's Lure*), and many others.

There is speculation about a lost play by Calderón de la Barca with this Celestinesque character. Menéndez Pelayo, in his study *The Origins of the Novel*, analyzed the possibility that *The Second Celestina* by Salazar y Torres could be the lost play by Calderón, since coincidentally Vera Tassis was the editor of Calderón's works and he mentioned "The Celestina" among the works about to be published in the "tenth part," which never went to press (Menéndez Pelayo, *Obras completas*, 15:450; Barrera, 55).

20. The name of the servant Tacón in this play is reminiscent of the servant in *The Look-Alike at Court*, by Agustín Moreto. Moreover, this character bears a similarity to Castaño, Atún, and Racimo, the comic foils in the other plays by Sor Juana; the name Racimo matches the pseudonym of the comic foil in *It Cannot Be*, by Moreto.

21. Following the analysis by Williamsen of the bilateral symmetry in Sor Juana's plays, I find that *The Second Celestina* has a similar structure. This critic structures plays for his study into subscenes of dramatic unity different from those that I propose in the present study. The following is the structure of *The Second Celestina* according to Williamsen's criteria (see also fig. 4):

Act I

1. Along the shore of the Betis (Guadalquivir River) don Juan meets doña Beatriz on a hunt, but she leaves without telling him her name.

2. Don Juan explains to Muñoz and Tacón his reasons for going to Flanders: a street duel and the need to flee to Flanders to protect a lady. Muñoz suggests to his master that he visit Celestina, a woman versed in the art of love and perhaps a fortune-teller, so that she can reveal the mystery of the huntress.

3. Celestina's house. Doña Ana asks Celestina if don Juan will return. The old woman promises her news of her absent beloved.

4. Celestina's house. Don Juan asks Celestina to help him find the huntress.

5. A fight in the street. Don Juan saves don Diego without knowing his identity.

6. In the house of Don Luis, doña Ana's father. Don Luis welcomes his niece, doña Beatriz, and then exits. Celestina tells doña Ana that she will soon see don Juan, whom she has identified as the nobleman who had visited her. With doña Ana off stage, don Juan arrives and doña Beatriz refuses to speak to him.

Act II

1. Doña Ana's father suspects that someone is prowling around his house (unaware that it is don Diego), and he exits. Doña Beatriz

confesses to doña Ana that she has come to Seville in search of her love, since her father wished to marry her to another in Cadiz, and she tells about her encounter with a nobleman along the Betis. Antonia reports that Celestina is hidden in her room.

2. Tacón announces the arrival of don Juan. Doña Ana gives Tacón a jewel as a reward (the jewel had been given her by doña Beatriz's father).

3. Don Juan has a conflict over not accepting doña Ana's explanations. Doña Beatriz enters and reveals to her cousin that the nobleman she encountered is don Juan. Doña Ana accuses him of infidelity. Tacón attacks don Juan. Celestina and the servants come on stage. Don Luis enters. Celestina saves the moment by accusing Tacón of theft, for which don Luis makes him return the jewel. Don Luis exits.

4. Don Diego arrives with the intention of seeing doña Ana, and he also finds doña Beatriz.

5. When don Luis arrives, they hide don Diego. Doña Ana and doña Beatriz implore Celestina to get rid of don Diego. Celestina tricks don Luis by pretending to show the image of the man he saw in his house (don Diego) in a mirror, which reflects don Luis as he is leaving the house.

Act III

1. Celestina's house. Don Luis visits Celestina in order to solicit her help in discovering who is prowling around his house. When Tacón arrives, Celestina hides don Luis. Tacón wants to take the jewel from Celestina, and when the old woman cries out don Luis comes to her aid, and the old woman now tells a lie by stating that Tacón has stolen 100 coins from her (the ones that doña Ana had given to the page). Don Luis forces Tacón to return them to Celestina. The old woman tells don Luis that it is don Diego who has been prowling around his house.

2. (Ending written entirely by Sor Juana) Don Luis's house. Doña Ana and doña Beatriz talk about their loves. Muñoz enters to report that Tacón has gone for the police and that don Luis visited Celestina.

3. Outside of Celestina's house. Don Diego finds Muñoz. Don Juan arrives. The two noblemen identify each other as enemies and challenge one another to a duel.

4. Outside of Celestina's house. Doña Ana and doña Beatriz go in disguise to Celestina's house to find out what happened to don Luis. Muñoz tells them about the duel between don Juan and don Diego. Celestina promises to help the women.

5. A place near Seville. Don Diego and don Juan challenge each other to a duel. The ladies arrive in order to prevent it and they manage to do so. The women depart because they know don Luis is pursuing them. Don Luis, who had been informed about things by Antonia, appears. Don Luis attempts to challenge don Diego, but don Juan stops it. Don Luis realizes that the two noblemen were fighting over doña Ana, and he also challenges don Juan. The three refrain from fighting.

6. Celestina's house. Doña Ana and doña Beatriz go with Celestina to ask for help. The police arrive. Don Luis enters, followed by don Diego and don Juan. The entanglements are resolved and the charms by Celestina are explained. Celestina falsely accuses Tacón of breaching a promise of marriage. The questions of honor reach their conclusion. Triple wedding: Beatriz/Diego, Ana/Juan, and Antonia/Muñoz.

The bilateral symmetry has been demonstrated for the majority of the scenes in spite of the fact that the play was written by two dramatists. This is another argument to prove that Sor Juana *perfected* the work in its entirety.

Fifth Critical Act

1. *The Traps of Faith*, by Paz, is an admirable book in more than one sense, but it is an example of the critical deviation regarding the method of analysis of Sor Juana's dramatic work, since this analysis is done from the point of view of poetics and not from the perspective of dramatic theory. Thus the interest in Sor Juana's theater is conditioned to an interpretation of the text as poetry or to the biographical similarities between the characters or dramatic circumstances and the author.

2. We have been able to list a total of 358 performances of Calderón in colonial Mexico, but with much greater frequency after the death of Sor Juana (Hesse, 15). *The Great Prince of Fez* was staged in Querétaro in 1680 as part of the celebrations for the dedication of a church in honor of the Virgin of Guadalupe. We also know of a performance of *It's Worse Than It Was Before* in June 1692 and in January 1694, at the Colegio de San Gregorio [Saint Gregory's College] in Mexico City, and of *Life Is a Dream* in Guadalajara in 1702.

3. For my analysis of the typical traits of the protagonists, I have relied on those mentioned by Ruiz Ramón, 138.

4. In the language of Sor Juana it would be more appropriate to call this subgenre the *comedia de saya y empeño* [*petticoat and perseverance play*], but I chose the other because it is easier to understand today.

5. For an explanation of the origins of the tragedy see Flickinger, 1-35.

6. In Salceda's edition of this play, the title of the song is identified erroneously with the title "Lyrics for 'Beautiful Narcissus . . .'" ([26] 4:63).

7. According to the *Dictionary of Authorities*, the Terrero is "the place or spot where Ladies were courted at Palace," as Salceda has explained it ([26] 4:543).

8. Méndez Plancarte includes several parodies of "Foolish Men" in Complete Works; see [26] 1:489-90 and [26] 2:528-30. There exists an anonymous poem entitled "Foolish Masters."

9. Cavite prison is also mentioned by the protagonist in *The Misfortunes of Alonso Ramírez*, by Carlos de Sigüenza y Góngora (1690).

10. The work by Acevedo, performed in the year following *The Trials of a Noble House*, was denounced to the Holy Office ([26] 4:xxvi). Méndez Plancarte also cites from the same author the *Villancico for the Assumption*, 1689 ([26] 2:xvi).

11. The winning gloss was inspired by the Góngora ballad: "While he gazes amazed / at her beauty, she multiplies / many powerful wounds / but none of them felt" (Sigüenza, 261, 270). Neither Salceda ([26] 4:557) nor I have been able to locate this sonnet in assonance in the work of Góngora.

12. The Italian author undoubtedly influenced the dramas of Monterde (1894-1985), to the point where the "The Group of Seven," to which he belonged, was given the nickname of the "Pirandellos" (Schmidhuber, *Flowering of the Mexican Theater*, 21-28).

13. I am substituting *Sor Juana* for *Moreto* in this line of *The Trials of a Noble House*.

14. In the second *sainete* there is another allusion to the art of bullfighting, when Acevedo defends himself against the booing: "Damned hissers, / I am disposed to die; / hisses were made / for the bulls" ([26] 4:123). One would also have to mention the sonnet by Sor Juana with the same theme, with the subtitle "To a noble bullfighter, his horse having killed a bull" ([26] 4:305). Bullfighting was highly appreciated by the inhabitants of New Spain, as proven by the numerous bullfights recorded in the *Diary of Notable Events* by Antonio de Robles.

15. I concur with what Celsa Carmen García Valdés states in her excellent edition of *The Trials of a Noble House* concerning the importance of this festival for being the only one to have come down to us in its complete form ([28], 80-81).

16. In order to make up for the absence of complete baroque festivals, Francisco Rico published *Disdain in Exchange for Disdain*, by Moreto, together with two of his interludes (Madrid: Castalia, 1972) and José María Díez Borque published *A Baroque Sacramental Festival* with the works of Calderón de la Barca (Madrid: Taurus, 1984). Another of the very rare original baroque festivals that has been preserved is *A Burlesque Festival*, celebrated before Charles II in 1684 (see Javier Huerta Calvo).

Sixth Critical Act

1. Abreu Gómez cites this author among those included in Sor Juana's library (344).

2. A verse is possibly missing between lines 58 and 59, since the ballad should not begin with the á-o assonance of the even-numbered lines. Salceda makes no mention of this in his notes.

3. For an explanation of this numbering system, see Salceda, [26] 4:574.

4. Athanasius Kircher was a prolific German writer and musicologist born in Geysen (Fulda) in 1602. He joined the Jesuits in 1618. He taught music, mathematics, oriental languages, and philosophy at the College of Wurzburg. He was the first European to study hieroglyphics. He used magnetism as a cure. He accompanied Cardinal Federico de Sajonia to Malta, as his secretary. He was professor of Hebrew and mathematics in Rome, where he died in 1680. His principal works are *Lingua aegyptiaca restituta* (Rome, 1643); *Ars magna lucis et umbrae* (Rome, 1644); *Mundus subterraneus* (Amsterdam, 1664); see Federico Carlos Sainz de Robles, *Dictionary of Literature* (Madrid: Aguilar, 1964), 3:678. Paz cites Kircher as one of the sources of Sor Juana's hermetic Neoplatonism (*The Traps of Faith*, 224-39). A book by Kircher is among the books painted in Sor Juana's portrait by Juan de Miranda and Miguel Cabrera.

5. Kircher also proposed a correspondence between musical notes and letters (*Musurgia Universalis*, 2:94): G = 8, F = 7, E = 6, D = 5, C = 4, B = 3, A = 2, G = 1. Just as the hands indicated the year (1688) in the same *loa*, so too the character EDAD [age] contained in his very name the day of the viceroy's arrival: EDAD = 6 + 5 + 2 + 5 = 18 (November 18). I confess that I do not know whether to interpret these numbers as obscure coincidences. It is worth recalling, as a similar example, the complicated number system included in the two poems written on the portrait of Sor Juana by Miguel Cabrera: the letters I, V, L, M of the lines are considered Roman numerals that when added together total, in one quartet, Sor Juana's birth year (according to Father Calleja); in another, her age at death; and in a third, the date of her death:

Mane lucet

NaCIó JVana haCIenDo Ver	0713
a Vn Phebo LenDo a SalIr	0557
qVe no fVe Vn soL en LVCIr	0221
pVes me fVe sóLo en naCer	0160
	————
Sor Juana was born in the year	1651

In Meridie fervet

JVana es Phebo I se enseñó	07
en Phebo JVana, PVes qVe	16
Phebo presVrosa fVe	10
pro breVe en aVanto gIró	11

Sor Juana lived	44 years

Vespere autem pallet

JVana a sV oCaso LLegó	0211
Vn soL soLo LVCIrá	0261
qVe otro soL no se haLLará	0155
sI Vn sol en JVana MVrIó	1068

Sor Juana died in the year	1695

6. Compare this phrase from the second act: "I am a tunafish, and I want to be a turtle" ([26] 4:256) with the phrase from the third act: "I am a tunafish and not an octopus" ([26] 4:306). Both belong to the humorous style of a single author: Sor Juana.

7. Salceda has also noted other similarities among some of the expressions relating to the sash (line 199) and to the feathers (line 250) with regard to phrases from the *Villancicos for the Assumption* ([26] 3:244), in lines 19 and 58-59. Upon finding these similarities Salceda notes that it is an indication—"although vague"—that these *villancicos* are by Guevara ([26] 4:588), but he does not study the possible authorship by Sor Juana of some parts of the second act of *Love Is Indeed a Labyrinth*, as I propose here.

8. Ce!, an interjection to call someone, to make someone stop or to get the attention of a person. From the fricative or affricative consonant *sss* or *tss*, which is generally used in these cases (Corominas, 141-42). It has remained in the language of the southern cone.

9. This alteration of the original myth, in the opinion of Peden, causes the play to have an imbalance, since the plot focuses on the love between Theseus and Phaedra, while the poetry focuses on Ariadne. I do not agree with her on this point because I believe that the play makes use of these digressions about Ariadne in order to extend the denouement, as Lope de Vega suggested in his *The New Art of Writing Plays*: "But the denouement does not allow it / until the last scene; / because if the audience knows the end / they will turn their faces towards the door, and their backs / toward what they have been watching for three hours," and "Surprise the audience, so that they see something they don't expect" (895).

Seventh Critical Act

1. Ruiz Ramón analyzes the "feminism" of Tirso: "His heroines, in that gallant war between the sexes that constitutes one of the principal love elements in the play, resist adopting a passive role vis-á-vis male aggression. Dissatisfied and opposed to the subordinate position that society, governed by masculine principles, has imposed upon them, they attempt to affirm their spirit of independence" (196). Rojas Zorrilla presents a new vision of women in his theater, in his plays about honor defended through feminine integrity, as in *Everybody's Due*, and in the tragedies *Progne and Filomena* and *Dying Thinking about Killing*; and Moreto has a collection of female characters—Diana from *Disdain in Exchange for Disdain* and the noblewomen Ana and Inés from *It Cannot Be*—who are doubtlessly precursors of Sor Juana's Leonor.

2. In May 1992, I visited the Art Museum of Philadelphia, in Pennsylvania, USA, to see the anonymous portrait of Sor Juana that is kept there. During my visit I proposed to the directors of that institution the idea of an exchange of the portrait for modern Mexican paintings more in line with the artistic and nonhistorical and nonliterary objectives of that museum. I received hopeful responses. I took my idea to Octavio Paz, who in turn told it to Mr. Rafael Tovar y de Teresa, Director of the National Council for Culture and the Arts, as Paz related to me in a telephone conversation. The government of Mexico has presented an official petition to that North American institution with the hopes that the portrait of Sor Juana, the one that most humanizes her, can be returned to Mexico. For a study on the pictography of Sor Juana see Aureliano Tapia Méndez's, *Letter from Sor Juana Inés de la Cruz to her Confessor: Spiritual Self-Defense*, a book that incorporates the best of the Sor Juana gallery and that includes the *Letter from Monterrey*, a discovery about Sor Juana carried out by this editor.

3. Usigli proposes the following triad as a condition *sine qua non* for the dramatist: "By disposition and by volition and by vocation" (*Teatro completo*, 3:497).

Bibliography

Primary Sources

First Editions of Sor Juana's Works

[1] The first volume: *Obras completas: Inundación castálida* [*Castalian Flood*] *de la única poetisa, musa décima, Sor Juana Inés de la Cruz, religiosa profesa en el monasterio de San Gerónimo de la Imperial Ciudad de México, que en varios metros, idiomas y estilos, fertiliza varios asuntos: con elegantes, sutiles, claros, ingeniosos, útiles versos: para enseñanza, recreo y admiración. Dedícalos a la Excelma. Señora D. María Luisa Gonzaga Manrique de Lara, Condesa de Paredes, Marquesa de la Laguna, y los saca a la luz D. Juan Camacho Gayna, caballero del orden de Santiago, Mayordomo y Caballerizo que fue de su Excelencia Gobernador actual de la Ciudad del Puerto de Santa María. Con privilegio. En Madrid: Por Juan García Infanzón. Año de 1689.*

[2] The second volume: *Obras completas: Segundo volumen de las obras de Sor Juana Inés de la Cruz, monja profesa en el monasterio del señor san Gerónimo de la ciudad de México, dedicado por su misma autora a D. Juan de Orue y Arbierto caballero de la orden de Santiago. Año 1692. Con privilegio, en Sevilla, Por Tomás López de Haro, impresor y mercader de libros.*

[3] The third volume: *Obras completas: Fama y obras póstumas* [*Reputation and Posthumous Works*] *del Fénix de México, décima musa, poetisa americana, Sor Juana Inés de la Cruz, religiosa profesa en el convento de San Gerónimo de la Imperial Ciudad de México: que sacó a luz el Doctor Don Juan Ignacio de Castorena y Ursúa, Capellán de Honor de su Majestad, Protonotario Juez Apostólico por su Santidad, Teólogo, Examinador de la Nunciatura de España, prebendado de la Santa Iglesia Metropolitana de México. Consagradas a la majestad católica de la Reina nuestra señora Doña Mariana de Neoburg Baviera Palatina del*

Rhin, por mano de la Excma. Señora Doña Juana de Aragón y Cortés,
Duquesa de Monteleón y Terra Nova, Marquesa del Valle de Oaxaca,
etc. El doctor Don Juan Ignacio de Castorena y Ursúa, Capellán de
Honor de su Majestad, Protonotario Juez Apostólico por su Santidad,
teólogo, examinador de la Nunciatura de España, prebendado de la
Santa Iglesia Metropolitana de México. Con privilegio. En Madrid: en
la calle de la Habana. Año de 1700.

[4] *Fama y obras póstumas [Reputation and Posthumous Works] del Fénix*
de México, Décima Musa, poetisa americana, Sor Juana Inés de la Cruz,
religiosa profesa en el convento de San Gerónimo de la Imperial Ciudad
de México: que sacó a luz el Doctor Don Juan Ignacio de Castorena y
Ursúa, Capellán de honor de Su Majestad, Protonotario Juez Apostólico
por Su Santidad, Teólogo, Examinador de la Nunciatura de España,
Prebendado de la Santa Iglesia Metropolitana de México. Consagradas
a la Soberana Emperatriz de Cielo, y Tierra, María Nuestra Señora.
Con licencia. En Madrid: En la Imprenta de Antonio González de Reyes,
año de 1714. Ed. Fredo Arias de la Canal. México: Frente de Afirmación
Hispanista, 1989 [facsimile of the edition of 1714]. THIS EDITION IS CITED
IN THE PRESENT STUDY.

[5] *Auto sacramental del divino Narciso, por alegorías: compuesto por el*
singular numen y nunca bien alabado ingenio, claridad y propiedad
de frase castellana, de la Madre Juana Inés de la Cruz, Religiosa Profesa
en el Monasterio del señor San Gerónimo de la Imperial Ciudad de
México; a instancias de la Excma. Señora Condesa de Paredes,
Marquesa de la Laguna, virreina de esta Nueva España, singular patrona
y aficionada de la Madre Juana, para llevarlo a la Corte de Madrid
para que se representase en ella. Sácalo a la luz pública el Dr. D.
Ambrosio de Lima, que lo fue de Cámara de su Excia., y pudo lograr
una copia...En la Imprenta de la Viuda de Bernardo Calderón, 1690.
There are also two separate volumes without dates, published in Madrid;
see [26] 4:513.

[6] *Villancicos de Santa Catarina: Discurriólos la erudición sin segunda y*
admirable entendimiento de la M. Juana Inés de la Cruz... Puebla:
Imprenta de Diego Fernández de León, 1691.

[7] *La segunda Celestina.* A separate edition [*suelta*] quarto book with *loa*
and play, no date or place of publication, 48 pages. There are only two
copies: (1) the rare book collection of the University of Pennsylvania
(*Comedias Varias,* volumen 14, número 672); and (2) the British Museum (1964 Catalogue: *Madrid?: 1676?* 11728. f. 33, *cuarto*). There are
at least three later editions: (1) the National Library in Madrid, T 9222,
and (2) R 12162, both without the *loa* and publication date; and (3)
Jardín ameno, T-i 120 (1794). In the British Museum there is a copy

identical to T 9222 in Madrid (1964 Catalogue: *Sevilla?: 1700?* 11728. i. 2. 16). The National Library in Madrid has manuscripts of two revisions: *La segunda Celestina, hechicera de Triana,* MS 16.080, dated 1818 and anonymous; and the second, with the same title, MS 18.075, with no date but with the initials D. S. (Dionisio Solis, according to Castanien, 559). In the National Library in Paris there is an erroneous catalogue entry under the title of *Segunda comedia de Celestina... agora nuevamente impressa y corrigida.* (Anvers: A la enseña de la polla grassa. s.d.), but this is the novel of the same title by Feliciano de Silva (Yg. 3713, in-I 6).

[8] *Protesta de fe y renovación de los votos religiosos que hizo y dejó escrita con su sangre la M. Juana Inés de la Cruz, monja profesa de S. Jerónimo de México.* See Núñez de Miranda: *Testamento místico,* n.p.

[9] *Los empeños de una casa.* There are four separate editions [*sueltas*] without dates, three published in Seville and one in Barcelona; see [26] 4:531: (1) *Comedia Famosa. Los empeños de una casa.* De sor Juana Inés de la Cruz. Fénix de la Nueva España. Sevilla: En la Imprenta de Joseph Padrino. No date, 32 pages; (2) *Los empeños de una casa. Comedia famosa y del Fénix de la Nueva España, soror Juana Inés de la Cruz.* Sevilla: En la Imprenta de la viuda de Francisco Leefdael. 32 pages; (3) *Comedia famosa. Los empeños de una casa, por Iuana Inés de la Cruz, monja profesa en el monasterio del Señor San Gerónimo de la Ciudad de Mixico* [*sic*]. 43 pages; and (4) a *suelta*, published in Barcelona, with no date or publication data, 43 pages. There is a copy of an unsigned manuscript in the National Library in Madrid, Vv 708: "Comedia famosa. Los empeños de una casa," no date, 51 pages.

[10] *Amor es más laberinto.* A *suelta*, no date, published in Seville; see [26] 4:578.

First Editions of the Original Villancicos

[11] *Villancicos que se cantaron en la Santa Iglesia Metropolitana de Méjico, en honor de la María Santísima Madre de Dios, en su Asunción triunfante, año de 1676, en que se imprimieron.* Mexico: Viuda de Bernardo Calderón, 1676.

[12] *Villancicos que se cantaron en la Santa Iglesia Metropolitana de México. En los maitines de la Purísima Concepción de Nuestra Señora. A devoción de un afecto al Misterio. Año de 1676. En México. Compuestos en metro músico por el Br. Joseph de Agurto y Loaysa, maestro compositor de dicha Santa Iglesia. Por la viuda de Bernardo Calderón, en la calle de San Agustín.* Mexico. Viuda de Bernardo Calderón, 1676. This text contains the following hand-written note: "Composed by M. Juana Inés de la Cruz, a religious in the order of S. Gerónimo of Mexico."

[13] *Villancicos que se cantaron en los maitines del gloriosísimo padre S. Pedro Nolasco, fundador de la Sagrada Familia de Redentores del orden de Nuestra Señora de la Merced, día 31 de enero de 1677 años [sic].* Mexico: n.p., 1677. This text contains the signature "M. Juana Inés de la Cruz."

[14] *Villancicos que se cantaron en la Santa Iglesia Catedral de México, a los maitines del Gloriosísimo Príncipe de la Iglesia, el Señor San Pedro. Que fundó y dotó el doctor y M. D. Simón Estevan Beltrán de Alzate y Esquibel (que Dios haya) Maestre-escuela, que fue, de la S. Iglesia Catedral, y catedrático jubilado de Sagrada Escritura, en esta Real Universidad de México. Año de 1677. Dedícalos, el señor Licenciado. D. García de Legaspi Velazco Altamirano y Albornoz, canónigo desta Santa Iglesia Catedral de México.* Mexico: Viuda de Bernardo Calderón. This text contains a dedication by Sor Juana dated June 20, 1677.

[15] *Villancicos que se cantaron en la Santa Iglesia Metropolitana de México, en honor de María Santísima Madre de Dios, en su Asunción triunfante y se imprimieron, año de 1679.* Mexico: Viuda de Bernardo Calderón, 1679.

[16] *Villancicos que se cantaron en la Santa iglesia Catedral de México, en los maitines del gloriosísimo Príncipe de la Iglesia, el Señor San Pedro, año de 1683 en que se imprimieron.* Mexico: Viuda de Bernardo Calderón, 1683.

[17] *Villancicos que se cantaron en la Santa Iglesia Metropolitana de México: en honor de María Santísima Madre de Dios, en su Asunción Triunfante. Que instituyó y dotó la devoción del señor Dr. y M.D. Simón Esteban Beltrán de Alzate y Esquivel, catedrático jubilado de Prima de Sagrada Escritura en cita real Universidad, y dignísimo maestre-escuela de dicha Santa Iglesia. (Que Dios haya.) Púsolos en metro músico el Br. Joseph de Loaysa y Agurto, maestro de capilla de dicha iglesia. Con licencia en México: Por los Herederos de la Viuda de Bernardo Calderón. Año de 1685.* Mexico: Viuda de Bernardo Calderón, 1685. This text contains a hand-written note: "Composed by M. Juana Inés de la Cruz, a religious in the order of S. Gerónimo of Mexico."

[18] *Villancicos que se cantaron en la Santa Iglesia Catedral de la Puebla de los Ángeles, en los maitines solemnes de la Purísima Concepción de Nuestra Señora, año de 1689. Y los escribía para dicha S. Iglesia la Madre Juana Inés de la Cruz.* With music by Mateo Dallo y Lana. Puebla: Imprenta de Diego Fernández de León, 1689.

[19] *Villancicos que se cantaron en la Santa Iglesia Catedral de la Puebla de los Ángeles en los maitines solemnes del Nacimiento de Nuestro Señor Jesucristo, año de 1689.* With music by Miguel Mateo Dallo y Lana. Puebla: Imprenta de Diego Fernández de León, 1689.

[20] *Villancicos con que se solemnizaron en la Santa Iglesia Catedral de la Ciudad de la Puebla de los Ángeles los maitines del Gloriosísimo*

Patriarca Señor S. Joseph este año de 1690. Dotados por el reverente afecto y cordial devoción e un indigno esclavo de este felicísimo Esposo de María Santísima, y Padre adoptivo de Cristo Señor Nuestro. Discurriólos la erudición sin segunda, y siempre acertado entendimiento de la Madre Juana Inés de la Cruz religiosa profesa de velo y coro y contadora en el muy religioso convento del máximo doctor de la Iglesia San Gerónimo, de la Imperial Ciudad de México en glorioso obsequio del Santísimo Patriarca, a quien los dedica. Puestos en metro músico por el licenciado D. Miguel Mateo de Dallo y Lana, maestro de Capilla de dicha Santa Iglesia. Con licencia en la Puebla en la oficina de Diego Fernández de León 1690. Puebla: Imprenta de Diego Fernández de León, 1690.

[21] *Villancicos de la Asunción, 1690. En la Imprenta Plantiniana de los herederos de la viuda de Calderón, compuestos en metro músico por Antonio de Salazar.* Mexico: Imprenta Plantiniana de los Herederos de la Viuda de Calderón, 1690.

[22] *Villancicos con que se solemnizaron en la Santa Iglesia y primera Catedral de la ciudad de Antequera, Valle de Oaxaca, los maitines de la gloriosa mártir Santa Catarina, este años de 1691.* Puebla: Imprenta de Diego Fernández de León, 1691.

[23] *Villancicos que se cantaron en los maitines del glorioso Príncipe de la Iglesia, el Sr. S. Pedro, en la S.I. Metropolitana de Méjico. En la santa Iglesia Metropolitana de México. Que instituyó y dotó la devoción del señor doctor y M. don Simón Estevan Beltrán de Alzate y Esquibel, catedrático jubilado de la Prima de Sagrada Escritura en la Real Universidad, y dignísimo maestro-Escuela de dicha S. Iglesia. (Que Dios haya). Compuestos en metro músico: por el maestro Antonio de Salazar que lo es actual de Capilla de dicha Santa Iglesia. México: Herederos de la viuda de Bernardo Calderón, 1691.* Mexico: Imprenta Herederos de la Viuda de Calderón, 1691. There is one copy with an annotation attributing the work to Sor Juana; see [26] 2:facing 320.

[24] *Villancicos que se cantaron en los maitines del glorioso Príncipe de la Iglesia, el Sr. S. Pedro, en la S.I. Metropolitana de Méjico . . . : compuestos en metro músico por el M. Antonio de Salazar.* Mexico: Herederos de la Viuda de Calderón, 1692. Méndez Plancarte includes this work among the *villancicos* attributed to Sor Juana.

Contemporary Editions of Sor Juana's Works

[25] *Inundación Castálida [Castalian Flood].* Ed. Georgina Sabat-Rivers. Madrid: Castalia, 1982. CITATIONS ARE FROM THIS EDITION RATHER THAN THE ONE BY MÉNDEZ PLANCARTE (see [26]).

[26] *Obras completas* [*Complete Works*]. 4 vols. Mexico: Fondo de Cultura Económica, 1976. Lyric poetry is published in volume 1; the *villancicos* and sacred songs are published in volume 2; the *autos* and *loas* are in volume 3; and the plays, *sainetes*, and prose are in volume 4. The first three volumes are edited by Alfonso Méndez Plancarte; the fourth, by Alberto G. Salceda.

[27] *La segunda Celestina* [*The Second Celestina*]. Ed. Guillermo Schmidhuber and Olga Martha Peña Doria. Mexico: Editorial Vuelta, 1990. Prologue by Octavio Paz and Critical Study by Guillermo Schmidhuber.

[28] *Los empeños de una casa* [*The Trials of a Noble House*]. Ed. Celsa Carmen García Valdés. Barcelona: Promociones y Publicaciones Universitarias, 1989.

Secondary Sources

Abel, Lionel. *Metatheatre: A New View of Dramatic Form*. New York: Hill and Wang, 1963.

Abreu Gómez, Ermilo. *Sor Juana Inés de la Cruz: Bibliografía y biblioteca*. Mexico: Relaciones Exteriores, 1934.

Alatorre, Antonio. "Para leer la [*sic*] *Fama* [Reading the *Fama*] y *Obras Póstumas* de Sor Juana Inés de la Cruz." *Nueva Revista de Filología Hispánica* 29, no. 2 (1980):428-508.

———. "*La segunda Celestina* de Agustín de Salazar y Torres: Ejercicio de crítica." *Vuelta* 169 (1990):46-52.

Alcántara, Pedro de. *Historia de la literatura española*. Madrid, 1884.

Arrom, Juan José. "Cambiantes imágenes de la mujer en el teatro de la América virreinal." *Latin American Theatre Review* 12, no. 1 (1978) 5-15.

Arroyo, Anita. *Razón y pasión de sor Juana*. Mexico: Porrúa, 1952.

Atamoros, Noemí. *Sor Juana Inés de la Cruz y la Ciudad de México*. Mexico: Departamento del Distrito Federal, 1975.

Barrera y Leirado, Cayetano Alberto de la. *Catálogo bibliográfico y biográfico del teatro antiguo español, desde sus orígenes hasta mediados del siglo XVIII*. Madrid: Rivadeneyra, 1860.

Beristáin y Sousa, José Mariano. *Biblioteca hispanoamericana setentrional* [*sic*]. 3 vols. Amecameca: Colegio Católico, 1883.

Blanco, José Joaquín. *Esplendores y miserias de los criollos: La literatura en la Nueva España*. Mexico: Cal y Arena, 1989. Salazar y Torres on pages 40-45; Sor Juana on 45-89.

Bryant, William C. "Estudio métrico sobre las dos comedias profanas de sor Juana Inés de la Cruz." *Hispanófila* 19 (1963):37-48.

Calderón de la Barca, Pedro. *Comedias*. Biblioteca de autores españoles. 4 vols. Madrid: Ediciones Atlas, 1945.

————. *La vida es sueño* [*Life Is a Dream*]. *Calderón de la Barca: Tragedias 1*, ed. Francisco Ruiz Ramón, 37-159. Madrid: Alianza Editorial, 1967.

Campoamor, Clara. *Sor Juana Inés de la Cruz*. Buenos Aires: Emece, 1944.

Castanien, Donald G. "La segunda Celestina; XVIIth and XIXth Centuries." *Hispania* 43 (1960):559-64.

Castañeda, James A. "'Los empeños de un acaso' y 'Los empeños de una casa': Calderón y Sor Juana, La diferencia de un fonema." *Revista de Estudios Hispánicos* 1 (1967):107-16.

Castorena y Ursúa, Juan Ignacio de. "Prólogo a quien leyere." In *Fama y obras póstumas* [4].

Catalá, Rafael. *Para una lectura americana del barroco mexicano: Sor Juana Inés de la Cruz y Sigüenza y Góngora*. Minneapolis: Prisma Institute, 1987.

Chang-Rodríguez, Raquel. "Relectura de *Los empeños de una casa*." *Revista Iberoamericana* 44, no. 104-5 (1978):409-19.

Chávez, Ezequiel A. *Sor Juana Inés de la Cruz: Ensayo de psicología y deestimación del sentido de su obra y de su vida para la historia de la cultura y de la formación de México*. Mexico: Editorial Porrúa, 1970.

Corominas, Joan. *Breve diccionario etimológico de la lengua castellana*. Madrid: Gredos, 1967.

Cossío, José María de. "Observaciones sobre la obra de Sor Juana Inés de la Cruz." *Boletín de la Real Academia Española* 32, no. 85 (1952):27-47.

Daniel, Lee Alton. "A Terra Incognita: Sor Juana's Theatre." Diss., Texas Tech Univ., 1979. 7920368.

————. "The *Loa:* One Aspect of the Sorjuanian Mask." *LATR* 16, no. 2 (1983):43-50.

————. "The Use of the Echo in the Plays of Sor Juana." In *La Chispa '83: Proceedings of a Conference on Hispanic Languages*, 71-78. New Orleans: Tulane Univ., 1983.

————. "Sor Juana's Pentad of Carlosian *Loas*. In *Sor Juana Inés de la Cruz: Selected Studies*. Asunción, Paraguay: CEDES, 1989.

————. "Encuentran *La Celestina* de Sor Juana." *Hispania* 73, no. 4 (1990):1035.

De la Maza, Francisco, ed. *Sor Juana Inés de la Cruz ante la historia*. Mexico: UNAM, 1980.

Delano, Lucille K. "Lope de Vega's Influence upon Sor Juana Inés de la Cruz." *Hispania* 13 (1930):79-94.

Diccionario de Autoridades. Madrid: Gredos, 1976. Facsimile of the edition of 1726.

Díez Borque, José María, ed. *Teatro y fiesta en el barroco: España e Iberoamérica*. Madrid: Ediciones del Serbal, 1986.

Eguiara y Eguren, Juan José de. *Sor Juana Inés de la Cruz*. Ed. Ermilo Abreu Gómez. Mexico: Porrúa, 1936.

———. *Biblioteca mexicana*. Ed. Benjamín Fernández Valenzuela, Ernesto de la Torre, and Ramiro Navarro de Anda. 3 vols. to date. Mexico: UNAM, 1986.

Feustle, Joseph A. "Hacia una interpretación de *Los empeños de una casa de Sor Juana Inés de la Cruz." Explicación de Textos Literarios* 1, no. 2 (1973):143-49.

Flickinger, Roy C. *The Greek Theater and Its Drama*. Chicago: Univ. of Chicago Press, 1973.

Flynn, Gerard. *Sor Juana Inés de la Cruz*. New York: Twayne, 1971.

Góngora y Argote, Luis de. *Obras completas*. Madrid: Aguilar, 1967.

González Peña, Carlos. *Historia de la literatura mexicana*. Mexico: Porrúa, 1928.

Gorham, Sarah. "The Celibate Matriarch." *Et Ultra* (winter/spring 1991):10-12.

Guardia, Alfredo de la. *Visión de crítica dramática*. Buenos Aires: Editorial La Pléyade, 1970.

Guijo, Gregorio Martin de. *Diario de sucesos notables (1648-1664)*. Documentos para la historia de Méjico. Mexico: Imprenta de Juan R. Navarro, 1853.

Hauser, Arnold. *Historia social de la literatura y el arte*. 3 vols. Madrid: Ediciones Guadarrama, 1969.

Hesse, Everett W. "Calderón in the Spanish Indies." *Hispanic Review* 23 (1955):12-27.

———. *La comedia y sus intérpretes*. Madrid: Castalia, 1972.

Holman, C. Hugh. *A Handbook to Literature*. Indianapolis: Odyssey Press, 1975.

Hornby, Richard. *Drama, Metadrama, and Perception*. London: Bucknell Univ. Press, 1986.

Huerta Calvo, Javier. "Anatomía de una fiesta teatral burlesca del siglo XVII." In *Teatro y fiesta en el barroco*, ed. J.M. Díez Borque, 115-36.

Jiménez Rueda, Julio. "Prólogo." In *Los empeños de una casa*. Ed. Julio Jiménez Rueda. Mexico: UNAM, 1940.

Johnson, Julie Greer. *Women in Colonial Spanish American Literature: Literary Images*. Connecticut: Greenwood Press, 1983.

Kircheri, Athanasii, Fuldensis Soc Iesu Presbyteri. *Musurgia Universalis sive ars magna consoni et dissoni*. 2 vols. Rome: Typis Ludouici Grignani, 1650.

Lapesa, Rafael. *Historia de la lengua española*. Madrid: Escelicer, 1968.

Lázaro Carreter, Fernando. *Teatro medieval*. Madrid: Castalia, 1965.

Leal, Luis. "El Tocotín mestizo de Sor Juana." *Ábside* 18 (1954):51-64.

León Mera, Juan de. "Prólogo." In *Obras selectas de la célebre monja de México, sor Juana Inés de la Cruz*. Ecuador: Imprenta Nacional de Quito, 1873.

Libro de las profesiones [*Book of Vows*] *que hacen las religiosas del monasterio de Santa Paula de la Orden del glorioso padre muestro san Jerónimo, de esta ciudad de México.* Ms. 1586 to 1713. The Benson Latin American Collection, University of Texas. Page 274 is signed by Sor Juana as number 251 in making her vows; additionally, the manuscript contains the majority of entrances to the order between 1680 and 1695 and the names of the prioresses.

Luiselli, Alessandra. *El sueño manierista de sor Juana Inés de la Cruz.* Mexico: Gobierno del Estado de México, 1993.

Luzán, Ignacio de. *La poética o reglas en general y de sus principales especies.* Madrid: Imprenta de Antonio de Sancha, 1789. [Book 3: *On Tragedy and Comedy, and Other Dramatic Poems*].

MacCurdy, Raymond R. *Spanish Drama of the Golden Age.* New York: Appleton Century Crofts, 1971.

María y Campos, Armando de. *Guía de representaciones teatrales en la Nueva España.* Mexico: Costa-AMIC, 1954.

Méndez Plancarte, Alfonso. *Poetas novohispánicos: Segundo siglo (1621-1721).* Mexico: UNAM, 1944.

Menéndez Pelayo, Marcelino. *Historia de la poesía hispanoamericana.* Madrid: Santander-Aldus, 1948.

———. *Orígenes de la novela* [*Origins of the Novel*]. In *Obras completas.* Madrid: Consejo Superior de Investigaciones Científicas, 1961.

Merrim, Stephanie. "*Mores Geometricae*: The 'Womanscript' in the Theater of Sor Juana Inés de la Cruz." In *Feminist Perspectives on Sor Juana Inés de la Cruz*, ed. S. Merrim, 94-123. Detroit: Wayne State Univ. Press, 1991.

Mesonero Romanos, Ramón de. *Dramáticos posteriores a Lope de Vega.* Vol. 49 of Biblioteca de autores españoles, ed. Ramón de Mesonero Romanos. Madrid, 1859.

Monterde, Francisco. *Sainetes de sor Juana.* Mexico: Editora Intercontinental, 1945.

Moreto y Cabaña, Agustín. *Comedias escogidas.* Ed. Luis Fernández-Guerra. Madrid: Biblioteca de Autores Españoles, 1950.

Nervo, Amado. *Juana de Asbaje.* Madrid: Biblioteca Nueva, 1910.

Núñez de Miranda, Antonio. *Sermón de santa Teresa . . . en presencia de . . . Fray Payo de Ribera, Arzobispo de México.* Mexico: Por la viuda de Bernardo Calderón, 1678.

———. *Testamento místico de una alma religiosa* [*Mystical Testament of a Religious Soul*] *que agonizante de amor por su divino esposo, moribunda ya, para morir al mundo, instituye a su querido, voluntario heredero de todos sus bienes. Dispuesta por el M.R.P. Antonio Núñez, prefecto que fue de la Congregación de la Purísima.* Mexico: Joseph

Bernardo de Hogal, ministro e impresor real y apostólico tribunal de la Santa Cruzada, 1707 and 1731. No pagination. We have only references to the first edition; but there are two copies of the second edition in the library of Indiana University, in Bloomington. The Hispanic Society of Nueva York also has a copy.

————. *Cartilla de la doctrina religiosa* [*Primer of Religious Doctrine*] . . . *en obsequio de las llamadas a religión y para alivio de los maestros que las instruyen.* Mexico: Por la viuda de Miguel de Ribera, 1708. This volume was reprinted as *Cartilla de la doctrina religiosa . . . para las niñas que se crían para monjas, y desean serlo con toda perfección.* Mexico: Imprenta de la Biblioteca Mexicana, 1766.

O'Connor, Thomas Austin. "Structure and Dramatic Techniques in the Works of Agustín de Salazar y Torres." Diss., SUNY, Albany, 1971.

————. "A Bibliographical Note on Salazar y Torres' *Cythara de Apolo.*" *Romance Notes* 15, no. 1 (1974):1-3.

————. "On the Authorship of *El encanto es la hermosura*: A Curious Case of Dramatic Collaboration." *Bulletin of the Comediantes* 26 (1974):31-34.

————. "Don Agustín de Salazar y Torres." *Bulletin of Bibliography* 32, no. 4 (1975):158-61, 167, 180.

————. "Language, Irony, and Death: The Poetry of Salazar y Torres' *El encanto es la hermosura.*" *Romanische Forschungen* 90 (1978):60-69.

————. "On Dating the *Comedias* of Agustín de Salazar y Torres: A Provisional Study." *Hispanófila* 67 (1979):73-81.

————. "Los enredos de una pieza [The Entanglements of a Play]. El contexto histórico-teatral de *El encanto es la hermosura* o *La segunda Celestina* de Salazar y Torres, Vera Tassis y Sor Juana." *Literatura Mexicana* 3, no. 2 (1992):283-303.

Olavarría y Ferrari, Enrique de. *Reseña histórica del teatro mexicano 1538-1911.* 5 vols. Mexico: Porrúa, 1961.

Oviedo, Juan Antonio de. *Vida ejemplar . . . del padre Antonio Núñez de Miranda.* In *Sor Juana Inés de la Cruz ante la historia,* ed. Francisco de la Maza, 278-82.

Pasquariello, Anthony M. "The Evolution of the *Loa* in Spanish America." *Latin American Theatre Review* 3, no. 2 (1970):5-19.

Pavis, Patrice. *Diccionario del teatro.* Barcelona: Paidós, 1980.

Paz, Octavio. *Sor Juana Inés de la Cruz o Las trampas de la fe* [*The Traps of Faith*]. Mexico: Fondo de Cultura Económica, 1985.

————. "¿Azar o justicia? [Chance or Justice?]" *La segunda Celestina.* [27], 7-10.

————. "*La segunda Celestina* ante sus jueces [*The Second Celestina* and Its Critics]." *Vuelta* 169 (1990):44.

Peden, Margaret Sayers. "Sor Juana Inés de la Cruz: The Fourth Labyrinth." *Bulletin of the Comediantes* 27, no. 1 (1975):46-47.

Pérez, María E. *Lo americano en el teatro de Sor Juana Inés de la Cruz.* New York: Eliseo Torres, 1975.

Pimentel, Francisco. *Reseña crítica de la poesía en Méjico.* Mexico, 1892.

Puccini, Darío. "Los *Villancicos* de Sor Juana Inés de la Cruz." *Cuadernos Americanos* 24 (1965):223-52.

Rabell, Malkah. *Decenio de teatro 1975-1985.* Mexico: Publicaciones Mexicanas El Día, 1986.

Ramírez España, Guillermo. *Cuatro documentos relativos a Sor Juana.* Mexico: Imprenta Universitaria, 1947.

Ramos, Duarte F. *Diccionario de mejicanismos.* . . . Mexico: Herrero Hermanos, 1898.

Regueiro, José M. *Spanish Drama of the Golden Age: A Catalogue of the "Comedia" Collection of the University of Pennsylvania.* New Haven: Research Publications, 1971.

Reichenberger, Arnold G. "The Counts Harrach and the Spanish Theater." In *Homenaje a A. Rodríguez-Moñino,* 97-103. Madrid: Castalia, 1966.

Robles, Antonio de. *Diario de sucesos notables (1665-1703).* Documentos para la historia de Méjico. vols. 2 and 3. Mexico: Imprenta de Juan R. Navarro, 1853.

Routt, Kristin. "Lo andrógino en *La segunda Celestina.*" *Torre de Papel* 3, no. 1 (1993):45-55.

Ruiz Ramón, Francisco. *Historia del teatro español* [History of Spanish Theater] *(Desde sus orígenes hasta 1900).* Madrid: Ediciones Cátedra, 1983.

Sabat-Rivers, Georgina. *The "Dream" of Sor Juana Inés de la Cruz: Literary Traditions and Originality.* London: Tamesis, 1977.

———. "Biografías: Sor Juana vista por Dorothy Schons y Octavio Paz." *Revista Iberoamericana* 132-33 (1985):927-37.

———. "Sor Juana Inés de la Cruz." In *Latin American Writers,* ed. Carlos A. Solé y María Isabel Abreu, 85-105. New York: Charles Scribner's Sons, 1989.

———. Book review of *La segunda Celestina. LATR* 26, no. 1 (1992):193-96.

———. "Los problemas de *La segunda Celestina.*" *Nueva Revista de Filología Hispánica* 40 (1992):493-512.

———. Reseña a *La segunda Celestina. Hispania* 75, no. 5 (1992):1186-88.

Sainz de Robles, Federico. *Ensayo de un diccionario de la literatura.* Madrid: Aguilar, 1964.

Salazar y Torres, Agustín de. *Cítara de Apolo* [Apollo's Lyre]. Ed. Juan de Vera Tassis. Madrid: 1694. The references to *El encanto es la hermosura* are from this edition.

————. *El encanto es la hermosura* [*Charm Is Beauty*]. In *Dramáticos posteriores a Lope de Vega*, ed. Ramón de Mesonero Romanos, 241-64. Biblioteca de autores españoles. Madrid: Editorial Rivadeneyra, 1951.

Salceda, Alberto G. "Cronología del teatro de sor Juana." *Ábside* 17 (1953): 333-59.

————. "Introducción." In *Obras completas*, [26] 4:vii-xlviii.

Schechner, Richard. *Performance Theory*. London: Routledge, 1988.

Schilling, Hildburg. *Teatro profano de la Nueva España: Fines del siglo XVI a mediados del siglo XVIII*. Mexico: UNAM, 1958.

Schmidhuber, Guillermo. "Búsqueda y hallazgo de una comedia perdida de Sor Juana." In *La segunda Celestina* [27], 11-26.

————. "*La segunda Celestina*: Sor Juana y la estilometría [Measurement of Style]." *Vuelta* (Mexico) 15, no. 174 (1991):54-60.

————. *El teatro mexicano en cierne* [*Flowering of the Mexican Theater*] *1922-1938*. New York: Peter Lang, 1992.

————. "Elementos biográficos en una comedia desconocida de Sor Juana, *La segunda Celestina*." *Hispanófila* 107 (1993):59-69.

————. "Hallazgo y significación [Discovery and Significance] de un texto en prosa perteneciente a los últimos años de sor Juana Inés de la Cruz." *Hispania* 192, no. 76 (1993):189-96.

————. "Hallazgo de dos obras perdidas de sor Juana Inés de la Cruz: la comedia *La segunda Celestina* y una *Protesta de la fe*." *Mairena* (Puerto Rico) 39 (1995):105-15.

————. "Un texto desconocido de sor Juana." *Cuadernos Hispanoamericanos. Los Complementarios* (Madrid) 16 (Nov. 1995):25-30.

Schons, Dorothy. "Some Obscure Points in the Life of Sor Juana Inés de la Cruz." *Modern Philology* 24 (1926-27):141-62.

————. *Bibliografía de Sor Juana Inés de la Cruz*. Mexico: Monografías Bibliográficas Mexicana, 1927.

Serrano y Sanz, Manuel. *Apuntes para una biblioteca de escritoras españolas*. Madrid: Rivadeneyra, 1903.

Sigüenza y Góngora, Carlos de. *Triunfo parténico que en glorias de María Santísima, inmaculadadamente concebida, celebró la pontificia, imperial y regia Academia Mexicana en el bienio que como su rector la gobernó el doctor don Juan de Narváez, tesorero general de la Santa Cruzada en el Arzobispado de México, y al presente catedrático de la prima de sagrada escritura. Descríbelo don Carlos de Sigüenza y Góngora, mexicano, y en ella catedrático propietario de matemáticas*. Ed. José Rojas Garciodueñas. Mexico: Ediciones Xóchitl, 1945. A new edition from the original (1683).

Simón Díaz, José. "Apuntes para la bibliografía de Agustín de Salazar y Torres (1642-1676)." *Celtiberia* 25 (1975):245-71.

Spaulding, Robert K. *How Spanish Grew*. Berkeley: Univ. of California Press, 1962.

Suárez Radillo, Carlos Miguel. *El teatro barroco hispano-americano*. Madrid: Porrúa Turanzas, 1981.

Tapia Méndez, Aureliano. *Carta de sor Juana Inés de la Cruz a su confesor: Autodefensa Espiritual*. Monterrey, Mexico: Producciones al Voleo El Troquel, 1993.

Teatro griego. Madrid: E.D.A.F., 1974.

Usigli, Rodolfo. *México en el teatro [Mexico in Its Theater]*. Mexico: Imprenta Mundial, 1932.

———. *Teatro completo*. Vol. 3. Mexico: Fondo de Cultura Económica, 1979.

Varey, J.E., and N.D. Shergold. *Comedias en Madrid: 1609-1709: Repertorio y estudio bibliográfico*. London: Tamesis, 1989.

Vega y Carpio, Lope de. *Obras escogidas*. Vol. 2. Madrid: Aguilar, 1961.

Villarrutia, Xavier. "Sor Juana Inés de la Cruz." *Revista de la Universidad Michoacana* (Mar.-Apr. 1942).

Vossler, Karl. "La Décima Musa de México: Sor Juana Inés de la Cruz." In *Escritores y poetas de España*, 113-29. Buenos Aires: Espasa-Calpe, 1947.

———. *Investigaciones lingüísticas*. Mexico: III, 1930.

Williamsen, Vern G. "La simetría bilateral [Bilateral Symmetry] de las comedias de Sor Juana Inés." In *El Barroco en América*, 1:217-28. Madrid: Ediciones Cultura Hispánica del Centro Iberoamericano de Cooperación, 1978.

———. *The Minor Dramatists of Seventeenth-Century Spain*. Boston: Twayne, 1982.

Wöfflin, Heinrich. *Renaissance und Barock*. Munich, 1888.

Index

metatheater in, 65, 66–67, 114, 122–23; Mexican quality of, 69, 70

Castorena y Ursúa, Juan Ignacio, 9–10, 20, 74–75, 83, 168n. 4

Catalá, Rafael, 68

Cavite prison, 116

Celestina, 56–57, 80–82, 98

Celia, 113

Cerberus, 60

Cerda y Aragón, Tomás Antonio de la, 25, 26, 114, 125

ceremony within theater, 65. *See also* metatheater

Cervantes, Saavedra: Sor Juana's allusions to, 168–69n. 7

Chang-Rodríquez, Raquel, 16, 121

characters: changing roles with in, 65–66; in Sor Juana's theater, 48–50. *See also* allegorical characters

Charm Is Beauty, and Charm without Witchcraft (Salazar y Torres), 33, 83, 89–92, 170n. 14. *See also* The Second Celestina

Charm without Enchantment, The Weapons of Beauty (Calderón), 90

Chávez, Ezequiel A., 16, 113, 121, 161n. 13

Choosing the Enemy (Salazar y Torres), 33, 164n. 7

Cintia, 36

classical allusions: in Sor Juana's plays, 60, 148

climax: in Lope de Vega's scheme of dramatic action, 53; in *Love is Indeed a Labyrinth*, 140; in Sor Juana's plays, 53–54

"cloak and dagger" plays: elements of metatheater in, 65–66; Sor Juana's structuring of, 38

co-authorship, 158–59n. 7; in *Love is Indeed a Labyrinth*, 129, 136, 143; in *The Second Celestina*, 73–89, 171n. 17

codes of reception. *See* theatrical reception codes

Coliseum of Plays: plays of Acevedo at, 118; plays of Salazar y Torres at, 33, 76; professional actors at, 164nn. 2, 3; *The Second Celestina* at, 26

collaborative writing, 158–59n. 7. *See also* co-authorship

comedias: written by Sor Juana, 7

comic foils: changing of roles within the character, 65; Mexican quality of, 69–70; of Moreto, 55; names of, 145, 172n. 20; self-reference and, 66–68; in Sor Juana's theater, 49–50; in *The Trials of a Noble House*, 113, 123. *See also* servants

complication: in Lope de Vega's scheme of dramatic action, 53

"Conch Shell, The" (Sor Juana), 133–34

conflict: in the *Loa for the Viceroy Marquis de la Languna's Birthday*, 131; in "*Sarao Of Four Nations*," 124; in Sor Juana's theater, 50–52

conga, 5

Conjecture (character), 49, 51, 52 table 4

conjectures: conflict of ideas and, 50

Conti, Natal, 35, 36

conujeturas, 50

coplas de arte menor, 40 table 1

Corneille, Pierre, 11

Country Houses of Toledo, The (Molina), 45

Courtesy (character), 110–11

Creon, 36, 60

Cretan labyrinth, 130

Crete, 60, 146